Writing for the Stage

A Practical Playwriting Guide

Leroy Clark

Florida International University

PEARSON

Boston   New York   San Francisco
Mexico City   Montreal   Toronto   London   Madrid   Munich   Paris
Hong Kong   Singapore   Tokyo   Cape Town   Sydney

Series Editor: Molly Taylor
Series Editorial Assistant: Susanne Stradley
Senior Marketing Manager: Mandee Eckersley
Senior Production Administrator: Donna Simons
Composition Buyer: Linda Cox
Manufacturing Buyer: JoAnne Sweeney
Cover Administrator: Joel Gendron
Editorial-Production Service: Omegatype Typography, Inc.
Electronic Composition: Omegatype Typography, Inc.

For related titles and support materials, visit our online catalog at www.ablongman.com.

Between the time website information is gathered and then published, it is not unusual for some sites to have closed. Also, the transcription of URLs can result in typographical errors. The publisher would appreciate notification where these errors occur so that they may be corrected in subsequent editions.

Library of Congress Cataloging-in-Publication Data

Clark, Leroy
    Writing for the stage : a practical playwriting guide / Leroy Clark.
      p. cm.
    Includes bibliographical references and index.
    ISBN 0-205-41297-1
      1. Playwriting. I. Title.
  PN1661.C555   2006
  808.2—dc22

                                          2005048089

CONTENTS

PREFACE

My aim in writing this book, *Writing for the Stage,* is to provide a guide to understanding the basic principles and techniques of the craft. The reader may have a
play already in mind and use the different exercises as guides to write various
scenes, or the reader may have no specific play in mind but use the exercises to
explore a number of different characters in a variety of situations. After writing
about six exercises, the writer should begin to focus the rest of the exercises on specific characters and develop a complete play. There are over one hundred exercises
divided into three levels: a level for the beginning writer and the intermediate level
and advanced level for those with more writing experience. This book is not
intended to be prescriptive but uses the information and techniques I have developed over the last thirty years as a professor, a director of about ninety stage productions, and a playwright of a dozen or so plays produced in twenty productions
at educational, community, and professional theatres.

    Writing for the Stage is unique in that it has three levels of specific exercises to
lead the beginning, intermediate, or more experienced writer through the process
of creating a stage-worthy script. There is extensive material on developing character and plot and dialogue. The book contains a wide variety of examples from
plays to clarify the major points. Another noteworthy feature is the relationship of
writing to the practical realities of theatre. Because of my experience in dealing
with writers' problems and questions, I have tried to provide practical advice and
information to cover many areas. A sample syllabus is provided in Appendix A to
help teachers in organizing a playwriting course, and a section on outcomes and
assessment is provided in Appendix B.

    From using these exercises in my own playwriting classes, I know they are
helpful for the majority of students. Usually, when an excercise is not helpful, it is
because the student didn't quite understand it. There is no way to please everyone
or to anticipate every need. This book is intended as a guide, not the ultimate
answer to every playwriting question. Take what works for you and your students.

    Within this book, you will find many references to plays. It is unlikely that
you have seen or read many of them. Most theatre majors at American universities
and graduate students in creative writing do not have a strong background in dramatic literature. Nevertheless, the examples provided should make some sense in
illustrating the basic point being made. I encourage you to see and read as many
plays as possible. I especially recommend the following short list of ten plays:

    How I Learned to Drive, by Paula Vogel
    A Long Day's Journey into Night, by Eugene O'Neill
    Getting Out, by Marsha Norman
    A Streetcar Named Desire, by Tennessee Williams

Killer Joe, by Tracy Letts

Fences, by August Wilson

The Miracle Worker, by William Gibson

Zoo Story, by Edward Albee

The Beauty Queen of Leenane, by Martin McDonagh

Proof, by David Auburn

When you write, write about stories you care about and people you want to spend time with. Write about what makes you happy, what you believe in, what you feel strongly about—and have fun!

Acknowledgments

I am very grateful to my students. I have learned much from them, and I have taken great pleasure in their successes. I owe special thanks to several students who read the manuscript and gave me suggestions: Hal Wyman, William Whitehurst, George Tucker, Hector Ramos, Jennifer Runberger, and Ramon Veunes. I am also very grateful to Molly Taylor and Michael Kish, of Allyn and Bacon, whose expertise and wisdom made this book possible. I would also like to thank the reviewers of this book for their helpful comments: Randall Cluff, Southern Virginia University; David Kahn, San Jose State University; Richard Kalinoski, University of Wisconsin Oshkosh; Carlos Morton, University of California, Santa Barbara; Michael Roos, University of Cincinnati; and David Wagoner, University of Washington.

CHAPTER

1

The Essence of Drama

The essence of drama is action. The word *drama* comes from the Greek word *dram,* which means "to do." A dramatic work presents a protagonist who acts—who does something. He takes the initiative to act upon a situation which results in something happening—an event that has consequences. He encounters strong resistance from the antagonist and either wins or loses. This is the traditional view of a play. Naturally, in the theatre, where rebels thrive and creative artists may reject the traditional, there are exceptions. Nevertheless, it is a starting place.

Conflict

In this chapter, we will explore a number of concepts related to conflict, including the inciting action, the protagonist's goal inspired by the inciting action, the central action or conflict that the protagonist experiences as he or she seeks to achieve that goal, the turning point, and the climax. There are three levels of conflict—internal conflict, personal conflict with another character, and external conflict dealing with issues affecting the larger community. We will also explore the need to create ever-increasing obstacles for the protagonist, as well as the pitfall static conflict. Finally, we will explore some common problems that lead playwrights astray and some solutions for correcting those problems.

Throughout this book, there are many exercises designed to help you put your ideas into practice. There are three levels of each exercise, moving from the beginning to intermediate and advanced levels, each designed to help you apply your ideas.

The Inciting Action

The *inciting action* is the first significant event of the play. It begins the plot and leads to the cause of the action. It may happen before the play begins, or it may occur at the opening of the play. Because of a change in the main character's situation, her world becomes unbalanced. Something is rotten in the state of Denmark or wherever the play takes place. This is the inciting action that creates a need within the protagonist that makes her want to do something about it. The action

1

may be taken to find an object, to achieve a position in society, to get money, to get the girl or the guy, to get revenge, or to find justice—the list goes on.

In many ways, the need leads the protagonist on a quest. In Sophocles' *Oedipus the King*, the city is suffering from a plague. Oedipus, a kind ruler, seeks to find the cause. In Shakespeare's *Othello*, Iago is motivated by revenge and seeks to make Othello jealous of his own wife. In Tennesee Williams's *The Glass Menagerie*, Tom is driven by his mother to find a gentleman caller for his sister. In Shakespeare's *Romeo and Juliet*, the two young lovers fall in love and get married, defying their parents, who are enemies. The protagonist's overall objective is "I want . . ."

The protagonist must initiate the action. In seeking to achieve his objective, the protagonist encounters a series of obstacles—in other words, resistance or opposition—that comes in the form of the second character, the *antagonist*. Obstacles create risks that bring physical and emotional danger to the protagonist. The bigger the obstacle, the more compelling the struggle. Denali, the highest mountain in Alaska and North America, has the dangers of avalanches, sudden storms, thin air, and temperatures far below zero. A misstep could bring death at any moment. A molehill has none of these dangers. Climbing to the top of Denali has bigger and more dangerous obstacles. These make the stakes high, the suspense strong, and the struggle much more interesting and emotionally charged. As the protagonist initiates the action, she raises the question that the rest of the play must answer: Will she succeed?

The Goal

The protagonist is aroused by the inciting action to assert her conscious will and direct it toward a specific goal. Yet the goal must be sufficiently realistic that it is attainable. The audience must understand the goal and the possibility of its fulfillment. The inciting action has upset the balance of the protagonist's world. The protagonist then takes it upon herself to restore order, to set a goal and to reach it. She plans strategies and tactics to achieve that goal. She develops the ideal scenario of how everything will work out. But the ideal scenario in her mind isn't what happens in reality. This causes a gap, a surprise, a worse problem, and as the antagonist responds, the protagonist must adapt.

Most people begin with one small step. They may try to be nice. They may not want to make a fuss or upset another person. Whatever they do first, they do not expect the consequences. They hope their first small action will solve the problem in the easiest way possible. However, the protagonist then discovers the gap between expectation and reality, which only results in a bigger problem.

The strength of the will must be strong enough so that the character is determined to go the distance. If a character is weak and gives in or gives up easily, then the conflict will be over. The character must be willing to continue to pursue his goal no matter what the obstacles. And the antagonist must be equally strong and committed. The antagonist must be as strong as the protagonist. There needs to be a balance of wills, a balance of strength. If the adversary isn't strong enough, then the outcome favoring the protagonist will be obvious. There will be no surprise, no more suspense. If the protagonist reaches his goal too easily, then there won't be enough of a struggle and the audience will be left unsatisfied. The antagonist must, therefore, be equally clever in his opposition so that the outcome will be truly in doubt until the climactic moment. The effectiveness of the action doesn't depend on what the antagonist and protagonist do; it depends on the meaning of what they do. One of the strongest antagonists we have seen in recent years is "The Terminator." He is a machine. He does not feel. He will not stop.

In drama, the first small action only complicates the situation and makes it worse. Every conflict consists of attack and counterattack. After the failure of the first action, the protagonist must then take action number two. Each decision leads the central character into more and more trouble. Thus, each decision is bigger than the last one, and the consequences are greater. At each turn, the protagonist must face the possibility of losing. Each step increases the tension and leads us from one crisis to a worse crisis until the final showdown.

In *Oedipus the King*, Oedipus sends Creon to the Oracle for information. He brings in the blind seer Tiresias. He sends for the shepherd. Each action results in the unexpected. In *The Glass Menagerie*, Amanda nags Tom to bring home a "gentleman caller" for Laura. Amanda makes a big fuss in preparation. The gentleman caller arrives but turns out to be already engaged. In each case, there is a difference between expectation and result—a difference between what the protagonist thinks will happen (the ideal scenario in his or her head) and what actually occurs.

When this gap opens up for the character, it also opens up for the audience. The gap is that "Oh, no!" moment, where the audience says, "Oh, no, don't do it. Oh, he did it. I can't believe it." These are the moments the audience comes to the theatre to see.

The Central Action

The *central action* answers the question created when the protagonist takes his first action. This question is the chief business of the plot: Will Oedipus solve the problem of the plague? Will Iago succeed in his revenge against Othello? Will the "gentleman caller" be the one for Laura? Will Romeo find happiness with Juliet?

Either the protagonist or the antagonist may win, depending upon the climax. In tragedy, the protagonist loses the struggle but gains her soul. In comedy, the protagonist wins and there is a happy ending. In drama, the ending may be neither tragic nor happy. Sometimes the ending doesn't provide an explicitly clear resolution to all the questions, but it must somehow feel satisfactory to the audience.

The stakes must be high. What the protagonist wants must have great personal value, and that means he must take risks. The protagonist places himself in a situation where he may win or lose. The greater the significance of reaching his goal, the more the protagonist is willing to risk to get it. In *A Man for All Seasons*, by Robert Bolt, Thomas More refuses to bow down to the king and go against his beliefs in the Catholic Church. His action puts his life in jeopardy, yet he is willing to die for what he believes is right.

The Turning Point

Eventually, the conflict must lead to a *turning point*. This scene may not seem to be important. The turning point of the leading character's life is not always one of the great moments. Real crises are often concealed in trivial events. The turning point is the moment when the protagonist's future is made apparent, determining whether he will win or lose. The turning point always involves a deed performed by the protagonist—a deed that involves not the antagonist but a third person. It is the deed that makes the ending for the central character inevitable—the moment when there is no going back. Oedipus learns that he killed his own father and married his mother, and so he blinds himself. Othello strangles Desdemona. Romeo kills Tybalt and with that deed forfeits all hope of acceptance by Juliet's family. It is the key scene that leads us to the climax.

The Climax

The *climax* of a play brings the relationship of the protagonist and antagonist to a final confrontation. A relationship is established in the beginning, and as the play progresses, this relationship undergoes dynamic alterations. It is at the climax of the play where the most violent dislocation occurs in this relationship. This is the scene that must be shown on the stage for the play to be completely satisfying. This is the scene in which we see the protagonist win or lose in face-to-face action with the antagonist.

Three Levels of Conflict

There are three levels of conflict. The first level is *internal* conflict, that inner struggle between duty and desire, between responsibility to self versus responsibility to others, or between one's sense of right and wrong. The second level of conflict is *personal and external,* involving a character's relationships with other people. The third level of conflict affects the larger world of *society.* Conflict can come from any level. A play may embody one or two or all three levels. Generally, a successful play employing all three levels is more complex, more deep, and more highly regarded.

Inner Conflict

When a character wants something that meets resistance within himself, there is inner conflict. People feel guilt and have misgivings, doubts, and second thoughts when duty collides with fear, love collides with guilt, or ambition collides with conscience. When an audience experiences profound empathy with a character, it is because the character is in a struggle of intense inner conflict. Inner conflict is what separates worthwhile drama from lesser melodrama. Hamlet suffers from a conscience and self-doubt. The psychiatrist in Peter Shaffer's *Equus* also has doubts whether his treatments in making Alan normal are really beneficial. Perhaps it is better for Alan to keep his creative, wild passion than to cut it out of his brain and make him calm and passive.

Inner conflict can be caused by sociological or psychological problems: religion, cultural differences, ethics, a sense of justice, patriotism, cowardice, temptation, sexual desire and fantasy—anything a character might feel strongly about. To have inner conflict, the opposing forces do not need to be great or earth-shaking issues, but they have to be great in the mind of the character. One man may torture himself over stealing a fountain pen, while another man may think nothing of stealing a million dollars. The story of the man who steals the fountain pen may be far more dramatic if the theft means the loss of his honor, integrity, or self-esteem. If your protagonist is planning to marry, an internal struggle may result if the girl is of a different religion or class or culture or education. If your protagonist is going to leave her husband, make certain she is reluctant to do so because of a powerful reason. Because of her religion, Antigone wants to bury her brother, who has been left on the battlefield. Her uncle Creon, the king, has decreed that anyone who buries the traitor will be put to death. Antigone is faced with a dilemma: to bury her brother and face death or to obey her uncle.

Put your character to the test. "Impale your character on the horns of a dilemma." You have impaled your character when the character is torn between doing one thing, for very powerful and convincing reasons, or doing something else, for equally powerful and compelling reasons. Your character is impaled when she is ripped apart by equally powerful forces pulling in opposite directions—the abused wife who wants to leave her husband but fears what may happen to her if she does. Your character is impaled when he must make a decision and doesn't like any of the choices. As news reports have revealed, a number of Catholic bishops, learning that some of their priests were pedophiles, were faced with a dilemma. If they turned the priests over to the police, it would cause a scandal. If they did nothing, the pedophiles would continue to abuse children. Many of them reassigned the priests elsewhere and paid off the victims.

EXERCISE 1 _____

Beginning Level   Choose one of the following:

   A. Write a monologue or a scene in which Character A confides to Character B inner conflict over what she wants to do and believes is morally right. Find the voice for the character. Show the struggle not only by what the character says but also by her behavior and actions. Is the character articulate or one who struggles to find the words? What does the character have to lose? Freedom? A relationship? Honor? Integrity? Money? Position? Power? Friendship?

   B. Write a scene in which Character A confides to Character B the inner conflict he is experiencing because of Character C. Perhaps A is torn by a lack of trust for Character C. Perhaps A is in love with Character C but afraid to admit it.

Perhaps A has learned a secret about Character C. What does A want from B? from C?

Intermediate Level   Choose one of the following:

C. Write a scene with internal struggle about an issue that affects the larger society. Character B makes Character A tell what's bothering him—an internal struggle. Suppose your character suspects his sister's husband is involved in terrorist activities? He doesn't want to hurt his sister, but on human, moral, and patriotic levels, he wants to do what is best for his country. Does he talk to the sister first, follow the brother-in-law and try to get proof, confront the brother-in-law, or call the FBI?

D. Write a scene in which the protagonist encounters a situation that incites him or her to action. The action may be taken to find an object, to achieve a higher position in society, to get money, to get the girl or the guy, to get revenge, or to find justice.

Advanced Level   Choose one of the following:

E. Write a scene in which the protagonist takes action to correct a problem but finds that the ideal scenario she has created isn't what happens in reality. What does happen is that her action causes the problem to become worse. Thus, there is a gap between the expectation and the reality, and the protagonist is surprised and faces a new dilemma.

F. Write a conflict scene in which the protagonist must demonstrate the strength of her will and commitment and her refusal to compromise.

Personal and External Conflict

The protagonist initiates an action. The antagonist may oppose the protagonist for a variety of reasons—his own different needs, beliefs, goals, values, feelings, and wants. The central character must try to overcome the obstacles. Each tactic that the protagonist tries to get what he wants meets resistance or is counterbalanced by the antagonist. It is important to orchestrate the play with different kinds of characters. In Neil Simon's *The Odd Couple,* for example, Felix is a compulsively neat person, whereas Oscar is a slob. They have different outlooks and different values. They think differently, behave differently.

All people have physical things about themselves that they don't like: nose, chin, lips, teeth, arms, legs, stomach, and so on. People also have mannerisms that drive other people crazy: leaving the toilet seat up, hanging pantyhose in the shower, leaving dirty clothes on the floor, and the like. Tennessee Williams, for example, gives a vivid detail of character in *The Long Stay Cut Short* with the line "Stop sucking your teeth, Archie Lee." In Williams's *The Glass Menagerie,* Amanda rails at Tom about his manners at the dinner table. Oscar rails at Felix in Simon's *The Odd Couple* for being obsessively neat. People have done things in their past that they are ashamed of—things involving sex, greed, power, revenge, or status.

People have specific likes and dislikes concerning food, sleeping habits, and daily living. People have different rituals—procedures to face the day, dinner rituals, family rituals for holidays, and rituals when they come home from work. There are personal, social, religious, and public rituals. Physical aspects, mannerisms, and interrupted rituals can cause conflict between people. To get what he wants, one character will bring up such problems and use them as weapons against another character.

Characters use a variety of questioning tactics. *Open questions* ask for an answer of more than a few words—for example, "What do you think about this problem?" *Closed questions* ask for a very specific response, such as yes or no—for example, "Do you love me?" *Leading questions* tend to direct the respondent toward the specific answer the other person is looking for—"What do you think of this stupid policy?" *Mirror questions* simply rephrase a previous answer to elicit more information—for example, "You think you can help Mary? Tell me more." *Probing questions,* like mirror questions, attempt to get more information or the reasons behind opinions and feelings—"Why do you feel like that?" Consider an interrogation scene with a policeman and a suspect, a courtroom scene between a hick lawyer and a well-educated witness, or a scene between a wife and her husband who staggers home in the early morning hours.

Dramatic incidents lead somewhere. When a conflict scene ends, more is expected to result because of it. More questions are raised. A conflict scene may end with no resolution, but when it ends, the conflict should be worse. Each scene needs to have a change in the relationship of the characters. It needs to build to something worse—an action, an event, an explosion of some kind.

Sometimes physical movement may constitute dramatic action. A handshake isn't particularly dramatic, but slapping someone's face is. Stabbing someone, smashing someone's prize object, throwing a manuscript into the fire—such actions as these have been pivotal points in a number of plays, signaling a character's explosive release. In plays such as *The Miracle Worker,* by William Gibson, physical action provides the turning point of the play. When Helen Keller has her hand in water under the pump and Anne spells the word for *water,* Anne finally makes Helen understand. Anne's struggle up to that point to teach Helen has been a failure. Anne depends on this job to give her life meaning. She has invested her self-worth in this job. Helen's breakthrough is a turning point for Anne, as well. She has finally proven her worth. The dramatic action equals the deeds done during the course of the story.

In any relationship, there are taboos, subjects, or events that people don't mention. A husband doesn't bring up the fact that his wife is fat, has heavy thighs, and cellulite. A wife doesn't discuss the size of her husband's penis. A daughter doesn't discuss religious differences with her mother-in-law. If you care about another person, you don't bring up past indiscretions, physical limitations, and other flaws. When someone does touch upon these topics, the conflict becomes very personal and very destructive. However, when the stakes are high enough, these things may be brought up.

But what happens when two characters love each other? How do you develop conflict with characters that care about each other? They may love each other and still have different needs, wants, and desires. When such differences are encountered, people usually start the discussion by being reasonable: "You can't do this. It isn't practical." When that doesn't work, they use other tactics: "You keep this up, and you're really gonna piss me off." "How can you do this to me?" "What's going to happen to me?" "You do this, and I'm leaving." Look at *The Lion in Winter,* by James Goldman, in which characters try numerous tactics to manipulate and win.

The following are some of the kinds of tactics used by characters to get what they want:

factual analysis	bargaining	threats
appealing to sense of fair play	cajoling	stereotyping
attempt to heal	efforts at humor	avoidance
persuasion	ridicule	tears
emotional appeals	physical force	rationalizing
appealing to trust	blackmail	appeal to common beliefs
concern for the other person	anger	using physical contact
looking for support	name-calling	admitting one's faults

When an actor studies a scene, he tries to discover the tactics the character is using. The actor must analyze the character's intentions and objectives and the tactics that govern the character's actions. The playwright in writing the scene needs to be clear in her own mind what those tactics are to make sure there are playable intentions within the scene.

Sometimes we may play different roles to get what we want. We play the child who needs to be cared for, the student, the teacher, the wife, the authority figure, the underdog, the understanding friend, the victor, the sick person, the misunderstood, or the maligned. In each episode of the *I Love Lucy* show, Lucy had a goal, usually opposed by her husband. She would use any tactic or play any role to get what she wanted.

EXERCISE 2

Beginning Level   Choose one of the following:

A. Write a scene in which the protagonist and antagonist battle over something personal and use a variety of tactics or play different roles to try to reach their individual objectives. For example, two sisters may fight if one of them wears the other's clothes without permission. What if someone eats your protagonist's chocolates, takes off in his car, or takes money from his wallet without his knowledge?

B. Write a scene in which the protagonist and antagonist battle over a physical object. The scene should involve physical action. The goal: to get the object by any means. The scene also should involve at least one character lying to the other. The protagonist should use at least six different tactics within the scene; the antagonist should counter with her own tactics. Bring in a third character that each of the other two tries to win to his or her side.

Intermediate Level   Choose one of the following:

C. People employ different rituals as a way of dealing with life: personal morning rituals; family rituals for dinners, holidays, and anniversaries; and social rituals such as religion and marriage. What happens when a ritual is interrupted? What happens when a secret ritual is discovered? Write a conflict scene between two or more characters that involves a ritual, a secret ritual, or an interrupted ritual. Chose an offbeat locale. Use music, sound effects, and props.

D. Write a conflict scene between two characters who love each other but disagree over a very important issue, such as whether to have a child, to invite their parents for Christmas, to buy a house, to have an abortion, or to borrow money. Give them conflicting perceptions, beliefs, and goals.

Advanced Level   Choose one of the following:

E. Write a scene in which two characters violate the rules and breech a taboo subject, involving past indiscretions, physical limitations, character flaws, or other weaknesses. When the taboo is brought up, the conflict should become personal and destructive.

F. Write a scene using ten of the sample tactics listed in the preceding section. Explore the variety of questioning techniques: open, closed, leading, mirror, and probing questions. Make sure the antagonist puts obstacles in the way to prevent the protagonist from reaching her goal. Who wins, who loses, and what are the consequences?

Conflict within Society

The third level of conflict involves issues that affect society, such as the family concerned that the electrical lines running overhead are causing children in the community to have leukemia, the man who takes a stand for justice, and the mother who joins MADD. Any issue can cause conflict. The protagonist is upset about a problem that affects the whole community and takes it upon himself to do something about it. He first takes a simple conservative action, but each subsequent step makes the matter worse. Each new obstacle creates higher risk. For example, in *An Enemy of the People* by Henrik Ibsen, Dr. Stockman has been a town hero for discovering that the local water was favorable for health baths, turning the town into a tourist center. At the opening of the play, however, he has learned that wastes from a tannery are polluting the baths. He demands that the condition be corrected and makes a desperate appeal at a public meeting, but the mob turns violently against him. Each action results in a situation he doesn't expect, which in turn forces him to take more and more drastic measures. By the end of the play, his whole world has crumbled.

Common Problems

The attention span, like the growth of technology, has changed over the years. Shakespeare couldn't afford to be dull, but playgoers then were willing to stand and listen to a play for several hours in an open-air theatre. The Elizabethans didn't bathe much, and the stench was considerable; sometimes it rained. On the other hand, theatregoers today have grown up with television, video games, and the Internet. People are used to seeing images change every twenty seconds. It is a challenge simply to get people to the theatre, and the greatest offense is to take their money, waste their time, and bore them. A dull play not only offends an audience, but it also scares them away from other future plays, including your own.

But how do you write a compelling play and avoid writing a boring one? Boredom is most acutely experienced when the playwright makes one of three mistakes:

1. *There is too much exposition.* Exposition is information, and providing too much about a character, one's past, or the nature of something without any real motivation for doing so is deadly. Typical of this error is the monologue in which a character offers up her life history when no one has asked for it.

2. *There are too many details.* When a character raves about the beauty of the sky, the nature of pigeons, or the history of an event without a need to do so, that is also deadly. In short, providing information about a subject when it has nothing to do with the conflict and doesn't aid the characters in achieving their goals causes a play to drag. This is particularly a problem for the writer who does considerable research to write a historical play and includes too much of the research as unnecessary exposition that slows down the action.

3. *Unnecessary characters appear on stage.* If a character is brought on stage to have someone to bounce jokes off or doesn't relate to the central action, a play becomes confusing. The writer needs to know the purpose of each character in each scene and in the whole play. Why is the character there? Why is he necessary?

Note that the common element in all three problem situations is the *absence of conflict.* Lack of conflict equals lack of energy. When a positive force meets a negative force, this causes sparks. For example, when polar opposites, such as a wife and her mother-in-law, clash over the husband/son, this causes sparks. The stakes are high. Both women are fighting for the man's love. If the wife and her mother-in-law do not clash and stay safely away from each other, the result is a dull play. Most plays can struggle through occasional scenes that are low on conflict, but everyone in the theatre feels it. Although the audience won't know *why* the scene in question is dull, they'll note the dip in energy. You, the writer, should also notice.

And nobody should be harder on you than you. If you build a house that falls down, you should recognize your faults and figure out how to correct them before building the next one.

You can describe a character at the beginning of a play as clever, witty, charming, noble, or wise, but your character will not be those things unless you show it by her actions and dialogue. The character must be put to the test, forced to make decisions and act. She must initiate action, face obstacles, and encounter conflict. What a character does and how she does it under extreme pressure reveals her nature.

If a play is like a meandering, slow-moving and flat river, it will be boring. The conflict should be like a raging river, crashing over rocks, rushing through deep ravines, and cascading over waterfalls. At times, it will be dimly glimpsed darting through the depths, showing the potential energy awaiting release. At times, the water will leap from the surface; this is kinetic energy being released. Two characters may seem to be getting along, but we know their making nice is destined to end soon in a big fight. At all times, the tension will be there if the characters are polarized and have different goals. It also works far better to take one major incident and develop it in depth than to take fifteen incidents and deal with them in superficial ways.

To correct errors that threaten to render your play weak, follow these guidelines:

1. Stay focused on each character's goal and how it is in opposition to the other characters' goals. In other words, keep the conflict going.

2. Deliver exposition as conflict. If there is information you must convey, put it into the antagonist's mouth as a weapon and attack the protagonist. This simple technique makes the antagonist an accuser and makes the protagonist resist and fight back. That's conflict.

3. When writing about history, realize that the audience doesn't care about a long, highly detailed account. They only need enough to know what happened, how it relates to the characters, and why it is important to the action now.

4. A conversation is not dramatic. If there is no conflict and nothing changes in the relationships of the characters, the scene isn't necessary. Push the characters until something happens.

5. Because of the costs of paying actors, it is necessary to keep the number of characters to a minimum. There is no place for a walk-on in theatre today. If you have a waiter who only appears once with a few lines, cut it. The *Dramatists Sourcebook* (2004–2005) lists all U.S. theatres that produce new plays and their guidelines. Most theatres are looking for small casts. Eight is usually the maximum; six is okay, and four is better.

6. Make sure the stakes are high. There's a difference between the student who wants an A for his own ego and the student who will lose his scholarship and get dropped from the program if he doesn't get an A.

Plot Motivators

Any number of conditions can provoke conflict. Choose from the following:

Injustice	the desire for justice
Vengeance	the desire for revenge
Catastrophe	the desire to act positively or negatively to a humanmade or natural disaster
Love	the desire for a relationship
Hate	the desire to respond in kind or go in the opposite direction
The chase	the desire to capture a character, for whatever reason
Grief and loss	the desire to avoid reality
Rebellion	the desire to challenge the status quo
Betrayal	the desire to violate a trust
Persecution	the desire to cause suffering
Self-sacrifice	the desire to help others at one's own expense
Survival	the desire to survive a humanmade or natural disaster
Rivalry	the desire to beat another person
Discovery	the desire for education, information, or insight
Ambition	the desire for success
Greed	the desire for material goods

Rising Conflict

To make sure you have rising conflict, plan your play so that the protagonist faces ever-increasing obstacles. The problems need to multiply. The pressure put on the character needs to increase. In every play, there is a *central* or *core conflict*. That conflict may be man against woman (Shakespeare's *The Taming of the Shrew*), woman against man (Lillian Hellman's *The Little Foxes*), man against man (Peter Shaffer's *Royal Hunt of the Sun*), woman against woman (Maxwell Anderson's *Mary of Scotland*), man against himself (Steve Tesich's *The Speed of Darkness*), man against society (Arthur Miller's *Death of a Salesman*), man against the environment (Patrick Meyers' *K2*), or man against nature (William Hoffman's *As Is*).

Typically, that core conflict is arranged scene by scene in climactic order, moving from the least important to the most important. Each scene requires the protagonist to risk more. Each scene puts her in more peril. Each situation is more difficult than the last, until we get to the climax—the scene in which the protagonist and her opponent meet face to face and one of them wins and the other loses.

Static Conflict

Conflict that doesn't escalate or change anything is *static*. Two characters bickering is static. A static or nonrising conflict is caused by a series of scenes that repeat the same conflict, make the conflict general rather than specific, seem of equal importance, or are not strong enough to cause change. Consider the situation of two brothers—Sam and Tom—who run a business. Sam is unreliable and so Tom does most of the work. If all the conflict scenes focus on the issue of Sam's general unreliability, then they will soon begin to seem too similar. If neither brother changes because of the conflicts, then nothing will really happen. What the writer must do is focus on specific irresponsible actions that cause larger and larger problems. The writer must focus on each brother's specific actions that cause larger and larger problems. Sam's actions might include taking an extra long lunch, taking too many days off, rudely reprimanding an employee in front of a client, writing down an order incorrectly, ordering the wrong materials, or telling off a client and losing a large order. With each problem Tom needs to assert himself with Sam to correct the situation. Tom's every action must be met with resistance from Sam, who must fight back in even more destructive ways. The writer needs to select specific events and arrange them in climactic order—minor irritations to major problems—until eventually they result in a showdown.

If a wife nags and her husband's response is only to give lip service, nothing will change. It will be static. However, if the wife's nagging causes the husband to take an action, then there will be change. Once when my parents went camping, my father forgot to bring a table. My mother went on and on about it until finally, my father took a piece of two-by-four out of the boat and nailed it to the side of his station wagon. Then he got a piece of plywood from the boat, nailed it to the two-by-four, and propped up the open side of the plywood with a couple of sticks. Then he said, "There's your damn table!"

Solutions

Four words to remember when thinking about conflict are *goal, motivation, obstacles,* and *tactics.* Because of a situation (motivation), Character A wants something (goal), but Character B seeks to prevent Character A from achieving that goal (obstacles). If the character's motivation is strong enough, the character will try various means (tactics) to overcome the obstacles. Consider the following scene in a diner:

SCENE I

AT RISE: (BETTY is at the counter. SAM enters.)

SAM

Hi, Betty. What's cooking?

BETTY

Same old, same old.

SAM

Coffee fresh?

                                              BETTY
Not as fresh as you, but it'll do. Black?
                          (HE nods.)
Want a menu?

                                              SAM
No, just give me the usual.

                                              BETTY
Hamburger, raw onion, pickle, mustard, hold the mayo?

                                              SAM
Sounds great.

                                              BETTY
Fries?

                                              SAM
Sure.

                                              BETTY
Paper is on the table. The Chiefs lost.

                                              SAM
What else is new?

This scene is realistic, but it is boring. The characters are flat, dull, and lifeless because there is no conflict. We know very little about these characters. They have not shown through action what makes them tick. They are having a conversation. Consider the following:

                              SCENE I

              AT RISE: (BETTY is at the counter. SAM enters.)

                                              SAM
Hi, Betty. What's cooking?

                                              BETTY
Nothing's cooking. We're closed.

                                              SAM
Coffee fresh?

                                              BETTY
It's about three hours old and cold. Want some?

                                              SAM
Forget it.

BETTY

No, you forget it. You were supposed to be here an hour and forty-two minutes ago.

SAM

I didn't know you could count that high. I got held up.

BETTY

Yeah, well, I've had it. This is it, the end, the big finish. I don't want to see you anymore. I don't want to wait for you. I don't want you coming around. Is that clear enough for you? You get no more hamburgers from me.

SAM

Sure. Now give me some coffee.

BETTY

You want it. Here it is.
> (SHE grabs the pot and pours coffee in his lap.
> HE jumps, yells.)

SAM

Hey, Jesus, cut it out. You'll burn my dick.

BETTY

I told yah, it's cold, baby.

SAM

I'm gonna slap you silly.

BETTY

Out! I want you out!

SAM

Aw, you don't mean that. You don't wanna hurt Sammy Whammy!

Conflict is the collision of characters' desires with resistance from another; from nature, society, the environment, the spirit world, or outer space; or from within themselves. We learn who a character really is by the way he or she responds to the obstacles. Conflict highlights and exposes deep character. Conflict between characters always takes the form of insistence versus resistance. In Neil Simon's *Barefoot in the Park*, Corie Bratter wants her husband, Paul, to loosen up and have some fun. Paul resists because he is practical. In William Inge's *Bus Stop*, Bo wants to sweep Cherie off her feet, marry her, and take her off to his ranch in Montana. She resists being manhandled and forced. When characters have different goals and are intent on achieving them, conflict results. If the stakes are high and both sides are unyielding, you have the makings of high drama.

Nothing moves forward in a play except through struggle—the push and pull of different wants, needs, and goals. Complication should not only make life difficult for the protagonist, but each new problem should be more difficult than the last. *Subplots* are also used to complicate the life of the protagonist. They must relate to the main action either by supporting it or contradicting it. There must be a relationship between the main plot and a subplot. If there isn't a connection, the audience will try to make one anyway. The subplot also allows for contrast, such as adding comic elements in a serious drama or vice versa. In Tennessee Williams's *A Streetcar Named Desire*, the neighbors, Steve and Eunice, have scenes that provide comic relief. Their battle is in contrast to that of Stanley and Stella. The love story in a murder mystery is there to make life more difficult for the protagonist. It complicates the main story if the hero falls in love with the killer. The magnitude of a work depends on the number of actions. Three major actions and three major reversals are needed to take the character to the limit of experience.

Some plays and films are more interesting than others because of the complexity and depth of their characters. Plot-driven works such as the farces *The Twin Menachmi* by Plautus and *The Comedy of Errors* by Shakespeare and many melodramas have little depth or complexity. However, plays such as Tennessee Williams's *The Glass Menagerie,* Arthur Miller's *Death of a Salesman,* and Edward Albee's *Who's Afraid of Virginia Woolf?* have a complexity that goes beyond the dialogue. There is a deeper, richer subtext. The characters do not always say what they mean or mean what they say. Yet with their very subtle techniques, these authors are able to convey the true meaning behind the words. In Beth Henley's *Crimes of the Heart*, Lenny tells Meg about the recent history of Doc, Meg's former beau (Act I, p. 20):

MEG

Gosh, the last I heard of Doc, he was up in the East painting the walls of houses to earn a living.
          (Amused)
Heard he was living with some Yankee woman who made clay pots.

LENNY

Joan.

MEG

What?

LENNY

Her name's Joan. She came down here with him. That's one of her pots. Doc's married to her.

MEG

Married—

LENNY

Uh huh.

                              MEG
Doc married a Yankee?

                              LENNY
That's right; and they've got two kids.

                              MEG
Kids—

                              LENNY
A boy and a girl.

                              MEG
God. Then his kids must be half Yankee.

                              LENNY
I suppose.

                              MEG
God. That really gets me. I don't know why, but that really gets me.

                              LENNY
I don't know why it should.

                              MEG
And what a stupid looking pot! Who'd buy it, anyway?

    Although it isn't mentioned, Meg still loves Doc. She probably has hopes that since she's come back to town, they might get back together. Whereas she's characterized as a free spirit by unconventional actions and behavior in most of the rest of the play, in this scene, she reverts to the childhood prejudice against Yankees. However, it isn't that the woman is a Yankee that really upsets her. It is because the woman is married to Doc. Meg's anger, resentment, hurt, and love are all conveyed in her last line about the pot.

    In the film *Casablanca*, there's one scene that has always remained with me because of the subtext. The scene is set at a linen stall in a marketplace. Ilsa is looking at some napkins. There is a sign on the counter by the display that reads "700 francs." That is the price the Arab quotes to her. Ilsa sees Rick approach but pretends to be absorbed in the napkins to escape his notice. When Rick tells her she's being cheated, she reacts in a formal manner and the Arab jumps in. He keeps changing the sign, and the price gets lower and lower. During this, Rick asks her why she abandoned him at the railroad station in Paris many years ago. She eventually tells him that she was married to Victor Laszlo. At the end of this scene, Ilsa goes into the cafe to her husband after that last line. Rick walks off in another direction. In an amusing moment, the Arab rushes back in with his arms full of linens and is shocked to find they have both left. Then he puts the first sign, "700 francs," back up.

What does the overall scene really show? Rick wants to win Ilsa back, and he is feeling positive in the beginning. Ilsa is full of mixed emotions because of their encounter the previous night. She wants to push him away. Rick apologizes. Ilsa rejects his attempts. He tries to make her feel guilty about the railroad ticket. She does the same to him about the previous night. She gives him the "let's be friends and remember the good times." He doesn't hear it. She basically calls him a jerk, and he calls her a whore, saying she'll lie to Laszlo someday. She really surprises him with "Laszlo is my husband." This opens a wide gap between what he was expecting and the reality of what he hears. She wants to hurt Rick. She wins. Love is at stake but never mentioned. The subtext revealed is far more complex than what the lines say on the surface.

Avoid "writing on the nose." People are seldom completely honest. What they say is always filtered by their relationships with the people they are talking to, what they want, and what they want to hide. "Writing on the nose" is the phrase used to describe direct dialogue, in which the characters say exactly what they mean. This kind of writing doesn't have any subtext and results in flat characters. What is exciting about theatre, for both the actors and the audience, is figuring out the subtext—trying to understand what the characters are not saying. People don't say exactly what they mean. They try to be polite, they lie, they want to avoid conflict. Suppose a guy hits on your protagonist. He's smiling with yellow teeth, his breath smells of bourbon, and his nose hair needs to be trimmed. Your protagonist smiles and edges away or gives a polite answer and tries not to offend him because she doesn't want to create a scene. The creep leans forward, puts his hand on your protagonist's thigh, and whispers something obscene. He won't give up. Finally, your central character says something direct. This makes the situation worse.

EXERCISE 3 _____

Beginning Level   Choose one of the following:

A. Is there a social problem that concerns you? Date rape? Bureaucratic red tape? Abuse of children? Select an issue you care about at work or in your neighborhood. Write a scene in which Character A seeks to deal with this problem in society. Character B represents the other side of the issue and opposes Character A. For example, what if Character A found out about other workers stealing merchandise? What if Character A suspected a relative of child abuse?

B. Write a three-person scene in which Characters A and B seek to deal with a problem in society but are opposed by Character C. Consider an issue that you care about—perhaps a nearby atomic power plant, a proposed highway that will cut the community in half, a pollution problem, or teenagers drag racing that leads to a hit-and-run. Whatever Character A and B's objective, it must run into an obstacle provided by Character C.

Intermediate Level   Choose one of the following:

C. Write a scene about a social problem or issue in which there is a reversal. Character A has a goal that he believes in. Character B opposes that goal for private reasons. Character C is brought in, and her information causes the opposite of what is expected.

D. Write a scene with four or five short sequences in which the emotional temperature of at least one of the characters rises. Start the scene at normal, and increase the pressure step by step so that the emotions escalate. Perhaps Character A is manipulating Character B deliberately. Perhaps Character A is having to drag information out of Character B, and each new revelation causes increased anguish for Character A or increased anguish for Character B as he relives a terrible ordeal.

Advanced Level   Choose one of the following:

E. Write a scene of no-holds-barred conflict that centers on a ritual interrupted by the protagonist who believes what is happening is wrong. What is the ritual? A social, family, personal, religious, or secret ritual? What is the antagonist doing to a third character that the protagonist believes is wrong?

F. Write a conflict scene in which two characters seek to avoid overt conflict. The two characters should never say exactly what they mean. Make them lie, tell fibs, and offer half-truths. Have the characters avoid a particular word. Give the two characters a variety of subtle tactics to use. Find behaviors that reveal the mental processes of the characters. What motivates the conflict? What does each character want? The idea is to make whatever they're doing or talking about on the surface different from the subtext.

Summary

The *inciting action* begins the plot and leads to the cause of the action. It may happen before the play begins, or it may occur at the beginning of the play. Because of the environment, a situation, or a circumstance of some kind, the world of the protagonist becomes unbalanced. This is the inciting action that creates a need within the protagonist that leads him to want to do something about it.

The protagonist is aroused by the inciting action to assert his or her conscious will and direct it toward a specific *goal*. The goal must be sufficiently realistic that it is attainable. The character's will has to be strong enough so that he or she will pursue the goal no matter what the obstacles. And the antagonist must be equally strong and committed. The central character plans strategies and tactics to achieve the goal, but his or her ideal scenario isn't what happens in reality on encountering the antagonist. There is resistance, and every conflict consists of attack and counterattack. Each decision is bigger than the last one, and the consequences are greater.

The *central action* answers the question, Will the protagonist achieve her goal? The action shows us the struggle, the conflict, the complications the central character faces.

The *turning point* of the plot generally involves a third character, not the antagonist, but it leads to the final confrontation between the protagonist and antagonist and the inevitable end. The turning point of a life may seem mundane at the moment when it happens. Real crises are often concealed in trivial events. The turning point is the moment when the protagonist's future is made apparent. This is the moment when there is no going back.

The *climax* of a play brings together the protagonist and antagonist for a final confrontation. It is at the climax of the play where the most violent dislocation occurs in this relationship. It is in this scene that the struggle is won or lost, and it must be shown on the stage.

There are three levels of conflict. The first level is *internal* conflict, or conflict within—that inner struggle between duty and desire, between responsibility to self versus responsibility to others, or between right and wrong within one's own conscience. The second level of conflict is *personal and external*, involving a character's relationships with other people. The third level of conflict involves issues and situations that affect the larger *society*. Some plays employ conflict on all three levels.

Common problems that lead playwrights astray include (1) providing too much exposition, or giving information about a character or background story without any real motivation for doing so and without conflict; (2) including too many details found through research that have nothing to do with the conflict and don't aid the protagonist in achieving his or her goals, and (3) introducing a new character without a clear purpose.

Solutions to these problems and others are as follows: (1) Exposition should be delivered as conflict. If there is information that must be conveyed, put it into the antagonist's mouth in the form of accusations and attacks against the protagonist. (2) Realize that the audience only needs enough information to know what happened, how it relates to the characters, and why it is important to the action now. (3) If there is no conflict and nothing changes in the relationships of the characters, the scene isn't necessary. (4) Keep the number of characters to a minimum. There is no place for a nonessential character in theatre today.

To make sure there is a *rising conflict*, the playwright must make the protagonist face ever-increasing obstacles. The problems need to multiply. The pressure put on the character needs to increase. Plan your play so that the central or core conflict is arranged scene by scene in climactic order.

Conflict that doesn't escalate or fails to rise is *static*. A static play is caused by a series of scenes that repeat the same conflict over and over, make the conflict general rather than specific, seem of equal importance, or have conflicts that are not strong enough to cause any change

Four words to remember when thinking about conflict are *goal, motivation, obstacles,* and *tactics.* Because of a situation (motivation), Character A wants something (goal), but Character B and/or others seek to prevent Character A from achieving his goal (obstacles). If the character's motivation is strong enough, the character will try various means (tactics) to overcome the obstacles.

Conflict between characters always takes the form of insistence versus resistance. Nothing moves forward in a play except through escalating conflict. The magnitude of a work depends upon the number of complicating actions. Three major actions and three major reversals are needed to take the character to the limit of experience.

CHAPTER 2

Getting an Idea for a Play

A play begins with characters and language. The story is generated by the wants and needs of the characters, especially the central character, and the characters usually pursue those wants with words. For example, if a young man wants to seduce a pretty girl, he employs a velvet tongue. If a prosecutor wants to win a trial, he uses words to get convincing testimony to support his case. The action is in the words.

But where does the idea for a character or a play begin? Like the beginning of a pearl, it may begin with an irritation, a tiny grain of sand. For each author and each play, it is different. There are probably as many sources of ideas as there are plays. However, we can start with three categories: personal experience; observations of people, images, and events in our daily lives; and research.

Personal Experience

Just as the actor often finds it easier in the beginning of his training to play a character similar to himself or herself, the beginning playwright will also find it easier to tell a story by using his own experience. It is often said that a writer should write what he knows. This is fine up to a point, but it must also be strongly emphasized that a writer may use his creative imagination, observation, and research to increase what he knows. An actor may play a deranged killer without having actually killed someone by building on his knowledge and experiences with imagination. The writer does the same thing. There have likely been times in both the actor's and the playwright's life in which he has been angry with another person. Perhaps he has felt injustice, prejudice, rage, and a desire for revenge. He may not have acted on those feelings but can *imagine* what would have happened if he had. So, the writer, like the actor, is able to build upon real-life events with his imagination and exploit specific events for dramatic ends.

My play *Like Father, Like Son* was inspired by an incident in my family. After my wife and I were married, my mother had a small party for us that ended tragically: My father and his brother got in a fistfight that began in the kitchen and continued into the driveway, where my uncle was pushed backward against a sharp piece of metal. From this event, I created a play in which there is a similar fight and the uncle is impaled and then dies. The father then commits suicide just as his father had done, by putting a gun in his mouth and blowing the back of his head off. (My grandfather actually killed himself in this way.) Thus, I began with characters and a basic situation that I knew and built upon it with my imagination.

John Guare notes in an interview in *The Playwright's Art,* edited by Jackson R. Bryer (1995), that the first scene in his play *Bosoms and Neglect* was taken essentially word by word from an incident in his life. This event was very personal and shocking to him emotionally, and after it happened, he wrote it down because he didn't know what else to do with it. This event, which involved his mother in one of the darkest moments of her life, served as a springboard for the play.

In Mel Gussow's (1999) *Edward Albee: A Singular Journey,* a biography, the playwright describes the genesis of *Who's Afraid of Virginia Woolf?* and other plays. Albee says, "I will discover one day that I am thinking about a new play, which means that it's been in my unconscious and I am informing my conscious mind that I have been thinking about it. I'll put it back again. I'll forget about it. It will pop up again a few weeks later and I will discover that I have thought more about it" (p. 151). Albee explains that it is similar to the arrival of *Six Characters in Search of an Author,* by Pirandello. They sort of come to him and say, "Write us." Albee experiments with characters like an actor doing improvisations. He says, "I'll take a long walk on the beach with the characters, who I plan to have in the play I haven't written yet. I will put them in a situation that won't be in the play, and I will improvise dialogue for them to see how well I know them" (p. 151).

Our dreams may provide a useful starting place. Dreams are theatrical. They are free. They don't have to be rational. They aren't predictable. Many expressionist playwrights have used dreams to explore the subjective, internal reality of humans. Dream sequences are common in television and films, as well. Dreams provide a rich and exciting source of ideas for work in the arts. Nightmares can provide thrilling experiences. It is possible to use the images and energy of anger, fear, and frustration to show what is inside a character's mind.

Write down a favorite dream or nightmare and explore the possibilities. Combine several fearful events. Ask others about their dreams and nightmares. What do you fear? What do you know of the fears of other people close to you? Avoid psychological interpretations or judgments of actions in a dream scene. You do not need to explain the dream or tell the audience what it means, but a dream scene must make sense within the larger context of the play.

Orphée, by Jean Cocteau, is a short surrealistic play that has many strange details like a dream, and the author also explains in the stage directions how to stage them. *What's Wrong with This Picture?* by Dennis Margulies, was inspired by a dream that he had after his mother's sudden death in which she came home. He wrote in "Writers and Their Work," in the *Dramatists Guild Quarterly* (Margulies, 1995), that it doesn't conform to any preconceived rules about a person who comes back from the dead. Margulies calls it his most "personal play."

Watch out for autobiographical characters. A character based on the writer is often a passive character. It is difficult, if not impossible, for a writer to be able to observe himself and report truthfully. We all have many secrets we fear to expose, and our writing usually doesn't capture an honest portrayal. The character based on the author usually ends up as an observer, watching others in action. The other characters then become far more alive and interesting. The character standing in for the author in the following plays is overshadowed by the women. In Eugene O'Neill's *A Long Day's Journey into Night*, it is the mother who is the major figure. The same is true in Tennessee Williams's *The Glass Menagerie* and Neil Simon's *Broadway Bound*. In Arthur Miller's *After the Fall* and Simon's *Chapter Two*, it is the wives who emerge as the most colorful characters.

Don't think of your characters as *you*. The characters are not you. When they are not you, they are more free, more complex, more alive, and more outrageous. You may step into their shoes sometimes to get in tune with what they feel, and you may use some of your experiences, but make your characters different enough from you so that you can be honest.

Many little moments in a play may come from personal experiences, which the writer puts into the mouths and actions of characters. When Albee was about twenty-one, he worked as a messenger for Western Union. His best friend, William Flanagan, was also a messenger. In *Who's Afraid of Virginia Woolf?* (Act 3, p. 107) George tells Martha that a telegram announcing the death of their only child was delivered by "some little boy about seventy." Martha then asks, "Crazy, Billy?" and George says, "Yes, Martha, that's right. . . . Crazy Billy." As Gussow tells us in his biography of Albee, this was a joking reference to Flanagan.

So, to what extent should playwrights use their own experience? As some critics have noted, writers can be too self-preoccupied and too self-indulgent. Such charges have been leveled at Tennessee Williams and Edward Albee, both for their return to the same themes and their regular use of family members. Williams's *Glass Menagerie* used portraits of himself for Tom, his mother for Amanda, and his sister for Laura. In *A Streetcar Named Desire*, there were elements of both Williams's mother (the southern belle) and sister (allegations of rape and insanity) in the character of Blanche. Stanley is a version of his father. In *Suddenly Last Summer*, his sister Rose is also reflected in Catherine as is his mother in Mrs. Venable. Mrs. Venable wants the doctor to perform a lobotomy on Catherine. In real life, Williams's mother had his sister Rose lobotomized. Albee's parents, Reed and Francis Albee, are reflected in *Who's Afraid of Virginia Woolf? The American Dream, Three Tall Women*, and many others.

There is room for plays of all kinds, but no matter what the story, it will only work if the playwright taps an emotional core. All artistic expression is naturally a reflection of the artist, but the point is to select characters you can be honest with. If the playwright is uncomfortable about revealing too much of himself in a character, it will not work. The character will seem hollow, untrue, and incomplete. On the other hand, the playwright who gets too involved with the intellectual issues, rather than the character and the emotions, will put the audience at a distance. When a play focuses on the ideas at the expense of character, it often doesn't grab an audience emotionally. A good play intrigues us by finding the balance between the intellectual and the emotional. It has something to say and touches us where we live.

Observations of People, Images, and Events

A play may begin with a character based on someone you have observed. When I was in college, I had a philosophy teacher whose name was actually Dr. Virtue, and he inspired me to write a character that I called Dr. Soul in *Wine of This Year's Vintage,* a play about resisting conformity. The actor Michael Wager, a great opera fan and friend, inspired the character of Mendy in Terrence McNally's *The Lisbon Traviata. The Caretaker,* by Harold Pinter, was inspired in 1960 by two brothers in the author's apartment building and a homeless person that they allowed to live with them for three weeks. Although he did not know these people intimately, Pinter's creative imagination was able to build upon the various encounters he had with them in the hall and on the street.

A play also may begin with an image. According to Mel Gussow (1999) in his biography of Albee, *The Death of Bessie Smith* was inspired by an album cover. It was also a reflection of Albee's outrage over the racial prejudice in the South. Albee explored the story about the great blues singer's alleged automobile crash and death from loss of blood because she was refused admittance to a hospital due to her skin color. A play may also begin with a series of images, or a *collage.* Nilo Cruz often gathers photos from newpapers and magazines and creates a collage when he's writing a play. Anything that helps him in the visualization of the characters, locale, or action is added. Sometimes he even does drawings himself.

Playwrights may be inspired not only by situations they encounter personally or by people or events they observe but also by newspaper and magazine stories. *Equus,* by Peter Shaffer, was inspired by a newspaper story about a boy who blinded several horses. Tracy Letts's play *Killer Joe* was inspired by a newspaper story about a family in Florida. Garcia Lorca's *Blood Wedding* also took its plot from a newspaper account of the murder of a bridegroom. The musical *Godspell* took its inspiration from the Bible.

I read an article in *Teacher* magazine about a gay high school teacher who came out to his history class and whose job became jeopardized. The article discussed some of the issues involved in the case but offered few details about the people involved. Nevertheless, I was intrigued and spent the next six years writing and rewriting *Outburst* based on this incident. It was up to me to invent the characters and get inside them until I could feel their pain, hopes, and dreams. Issues may be important for essays and magazine articles, but it is the characters' wants and needs, actions and words, feelings and clashes that make a play compelling.

Godspell, *performed at Idaho State University. Directed by J. David Blatt, Set and Lighting Design by J. David Blatt, Costume Design by Sonja Nelson.*

A photograph, a painting, a poem, a stranger, a magazine article, an over-heard conversation, or something that the writer sees on the street—almost anything can trigger an idea for a play. By the time a play has been finished, however, there may no longer be a connection. A play has to start with an idea somewhere, but the actual writing may lead the writer in a totally unexpected direction. Lanford Wilson said in *The Playwright's Art* (Bryer, 1995) that the *Hot l Baltimore* started with an image of lost trains, abandoned railroad stations, and a once glorious hotel that had become run down. He didn't realize it was a whores' hotel until the character of April came down the stairs. Once she entered the play, the focus of what he was writing became clear.

Neil Simon's *Lost in Yonkers* was quite different when he first thought of the idea. He wrote twenty pages of it and then decided that it wasn't going anyplace. He put it aside and went on to other things, but it was starting to germinate and grow in his mind. When he went back to it, he realized what was wrong. In the first version, Bella was not retarded and the young boy who came to live there was alone. As Simon continued to work on the play, Bella became emotionally arrested because of her grandmother. The boy was joined by a brother so that he would have someone to talk to. Louie the Gangster turned into Bella's brother, who was there to show what the grandmother had done to the family and to encourage Bella to speak up against her.

John Guare (1992) has noted that his play *Lydie Breeze* was inspired by seeing two women on a beach one day when he went swimming. There, walking along the beach in the water, was a woman with more vivacity and energy than he had ever seen before. She was wearing a long dress, because she wore long clothes to mask herself, and pointing at a young girl and lecturing to her. That was the image that started the writing. The rest of the story came from Guare's desire to write about one of his ancestors, a very beautiful woman who had come from Poland and defected to the United States through an extraordinary chain of circumstances.

Disease can also serve as inspiration. The AIDS epidemic has been the source of many works, such as Larry Kramer's *The Normal Heart*, William Hoffman's *As Is*, Paula Vogel's *The Baltimore Waltz*, Tony Kuchner's *Angels in America*, and Craig Lucas's *The Dying Gaul*. *Wit* tells the story of a cancer patient. *Steel Magnolias* focuses on a diabetic.

Throughout human history, from the Peloponnesian War to Vietnam to the Israeli/Palestinian conflict, war has served as the source for numerous plays. Vietnam War experiences have been drawn upon for plays such as *Tracers*, which was conceived by John DiFusco and written by the original cast, and the trilogy by David Rabe including *Streamers, Basic Training of Pavlo Hummel*, and *Sticks and Bones. In the Heart of America*, by Naomi Wallace, is a recent play about the Gulf War.

Intolerance, injustice, and prejudice also have inspired plays. Clifford Odets voices his protest about unfair labor practices in *Waiting for Lefty*. Society's intolerant treatment of gays is the focus of plays such as *The Children's Hour*, by Lillian Hellman; *Boys in the Band*, by Mart Crowley; and *Gross Indecency* and *The Laramie Project*, by Moises Kaufman. Other plays showing an emerging tolerance in the last few decades include *Torch Song Trilogy*, by Harvey Fierstein; *The Lisbon Traviata*, by Terrence McNally; *Jeffrey*, by Paul Rudnik; and *Angels in America*, by Tony Kushner.

Racial discrimination has been portrayed in Lorraine Hansberry's *A Raisin in the Sun*, Leroi Jones's *The Dutchman*, and Charles Fuller's *A Soldier's Play*, among others. A broad range of the African American experience in the United States has been chronicled by writers such as the three just mentioned and August Wilson, Cheryl West, Susan-Lori Parks, James Baldwin, Langston Hughes, Charles Gordone, Joseph A. Walker, and George C. Wolfe. While few plays by Latin American authors have become well known nationally, the Hispanic world is represented by playwrights Nilo Cruz, Jose Rivera, Luis Veldez, Judith Perez, Severo Perez, Arthur Giron, Milcha Sanchez-Scott, and Jeremy Blahnik.

Conflict is readily apparent in social problems such as injustice, war crimes, hate crimes, rape, gender issues, sexual molestation, aging, the youth culture, drugs, adultery, abortion, discrimination, freedom of speech, euthanasia, suicide, terrorism, arson, and so on. However, a play must focus on characters, not just issues. If the characters are not developed enough to make the audience care about them, the audience won't care about the issues, either. Moreover, its best to avoid a protagonist who is a passive victim. A play that focuses on a person who has been wronged by society but fights back for her rights, justice, and dignity will be far more interesting because she takes action.

What situations in your own life make you really angry? Imagine waiting for a parking spot and having another driver zip around you and steal the space. What would happen if you took a tire iron from the trunk and smashed the driver's headlights? Imagine that you are at a university trying to find out why you lost your financial aid. You call the office but get a recording. You go to the office but are ignored; the clerk is indifferent, then hostile, and then rude. You are sent to the registrar's office, then the dean's office, then back to financial aid. You are given an appeal form and told it will take a month before it will be acted upon. What other situations have you experienced that might be useful in writing a play?

Research

Another very important element in the creation of plays is research. If writers write about what they know, that also means they can write about what they learn. Many plays are based on historical figures, such as Abraham Lincoln, Saint Joan, Queen Elizabeth I, Mary Queen of Scots, Becket, Shakespeare, Oscar Wilde, and Edgar Allan Poe, among many others. There are plays about 9/11, dropping the bomb on Hiroshima, hiding from the Nazis, and the destruction of the Native Americans in early U.S. history. There are plays about historical figures and events in nearly every country.

Biographies and autobiographies, diaries, letters, photos, newspapers, magazines, journals, transcripts of court trials—all of these may serve as source material. *Dear Liar,* by Jerome Kilty, is a play based on the letters of George Bernard Shaw and Mrs. Patrick Campbell. Probably the best-known play adapted from a diary is *The Diary of Anne Frank,* by Frances Goodrich and Albert Hackett. Transcripts of court trials were used in Moises Kaufman's *Gross Indecency* and Shaw's *Saint Joan.* Since the mid 1990s, there have been many one-person shows based on the lives of famous people. Katherine Hepburn in Matthew Lombardo's *Tea at Five,* George Burns in Rupert Holmes's *Say Goodnight, Gracie,* and the former prime minister of Israel in William Gibson's *Golda's Balcony,* are three examples.

I have written three plays based on historical events and people: *Shootout at Keystone Canyon, The Lady and the Gypsy,* and *Shakespeare's Journey.* With each succeeding draft, I had to throw out more and more history because all the little facts and anecdotes slowed down the action.

Shakespeare's Journey, *performed at Wichita State University. Directed by J. David Blatt, Set and Lighting Design by Dan Williams, Costume Design by Betty Monroe.*

In *Shakespeare's Journey,* I wanted to write about Shakespeare's adult life as a husband and father, actor/playwright, and successful businessman. The amount of material written about Shakespeare is enormous, and so I had a wealth of material. My major problem was deciding what to keep and what to omit. What I learned from writing these plays is that historical details do not a play make. You have to structure the events to tell the story effectively. Sometimes you have to omit details and add events to make it work—to make it stage worthy. You have to make the play meaningful. You may ask, If I have to throw out the history, then why do the research? It's important to know as much about the truth as possible. You should be faithful to the spirit of the truth yet provide an interpretation that will have a point of view and enlighten the audience. It is not the facts that are important; it's your interpretation of them. Select the details that make the story dramatic and meaningful.

Recently, several movies, including *Hurricane* (about the boxer Rubin Carter) and *A Beautiful Mind* (about the brilliant mathematician John Nash), have came under fire because the filmmakers left out some details in order to focus the stories.

Their intent was to make art, to tell a story in the most dramatic terms, not to provide every detail of the subject's life.

Contemporary people or situations may inspire a play as well as historical ones. Presidents, national heroes, movie stars, and various other real-life individuals in the United States have given rise to plays such as Dore Schary's *Sunrise at Campobello,* about Franklin Roosevelt; Kathryn Schultz Miller's *Amelia Earhart,* about the early woman aviator; and Moises Kaufman's *The Laramie Project,* about the effect of the murder of Matthew Shepard on the town. The film *Erin Brockovitch* came into being because of a situation involving industrial pollution and a real contemporary person.

A theme may inspire a play. If you have a particular message, something important to say, that may inspire you to write. Tennessee Williams's *Not about Nightingales* was inspired by an atrocity in Pennsylvania, in which convicts were locked in a steam-heated cell and roasted to death. David Rabe's play *A Question of Mercy* explores the issue of euthanasia, with each character battling with the moral and legal issues that attend helping an incurably ill person to die. Arthur Miller's *The Crucible* explores the hysteria and hypocrisy of religious fundamentalists. Although inspired by the hearings of Senator Joseph McCarthy, who sought to find communists in the United States in the 1950s, the play's theme remains timeless.

Observe your world to see what inspires your voice. You may find inspiration in a contemporary or a historical event, person, injustice, or ethical concern. What current events grab your attention? Which do you think could be developed into a story about a central character who has a strong goal and who is faced with great obstacles? Who would be the opposing characters? Do you foresee a way of structuring the idea? How can you best show the action? As Jeffrey Sweet (1986) notes in "Ethics and Responsibilities," in *Dramatists Guild Quarterly,* "Playwriting, by its very nature, is bound up in ethical concerns. As playwrights, we design behavior for the stage. That's what a script is—a program of words and actions which, when given life by actors, are evaluated by the audience" (p. 15). The evaluation of behavior is the evaluation of ethics.

All the wrongs and injustices of society, the business world, and politics may provide fodder for a play. However, the author must show what is happening and portray people in action, not just talk about it. If there is no conflict, there is nothing dramatic happening. As David Mamet (1993) wrote in *Dramatists Guild Quarterly,* "Anything in drama which is not dramatic is going to cause the audience to snore, and they won't tell their friends to come and see the play" (p. 13).

Any story may require you to do research on a particular name, event, disease or drug. Research may be needed to enhance your knowledge even for writing a contemporary play. For example, you might need to research tuberculosis because one of your characters has this illness. If you write a play about a specific kind of cancer, you had better know the symptoms and treatments. When you give a character a profession, you need to know the vocabulary and views of people in that profession. Police officers, firefighters, and accountants all have unique vocabularies and perspectives of society because of who they are and what they do.

Keeping a Journal

A journal is a helpful tool for the playwright to jot down the events of the day, descriptions of people he meets, a new word or a line of dialogue he hears, a scrap of conversation, or a sketch of an unusual place he sees. Sometimes the playwright may want to carry the journal with him, especially on going to a public place such as an airport, bus station, grocery store, or mall. It is also helpful to keep a file for newspaper clippings, magazine articles, pictures, letters, and even ads that might have dramatic possibilities. Later, the playwright can come back to the journal or the file for inspiration.

EXERCISE 4 _____

Beginning Level   Choose one of the following:

A. Consider a situation or event in your past that resulted in a change of perception and behavior. Such an event might include a divorce, a death, a hard-earned success, or discrimination. What happened? How did you feel? Write a monologue in which a character responds to such an incident. Have the character speak in an immediate conflict in which she uses the past event to achieve a current objective. To whom is she talking? Why?

B. Choose a character different from you in education, status, values, or lifestyle. Develop a second character that is the opposite of the first. Create a collage for each character, or a list of details—important, insignificant, meaningful, random, internal, external—that add up to a composite portrait of each character. Write a scene about one event in which the two different personalities clash.

Intermediate Level   Choose one of the following:

C. Write a monologue in which Character A talks about a significant object given to him by Character B, a person no longer in his life either because the person is dead, estranged, or moved away. Use an object that an actor can have in his hand when performing the monologue. The significance of the object is not its monetary value but its importance as a symbol of something the character values because it represents the relationship—the love, sadness, joy. Possible objects include a ring, key, pin, shirt, candy box, watch, photo, and letter.

D. Write a conflict scene inspired by a photograph, a painting, or an observation. Create two people whose personality and character traits are polar opposites.

Advanced Level   Choose one of the following:

E. Find a newspaper article that tells about an event that is inherently dramatic. It must deal with at least two people in a conflict involving intolerance, prejudice, or injustice related to race/ethnicity, color, religion, age, size, or sexual orientation. Write a scene focusing on the two people in conflict. Remember that a play must focus on characters, not just issues. We must care about the people in order to care about the issues. (See Chapter 4 for format guidelines.)

F. Do research on a historical figure that intrigues you. Write a scene in which two contemporary characters encounter the ghost of the historical figure. What is the conflict? What does the ghost want? Is the ghost one who provides obstacles or help?

Summary

Where does the idea for a play begin? For each author and each play, it is different. However, most sources fall into one of three categories: personal experience; observations of people, images, and events in our daily lives; and research.

Just as the beginning actor often finds it is easier to play a character similar to herself, the beginning playwright will find it easier to tell a story by using her own experience. It is often said that a writer should write about what she knows, but it must also be emphasized that a writer may add to what she knows with creative imagination and research. An actor may play a murderer without having actually killed someone by building upon her knowledge and experience with imagination. It is the same for the writer. A writer needs to be careful in this regard, however, for autobiographical characters are often passive observers. It is very difficult for writers to observe themselves and report truthfully because they fear exposing some aspects, making the writing often flat and dull.

Observations of people, images, and events may inspire a character or a story. A writer may be inspired by an image, a painting, a newspaper article, a poem, an interesting stranger, or an overheard conversation—almost anything can trigger an idea for a play.

Research is another important element in the creation and development of plays. If a writer writes about what he knows, then it can also be about what he learns. Many plays are based on historical figures and events. Biographies and autobiographies, diaries, letters, photos, newspapers, magazine, journals, transcripts of court trials—all may serve as source material.

A journal can be a helpful tool for the playwright, prompting her to jot down the events of the day, descriptions of people, a new word or a line of dialogue overheard, or a scrap of conversation. Keeping a file of newspaper clippings, articles, pictures, letters, and other material that catches the writer's eye also may provide inspiration for future plays.

CHAPTER

3

Planning the First Draft

Once a writer gets an idea for a play, it is unlikely that that idea will emerge exactly as planned. It is the approach in this book to encourage you to write nine or ten scenes based on some of the suggested exercises and then try to develop your idea for the play into a clearer scenario. With a clearer idea of the major action and conflict, the characters, the climax, and the ending, you can then focus your writing in the later exercises to accomplish the plan. Once you have completed the exercises, it will be time to put them together, add transitions, make changes, and create the first draft.

When John Guare (1992) began writing *The House of Blue Leaves,* he had an entirely different ending in mind. As he recalls, "I got sick when I saw what Artie was going to do, what had to happen. The lesson that it taught me was, if you go into a play knowing the ending, it's no fun to write. You can have a general idea of where you would like to have it end, but leave open the possibility of the character's running away with it" (p. 34).

When Lee Blessing gets an idea for a play, he asks himself what makes the seed of the play distinctive or different in point of view. "I want to find something special or unique about it," he says. "What's this idea going to do that others I've seen don't do?" (Albee, 1993, p. 11). By *do* he means the effect on the audience: How is this idea going to affect the way an audience thinks, feels, or dreams about a particular subject or a particular feature of the perceptual world around us? What can this play do to make them deal with it in a way they haven't before? How can it make them see the values they have and make them question those values? Blessing believes that "affecting the audience is why one writes a play to begin with. You don't write a play for yourself, the actors, or the director. You're there to do something to the audience" (p. 11).

Blessing's process is to walk around the lake eating chocolate bars and thinking about the problem confronting the main character and the solutions that character tries in order to solve the problem. He says, "It's fairly close to what an actor has to do in his or her process. Given the character's problem, how does he want to solve it, where does he go with the people he encounters, what gets in his way, and how does he shift to try to get around it" (p. 12). A lot of exploratory work goes on in his head. He says, "I think of the characters in the setting. I see them there, see a scene, hear some dialogue. The process that is occurring, I hope, is that the good ideas are staying in my head. The ones that aren't necessary go away" (p. 12).

In this chapter, we will explore the development of the working title, character names and descriptions, and first scene. We will also consider how to hold the audience's attention and create plot scenarios.

The Working Title

Finding the right title for a play may be difficult. A title should be relevant to the subject matter and fit what the play has to say. It needs to be brief. It also needs to grab our attention and arouse our curiosity and interest. It should not give away the ending. *The Hot l Baltimore* is an intriguing title because of the missing letter, which leads us to understand that the setting for the play is a rather seedy, run-down hotel. We also get author Lanford Wilson's suggestion that it is "hot," that the goings-on there are spicy. *Proof,* by David Auburn, is a very appropriate title for the mathematical connection to the story and what the leading character has done. The word means the act or process of testing or trying to establish the truth of something. Truth is also what the characters are seeking. *Fences* is another appropriate title both because of the literal fence being constructed on stage during the play and the metaphorical meaning playwright August Wilson wants to convey related to barriers created between people and the fences we build to keep others out.

Brainstorm and make a list of every title you can think of that may fit your play. Ask others for their opinions. Pick the title you think is the most special, will catch public attention, and is most appropriate for the content of the play.

Character Names and Descriptions

Write a brief description of each character in your play. What does an actor or director look for in a description of a character? Most contemporary playwrights give only minimal information, as Martin McDonagh did in *The Beauty Queen of Leenane:*

MAUREEN FOLAN	Aged forty, plain, slim.
MAG FOLAN	Her mother, aged seventy. Stout, frail.
PATO DOOLEY	A good-looking local man, aged about forty.
RAY DOOLEY	His brother, aged twenty.

Others give a slightly longer description, as did David Grimm in *Kit Marlowe:*

THOMAS WALSINGHAM	A trim and elegant young gentleman in his twenties. Born to a good family and raised with tradition. Though more pretty than handsome, there is nothing delicate about him. He is quick-tempered and impatient and deeply concerned with appear-

ances. Dark curly locks over soulful eyes. He dresses conservatively but expensively.

KIT MARLOWE   A playmaker. An athletically built, yet unhealthy-looking young man in his twenties. Lack of sleep and too much drink are running him to seed at an early age. A wild haystack of hair sprouts over a moonlike face which is capable of the wildest animation and the coldest stare. He is at once jester, scholar, thug, and seducer. His voice is quick and confident but undermined by a self-mocking laugh.

Names should be chosen carefully. A name often says a lot about a character. Marjorie, Margie, Madge, Marj, and Jorie all suggest different ages and personalities, as do James, Jim, and Jamie. Avoid having two characters with similar-sounding names. Millie and Mattie are of course different, but they look and sound too much alike. It will be easy for actors to read the wrong lines, and the names may be confusing to the audience. In descriptions, note each character's age, relationship to other characters, and what is special about him or her. Keep the information minimal.

The First Scene

Your first five to ten pages should grab the audience and make them want to discover the rest of the play. They should also give a feeling for the tone of the rest of the play. Make the dialogue fit the characters. For example, two students were reading a scene in class about two bank robbers. Suddenly, there came a line that stood out. One robber said, "I'm screwing this goat; you just hold onto the horns." This line struck a chord with the class. It fit the moment and said metaphorically exactly what the robber meant. It was a gem, like "What kind of a house is this it ain't got an orange?" from *Awake and Sing!*, by Clifford Odets, Blanche's line in Tennessee Williams's *Streetcar*, "I have always depended on the kindness of strangers," and even the famous line from Clint Eastwood's *Sudden Impact*, "Go ahead. Make my day." These lines grab us because they are so right. Make sure you don't lose important characters for long periods of time in your play. Keep important characters alive and involved during a scene.

EXERCISE 5 _____

All Levels

Write the first scene of your play. Select a relevant working title and the names of your characters. Give a brief description of each one. Visualize the setting. Try to jump into the conflict quickly. Put the exposition into the mouth of the antagonist, who uses it as a weapon. We need to know what the protagonist wants within the first five pages.

To provide depth to your character, focus on the journey she takes. Have a sense of your central character at the beginning of the journey and how she will change by the end of the journey. What are the obstacles? How does the character overcome them? Pay close attention to the key choices that your central character makes. All choices—from moral to expedient—define character. What are the character's major relationships in the story? How do these relationships help define her?

Answering the following series of questions for each character will provide further insight into his or her specific makeup:

1. What is the character's sign? Scorpio, Aries, Leo? A horoscope guide will provide an overview of the personality characteristics associated with each sign. Such a guide can give you ideas for character attributes, especially those that are polar opposites (fire and water or earth and air).

2. What music does he or she like? Music is very personal. People have strong likes and dislikes.

3. What is the tackiest thing in the character's life? Does he or she have plastic trinkets from Las Vegas, porn magazines under the bed, or underwear with holes?

4. What kind of advice would the character offer his or her best friend? Some people mean well but don't have a clue. Some try to be a savior figure, but their advice and actions are often more destructive than helpful. Others are jealous or resentful and provide advice that undermines others.

5. Where is he or she from? People from each part of the country have distinct characteristics, attitudes, concerns, and regionalisms. How do they affect this character?

6. What food reminds your character of home or of a pleasant time growing up?

7. If this character were stranded in a desolate place, what one item would he or she want to have? Why?

8. What is the first movie the character remembers? What is his or her favorite movie and why?

9. How does this character feel about holidays? What is his or her favorite one? Why?

10. What games does your character play?

In his book *Games People Play*, Eric Berne (1964) provides an analysis of social intercourse in which people respond either as an adult, a parent, or a child. A character may respond to his wife, for example, as if he were a responsible adult—an equal. He also may respond as a parent—in the same mindset as one of his parents and with the same posture, gestures, vocabulary, and feelings. This carries with it a sense of authority, of "I'm right and you're wrong." A character may respond inappropriately as a child. It is the role of the adult to regulate the activities of both the parent and the child. The transactions, roles, or "games" between any two characters in a scene may involve the following responses:

Character A		*Character B*
Adult	to	Adult
Adult	to	Parent
Adult	to	Child
Child	to	Adult
Child	to	Parent
Child	to	Child
Parent	to	Adult
Parent	to	Parent
Parent	to	Child

Each of us has these ego states within us. In some situations, we function and respond as adults and process data in order to effectively deal with the outside world. In other situations, something triggers us to respond like one of our parents did. At other times, we act like children. The child may operate on a positive level creatively and with enjoyment or on a negative level as a rebel who is angry, defiant, and destructive. If another person takes on the role of the child, we often take on the role of the parent.

Holding the Audience's Attention

Many contemporary plays, like *How I Learned to Drive*, by Paula Vogel, are ninety minutes straight through with no intermission. Today, people are used to seeing fast cuts and films that change the visual picture every twenty seconds. Fewer and fewer people have the concentration or patience for the long plays of the Elizabethan or Restoration periods. It is difficult for modern audiences, for example, to see a production of Shakespeare's *Hamlet* without cuts. Five-act, four-act, and three-act plays are forms of the past. Even today when they are produced, they are usually done in two acts and cut for shorter playing times. Audiences want shorter plays.

Audiences also want to know the point of a play, and they want to know it right away. This doesn't mean that we should directly *tell* them. Rather, it means that we should suggest the point of the play and do so in the first scene. If the play is about a vegetarian forced to eat meat at the hands of a sadistic butcher, then the first scene should have him or her in a fury about the evils of fast-food hamburgers. This conveys what the audience will need to know about the character and the probable challenges ahead. Moreover, there's immediate energy.

Begin with an interesting character in conflict. You also need to answer at least two other questions at the same time: What is the tone? Comic or tragic?

Lightly comic or darkly comic? Learn from so-called pulp writers. Their first chapter always grabs you with some odd situation that resists reasonable explanation until the final chapter, which you race breathlessly toward. Similarly, your play has only the first couple of pages to grab the viewer (or director, literary manager, or agent) and make the rest of the play irresistible. Don't spend those pages describing daffodils. Martin McDonagh's *The Beauty Queen of Leenane,* Neil LaBute's *The Shape of Things,* and David Auburn's *Proof* are just three examples of plays that grab you, take you to unexpected places, and make you re-examine what you thought was the truth.

EXERCISE 6

Beginning Level   Choose one of the following:
A. For several days, jot down in a journal descriptions of people and locales that you find intriguing and note bits of dialogue that you overhear. Select settings that are simple yet unique and dramatic. A dark basement, a place in the woods, a rooftop, a parking garage, a storage room, and an auto shop are all more interesting and unusual than a typical living room or kitchen. What characters and locales stand out? Pick any two of the most colorful people and one locale and write a five- to seven-page scene in which the characters clash. How does the locale affect them?
B. Write the answers to the preceding ten questions for two characters, and then write a scene of their first meeting. Do research on the characteristics of their astrological signs. Make your characters different and complex with contradictions, but give them strong wills.

Intermediate Level   Choose one of the following:
C. Write a scene in which one character acts like an adult but the other character switches his behavior from that of an adult to a parent to a child. What is the status of the main character? What does he know that the audience does not? Who in the story is in the superior position? When does your character discover something new and important? Does the audience learn the truth before the protagonist or at the same time?
D. Write a scene beginning with an immediate action and strong conflict that builds from one surprise to another. The pace must be fast. The lines must be short. The characters should be clearly different—different perspectives, quirks, looks, objectives, and voices.

Advanced Level   Choose one of the following:
E. Observe real-life individuals in a public setting. Note what they are wearing and look like, as well as their manners, attitudes, voices, and movements. Add these specific details to two of your characters. Imagine a situation in which one confronts the other to learn the truth, confirm a newly learned secret, expose a lie, or demand information about an event. Write a five-page scene. (See Chapter 4 for the proper format).

F.   Write a scene set in a hospital room about a young person who is unconscious from a drug overdose. In the scene, Character A—a doctor or a nurse—questions Character B—the patient's friend—about a rave and what drugs the patient ingested. Nexus, Liquid-X, Afterburners, rolling, speeding, 2-CB, MDMA, 4-PMA, and GHB are associated with the drug scene. Do some research about the symptoms and street slang. Make Character B reluctant to talk but finally have to confess.

Plot Scenarios

In preparation for writing and developing the structure of your play, you need to map out and describe the high points, or the major incidents. You need to plot the key events and write a brief narrative of the story. As noted earlier, while Lee Blessing, John Guare, and many other playwrights do not preplan by writing out a detailed plot synopsis, they do have a general plan in their heads of where they intend to go.

As you think about the scenes you have written, you may find the original scenes were in different locales. If so, you may need to translate and adapt them to work in one locale or a unit set. If you have many characters, you must limit the number to no more than three or four in a one-act play or six in a full-length play. You therefore may need to eliminate characters or combine several into one.

Perhaps at this point, having worked your way through the first few chapters, you have already written scenes that will be incorporated into your play. It is time now to fill in the gaps and to complete your scenario of the major incidents: the inciting action, what the central character wants, what tactics the character uses to get what he or she wants, what the antagonist wants, and the climax.

In a linearly structured story, the events are causal and chronological. Event B cannot happen unless Event A has already happened. In a nonlinear story, each scene leads to the next, but the story is not shown chronologically. Think of each scene as a railroad car. On the side of each car, write who is in the scene, what happens, and what is different at the end of the scene. What is the overall premise for your play? State in one sentence what you intend for the action of the play to show or say. Review the scenario of your play, and rewrite and edit so that it is no more than one or two pages. Make it exciting.

The following examples are based on the first three scenes in my play, *Shakespeare's Journey:*

Goodbye Scene

Scene 1: Stratford. Will, Anne, John, and Richard

Leaving to join the players in London, Will tries to convince his wife, Anne, that it is his opportunity to make something of himself. Although she doesn't want to be left alone to raise the kids, she gives in at the end.

Learning the Ropes Scene

Scene 2: London. Will, Richard, Cuthbert, Kempe, Pope, and Tooley

At the Theatre, Will is put to work with menial tasks while the more experienced players make fun of him and his shortcomings and rail against the Puritans. At the end of the scene, Will vows to keep his wife's Puritan background a secret.

Trouble at Home Scene

Scene 3: Stratford. Anne, Gilbert, Mrs. Crosse, John, Mary

Mrs. Crosse, a strict Puritan, considers Will a sinner and chides Anne for not disowning him. When the sinner comes home, Anne is greatly disappointed to learn that it's just a short visit. At the end she storms out.

EXERCISE 7 _____

All Levels

Write a scenario of your play. Your synopsis of the story should answer the following questions: What are the given circumstances in terms of place; time of day; economic/political/social/religious environment, if relevant, the inciting action; the complications; and major conflict scenes? When does the climax occur? What happens that changes the protagonist's course of action? How is the play resolved? Divide the play into its scenes and designate the nature of each with a title, such as the "drink scene," "sex scene," "no scene," "fight scene," and so on. Who is in each scene, what happens, and what is different at the end of the scene?

Summary

Develop a scenario of your play. Decide on the point of attack. You may begin by showing the audience a normal situation to introduce us to the main character, and then hit the character with a dilemma. You may begin after the world has become unbalanced—after the inciting incident—plunging the audience directly into the conflict. Include only the significant events.

In a linear structured story, the events are causal and developed chronologically. Event B cannot happen unless Event A has already happened. In a nonlinear structured story, each scene leads to the next scene, but the story is not chronological.

Rough out the order of the scenes or incidents in the play. Develop a working title. Write a list of characters' names and a brief description of each character. Choose names carefully to match or contrast with personality and avoid having names that sound similar. Use a single or unit set. Limit the number of characters to no more than six. For the scenario, divide the play into its scenes and note who is in each scene, what happens, and what is different at the end of the scene. To better understand your characters, provide answers to the following questions for each character.

1. What is the character's sign?
2. What music does he or she like?
3. What is the tackiest thing in the character's life?
4. What kind of advice would the character offer his or her best friend?
5. Where is he or she from?
6. What food reminds your character of home?
7. If this character were stranded in an isolated place, what one item would he or she want to have?
8. What is the first movie the character remembers?
9. How does the character feel about holidays?
10. What games does the character play?

Particularly for a short play, jump into the conflict quickly in the first scene to grab the audience and make them want to discover the rest of the play. The first scene should also set the tone and clarify the genre (comedy or drama).

CHAPTER

4 The Professional Format

Imagine what reading a book would be like if there was no standard for spelling. Imagine seeing a film in which no one paid any attention to the continuity—for instance, a character walks down the street wearing a coat, then suddenly comes around a corner without the coat, and then enters a store with the coat back on. Imagine seeing a play during which (totally unconnected with the play) a stagehand or a cat keeps coming on stage. Any of these distractions would take away from the story and lessen our enjoyment. The same is true in writing. A play with excessive spelling and punctuation errors or typos will distract and confuse the reader. You must learn and follow the professional format, or no actor, theatre director, agent, or producer will want to read your work.

The goal of proper manuscript form is to make it easier for literary managers, agents, actors, and directors to read. Most experienced theatre practitioners are used to seeing manuscripts that follow a professional format. A standard page layout, with at least one-inch margins on each side and at the top and bottom, is expected, and following that layout means you are conforming to traditional word counts.

Most directors and actors really don't care what font is used, as long as it easily readable. Choose a font in which the letters are simple, clear, and not too close together, such as Arial or Times New Roman, and use a 12-point size for the type. Single-space each individual character's speech and double-space between separate speeches. As for page and time estimation, you can generally assume that one page of dialogue averages one-and-a-half minutes. Long monologues may take several minutes, and really short speeches may fly by in a minute. The general length of a play—about seventy-five pages of script—is about two hours, including intermission. A one hundred-page script is two hours and forty minutes, with intermission. Today's theatre audiences expect a two-hour show or less, including intermission. A play that runs two-and-a-half or three hours is considered too long.

Format Guidelines

1. The name of the character (JOHN) speaking should be in capitals and centered above the speech. Set the tab for 3.0 inches.

2. Single-space speeches.

3. Double-space between the end of a speech and the name of the next speaker.

4. Single-space between the name of the speaker and his or her speech.

5. Put all stage directions on separate lines from the dialogue.

6. Put stage directions in parentheses. Set the tab for 1.5 inches.

7. Type the names of characters within the stage directions all in capitals (JOHN). Do the same for pronouns (HE, SHE, or THEY) referring to the characters. Do **not** put *him, her,* or *them* all in capital letters.

8. In general, avoid stage directions that tell an actor how to read a line, such as "quietly," "angrily," or "sarcastically." The line itself should convey the tone: "What in the hell do you want?" "Hi, it's nice to see you," or "Whatever it is, the answer is no." Give a clear impression of the character's state of mind.

9. Preceding the first page of the play, there are three pages without page numbers. First is a cover page with the name of the play and the author's name. Second is a page with the name of the play and the author's personal contact information in the lower-left corner: copyright date, name, address, telephone numbers, and e-mail address. Third is a page that includes the character names and descriptions, a description of the setting, and a specific listing of the time scene by scene.

10. When describing the characters, provide each character's age and note his or her relationship to others in the play. Put the character's name, all in capital letters, at the left margin. The description starts in the middle of the page, indented to 3.0 inches. For example:

MARJORIE

> The head of the household, a widow of thirty-five, with a slim figure and still youthful, long hair.

JIMMY

> Her son, a skinny fifteen-year-old, still in that rebellious stage.

11. Keep the description of the setting brief. Convey the general look of the place, the entrances, and the atmosphere. If specific items must be there, note them, but avoid highly detailed descriptions. Give enough so that the set and lighting designers have the information they need but the freedom to be creative. The following is an example from the beginning of *Betty's Summer Vacation,* by Christopher Durang:

> A summer cottage, breezy-looking, inexpensive but functional summer furniture. Pleasant, soft colors, inviting. An upstage door leads in from the front of the cottage. Inside there are a number of doors, leading off to bedrooms—four doors in a cluster, one by itself. (Some of the doors can be implied in an offstage hallway, if need

be.) There is a door off-left that leads to an outdoor deck and the outside. Primarily a living-room, but an open kitchen is also part of it. (Act 1, p. 1)

12. Note the time of the play. If there are various times, show a breakdown of the play scene by scene, and note the time of each.

13. The scene and number (SCENE 1) should be typed in all capital letters and centered at the beginning of each scene. END OF SCENE 1 should be centered at the end of the scene, again in capital letters.

14. If you are using Microsoft Word, set your tabs for 1.5 inches for stage directions, 3.0 inches for the characters' names, and 5.5 inches for act, scene, and page numbers. The pages should always be numbered consecutively.

15. On the first page of each scene under the scene designation (SCENE 1) and indented 1.5 inches, the same as the stage directions, type the words AT RISE: followed by a colon. On the same line, indented 3.0 inches, indicate who is on stage and what each character is doing at the beginning of the scene. Put this description on the top-right side of the page, single-spaced and in parentheses. If more than one line is needed, indent every line of the description to 3.0 inches.

16. Put all stage directions in parentheses and on separate lines from the dialogue. Generally, keep stage directions brief. Most stage directions are skipped over by actors and directors. They focus on the dialogue. Keep the stage directions limited to noting characters' entrances and exits and their physical actions. Do not describe characters' thoughts and feelings. Do not tell the actors how to act (sarcastically, angrily). The dialogue should convey the characters' emotions. If you feel stage directions are needed to understand what you want to show, rewrite so that it's clear in the dialogue. Stage directions should indicate action—what the characters are doing.

17. Use proper punctuation and spelling. Avoid typos, grammatical errors, and punctuation and spelling errors. Proofread several times. If you haven't mastered the rules of punctuation, grammar, and spelling, you will need to follow an English grammar guide.

18. In the following section, which shows a sample format of a scene, note that the page numbers indicate it is the first scene of a one-act play with several scenes. For a full-length play, the writer may need to include three numbers at the top-right of the page. The first is for the act, the second is for the scene, and the third is for the page number (for example, 1-1-1, 1-1-2, 1-1-3). If you are writing a one-act with no scene breaks, only the page numbers are needed (1, 2, 3, 4, 5, etc.). If there are scene breaks, the first number is for the scene and the second number is for the page (1-1, 1-2, 1-3 and 2-4, 2-5, 2-6). If there are several scenes, for Scene Two, the scene number changes to 2 but the page numbers continue to be numbered consecutively. A third scene is designated with a 3 and the pages continue to be numbered consecutively (3-7, 3-8, 3-9). Do not start over with number 1 for the first page of every scene. In all cases, no matter how long the play or how many scenes, the page numbers are consecutive, beginning at 1 on the first page of the actual script (1, 2, 3, 4, 5, etc.).

19. If you have a speech by one character (MARJORIE) that is interrupted by lengthy stage directions, particularly actions by another character, you may want to insert the character name again followed by (cont.) in parentheses to indicate that the character is continuing to speak:

MARJORIE

Stop it! No! Don't!

> (SHE tries to push him off, but RAFAEL forces her hands above her head. HE pulls up her shirt and licks her bellybutton. SHE tries to squirm out of his grasp, but HE slams her head onto the floor hard.)

MARJORIE (cont.)

Please, I have money. Just let me go. I won't say anythi—

20. If a character's line is interrupted at the end of a page, its continuance on the following page should be shown in the same way: MARJORIE (cont.). Avoid leaving a character's name isolated at the bottom of one page with the speech on the next.

21. When you have completed your play, have the manuscript bound. Copy centers can do this for you. The spiral plastic binder is the best. A three-ring binder is difficult to hold and the pages rip out. Loose pages get out of order easily, get lost, and are difficult to handle.

22. Manuscript format is different from that of a published script. When a play is published, the character's name is usually placed at the left margin, followed by the speech. Stage directions are also mixed into the speeches. The aim is to cram as much on a page as possible because that's the cheapest way to print it. That format is not acceptable for a manuscript. Manuscript format is designed to make it easy for actors to read by clearly separating the dialogue from the stage directions.

You can order online a handbook for professional manuscript format that is used by publisher Samuel French. Just go to the Samuel French website at www.samuelfrench.com and follow the directions. Feedback Theatrebooks also publishes professional playscript format guidelines. Go to www.hypernet.com/prospero.html. Both French and Dramatists Play Service have a terrific selection of plays that you can order online. Go to www.dramatists.com. Their catalogues also provide excellent examples of how to write a play synopsis that is brief and grabs the reader's attention.

Sample Scene

SAMPLE SCENE

By George Spelvin

CHARACTERS

JOHN   The Artistic Director of a professional
                            regional theatre in his mid-forties.

PAULINE   A student playwright in her early
                            twenties.

SETTING

The director's office is in an old theatre, cluttered and comfortable, with one window and a door to the outer office. The furniture which includes a table with a computer, a desk, an office chair, two arm chairs and an end table are of good quality but worn. There are colorful, framed posters on the walls, stacks of scripts, production photos and other theatrical items scattered about.

TIME

An afternoon in spring.

SCENE 1

AT RISE: (An afternoon in spring. JOHN is sitting
                            at his desk working. There is a knock at
                            the door. JOHN rises, comes around the
                            desk and opens the door. PAULINE
                            enters.)

JOHN

Come in. Welcome. So you're Mrs. Vernon's daughter. Pauline, right?
(HE offers his hand. THEY shake.)

PAULINE

Yes. Thanks for taking the time to see me, Mr. Church.

JOHN
(HE gestures for her to sit and crosses back to his chair.)
Call me, John. Your mother twisted my arm.

PAULINE

She's a strong lady.

JOHN

She's a rich supporter. So what are your questions?

PAULINE

(Opening her notebook)

Well, John, I'm taking a playwriting class—actually my second, and I'm doing a report on your theatre. What is your company's approach to producing new plays? If I decide to submit a play to your company, what do you base your decisions on whether or not to produce it?

JOHN

Given the number of submissions and the costs of mailing manuscripts, I suggest sending a letter of inquiry with 5–10 sample pages from the play first to see if we want to read it.

PAULINE

(Looks up from taking notes)

So if I just send a script, you may not even read it.

JOHN

Without being recommended by an agent, yours would go to the bottom of the pile. And it would stay there unless some intern happened to pick it up and read it on his own.

PAULINE

That's not very encouraging.

JOHN

Look, we get over 1,000 scripts a year, but we're lucky to find half a dozen of quality.

PAULINE

You're tough.

JOHN

It's a business. Listen, a good writer learns the craft, the skills needed for the job. He understands what makes a good play, understands character and conflict, and understands how to put it all together to make it clear on the page. If it's not on the page, it won't be on the stage.

PAULINE

I'll remember that.

(SHE rises, offers her hand.)

Thank you.

JOHN

(Shaking her hand)

Say "hello" to your mother.

PAULINE

I will.

(SHE exits. JOHN picks up the phone. Blackout.)

END OF SCENE 1

Summary

The goal of using a professional manuscript format is to make it easier for literary managers, agents, actors, and directors to read. Experienced theatre professionals and practitioners are used to seeing manuscripts that follow a professional format. The use of a simple and easy-to-read font, such as Times New Roman or Arial, and a standard page layout, with at least one-inch margins on each side and at the top and bottom, is expected.

Professional theatres have been inundated with so many scripts that most now require a script to be submitted by an agent. If a play is not in the proper format, many theatre directors, managers, and agents will not even read it. If you enter a play in a contest and it is not in proper form, it will also likely be discarded unread. The general feeling is that if the play follows a professional format, the author has at least some knowledge and training in theatre and playwriting. If it doesn't, the playwright is considered uninformed or ignorant. Who wants to read a script from someone who doesn't even know the proper format? Moreover, using the professional format makes it easier to see the difference between dialogue and stage directions and thus makes a script easier to read.

CHAPTER

5 Rhythm

Rhythm is a part of life, and the natural world is highly rhythmic. Consider the sounds of crickets chirping, dogs barking, a fire crackling, a fountain spraying water, and a brook babbling behind your house. Your heart beat is rhythmic. Your days have a rhythm in the ebb and flow of daily activities. One day starts off slowly with a morning coffee, speeds up as work takes over, slows down when the midafternoon "blahs" set in, and then picks up again when you have an evening play or ballgame to go to. Another day goes haywire when you drop the coffee pot on the floor, get chewed out by the boss, have a flat tire on the way home, and get some unexpected company that night just when you're ready to settle down for a quiet evening.

For a play, we telescope the events, eliminating the dull parts. It is important to plan the rhythm so that the play has variety. In this chapter, we will explore the use of rhythm, what influences rhythm, and the differences between vertical and horizontal development.

Creating Rhythm

Consider rhythm the heartbeat of your play—its pulse. The more excitement and the more action, the faster it beats. But it can't continue fast all the time because that's exhausting. Therefore, some scenes need to be fast, others need to be slow, and some need to be in between. Some should start softly and happily and end in agitation and anger. Rhythm is part of structure, and if you write with careful attention to the rhythm of your material, you should be able to come up with a play that is sound and solid.

Rhythm is not just a matter of the tempo of speech—fast or slow. It is also the variation of tempo and beat that provides emphasis. Rhythm provides emphasis by contrast. Edward Albee (cited in Bryer, 1995) notes that drama is made of two things: sound and silence.

> Each of them has its own very specific duration. Playwrights notice sound and silence, loud and soft, just as precisely as a composer does. There is a profound difference in the duration of pause between a semicolon and a period, for example, and the wise playwright knows that, in the same way that a conductor knows the difference between durations. I discovered that writing a play is very similar to

writing a piece of music. The psychological structure of a play is very similar to that of a string quartet. (p. 12)

A play is developed though a series of scenes that vary in length, rhythm, and mood. Like structure, rhythm creates a sense of forward movement. It provides the variety needed to hold audience attention and conveys a sense of progression. It also has the effect of helping us balance between advancing the action and deepening the characters. Orchestrating the rhythm of a play is in a sense like creating a symphony with words. If the last scene was a fast one, make the next one a slow one, the next one moderate with deep lows and high highs, and the next one staccato and jumpy.

What kind of scenes are slow? Perhaps a leisurely breakfast scene, a romantic love scene, or a death scene. What kind of scene is harsh, staccato, fast, and jumpy? A scene of excitement, a wacky party, people in and out, a battle, or a fight between lovers. What kind of scene has deep lows and high highs and swings from one extreme mood to another? Perhaps a manic-depressive woman waiting for her lover, a scene of deep emotion, or a scene of despair. What kind of scene is fast and light? Perhaps a comic scene, a farcical chase scene, or a comic lover's quarrel. Usually, as we move toward the climax of the play, the scenes get shorter and things happen more quickly.

Influences on Rhythm

A number of factor influence the rhythm of a play. For instance, the characters help in determining the rhythm. Rhythm of speech and movement both vary with the kind of character as well as with the attitude of that character in that situation. People also have their own individual rhythms. If we compare a waitress and a bus driver with a couple from the country club set, it becomes evident that each pair demands a different rhythm. The first couple are likely to be placid, tired, and less verbally astute while the sophisticated couple are likely to be sharp, rapid thinking, and poised. There are differences in social status, education, and income. Race/ethnicity may also affect rhythm. Different kinds of scenes call for different energy from the characters.

The locale also affects the rhythm. Each locality is different. If the play is set in the country, it is likely to be more casual and relaxed than a play set in a major city. The time of day, the season of the year, and the kind of climate or weather affect the rhythm. Two characters in bathing suits in Miami on a sunny day will have a different rhythm than two characters waiting at a bus stop in Chicago in the winter. A scene at the waterfront in thick fog will have a different feeling than a scene in full daylight. The time of day also affects the rhythm and mood. If you are alone in an isolated country house in the middle of the night, it may be frightening. Two characters in a beach house during a hurricane may be frantic.

Rhythm and mood are intertwined. The *mood* is the dominant emotional characteristic of a scene. If the mood is hard or soft or light or heavy, the rhythm of the scene will correspond. The tonal quality is varied by the lengths of lines and pauses as well as by emphasis, movement, vocal quality (the pitch of the voice, the resonance), and delivery of lines. There may be scenes of love, jealousy, argument, reconciliation, deceit, or death and so on in a play. Each of these scenes will have its own inherent mood.

What determines the rhythm has to do with both the emotional content and the lengths of the lines and speeches. A series of very short speeches, with only a word or short phrase in each, will suggest a fast rhythm. A majority of medium-length speeches (two or three lines) or short monologues with serious intentions will provide a moderate or slower rhythm. A scene with considerable conflict and a variety of tactics will contain a mixture of short and long speeches: abrupt and angry exchanges, apologies, further explanations, more anger. In short, it may have a harsh, staccato rhythm and build in intensity to a strong climax, an explosion. It is impossible to make a love scene seem real if it is rushed. Expressing deep emotion, kissing, and caressing are not fast activities. The words are less important than the responses and feelings they generate. A scene with deep emotion, such as one portraying a child dying and the anguish of the parents, may have deep lows and a slow pace. It has to be slow for the actors to capture the emotion.

Nilo Cruz, who won the Pulitzer Prize for his play *Anna and the Tropics,* pays careful attention to rhythm in his plays. His work usually features Cuban characters and poetic language, which are captured especially in the economy of words and use of rhythm in his work. Cruz met with my playwriting students the week before his award-winning play opened and noted that each scene has a different overall rhythm. "Language has to be re-created in the theatre. It is art. My plays are poetic," he told them.

The rhythm in poetry is more formal than the rhythm in prose. Poetry involves a heightened patterning of rhythm. It is more structured than prose, but most of the principles of poetry analysis are also applicable to prose. The general term for the patterning of poetic elements is *prosody,* and the name for analyzing rhythm syllable by syllable is called *scansion.* All words are made up of one or more syllables, some of which are emphasized or stressed and some of which are relatively unstressed. When these words are joined in a poetic line, their stressed and unstressed syllables work together to form an overall rhythmic pattern for the line.

Prose rhythms are usually not as heightened or as formalized as poetic rhythms, but they operate on much the same principle of variety within regularity—changes in the repetition of stressed and unstressed syllables. The rhythmic layers of prose are called *cadences.* Sentences are grouped into units of meaning, or paragraphs. A character's speech acts as a paragraph. We get a good impression of the tempo of a scene by looking at the density of the script. A mass of long speeches will be slower than an exchange of short back-and-forth dialogue. We call this *dialogue cadence.* A play is generally composed of a great variety of combinations: sequences of short speeches interspersed with monologues or longer speeches and sequences of moderate length mixed with short speeches.

The genre of a play generally dictates an overall tempo. Tragedy is usually slow, for instance. Greek and Roman tragedies are filled with long speeches and monologues, as are Elizabethan tragedies and histories and neoclassic tragedies. Romantic works from the late eighteenth and nineteenth centuries also contain long speeches, but they usually have a mixture of dramatic and comic scenes. A comedy has a faster tempo than a tragedy or drama. Farce calls for the fastest tempo. Situation comedies, comedy of manners, and romantic comedies generally provide a mixture of short and moderate speeches with perhaps a few long speeches. Comedy also calls for a heightened sense of timing in relation to the development of a joke as well as the comic physical activity. Drama generally calls for a moderate tempo.

Within each play, there is usually a mixture of serious and comic scenes. While each genre has an overall mood, there needs to be variety within it. The same tone throughout would be boring. Tennesse Williams's *A Streetcar Named Desire* is a serious drama, but it also has numerous funny moments. Blanche's scene with the newspaper boy has a poignant quality but is also funny. The early awkwardness between Mitch and Blanche has a similar quality. The squabbling neighbors, Steve and Eunice, add humor in their scenes.

Rhythm is also affected by the lengths of scenes. A series of short scenes gives a sense of rapid change and movement. Longer scenes seem slower. Speed conveys an emotional meaning. Short speeches generate quick, brisk, clipped speech and fast movement. Long speeches and monologues slow down delivery and call for slower movement. Scenes of excitement, anger, and violence move quickly. Scenes of love, tenderness, and grief move slowly. As the emotional key changes, the tempo changes.

Tempo is defined as the impression of speed, and the impression of speed depends upon audience involvement. If the actors feel, the audience will. If the actors are mechanical and race through their lines, they may speak and move quickly but the audience will find the play dull and boring. They will not be emotionally involved, and the impression of speed will be slow. Extensive exposition without conflict will also seem boring and slow.

Jump into conflict soon in every scene, and only bring in exposition when it is essential to the immediate conflict. Make sure long speeches are built in climactic order from the least important to the most important. There should be only one objective per speech. Ask yourself, What response does the character want? There should be one answer.

Horizontal and Vertical Movement

It may be useful to think in terms of two kinds of movement: horizontal and vertical. *Horizontal movement* is concerned with the action that takes the story from Point A to Point B. It is a scene that advances the plot. It is horizontal movement because it covers ground and takes us to a new point in the story.

Horizontal and vertical movement are also related to tempo. Horizontal movement is faster since it moves the plot forward. *Vertical movement* occurs when you slow the story down in order to explore character—what a character is thinking or feeling, some aspect of her back story or the past events that have shaped her. Vertical movement occurs in the scenes in which we learn something important to the story about the characters that we didn't know before. Instead of moving forward, you go deeper. It is vertical movement because it digs into the roots of the character.

Most melodramas and certainly many action movies have a lot of horizontal movement—amazing plot revelations, people getting killed, explosions, car chases, and so on—but not much vertical movement. In other words, plot is their primary focus. Anton Chekhov's plays, in contrast, have relatively little horizontal movement and primarily vertical movement—characters bewailing their plight or moping and not really able to do anything about it. As you watch *The Cherry Orchard*, it sometimes feels like little is happening, although by the end of the play, you may find it amazing how much ground has been covered.

Both kinds of movement are needed. If a play is all horizontal movement, its relentlessness will burn an audience out, and they may not care much about the characters anyway. Plays that emphasize plot over all else fall into this category. However, if a play is all vertical movement, it will put the audience to sleep.

You should be conscious of the movement of each scene. It may mean following a scene that drives the plot forward with one that explores character. It may mean knowing that if you've had three horizontal scenes in a row, then it's time for a vertical one. It's also important to vary the lengths of the scenes. It may mean allowing for both kinds of movement within a single scene. There is a pure theatrical pleasure to be drawn from simply contrasting the two—following a fast scene with a slow one or following a scene set in dazzling sunlight with one set in shadowy moonlight.

Was the last scene you wrote primarily horizontal or vertical? Does the scene present your protagonist with a new problem, or does it reveal something genuinely significant about him? Is the beginning of the scene positive or negative? What about the ending? Pay attention to positive and negative values at the beginning and end of scenes. Some scenes start on a positive note and end on a negative note. Some start negative and end positive. You may also begin and end on a negative note or begin and end on a positive note. If you are focused on varying the rhythms of the scenes, varying the movement from horizontal to vertical, you should also vary the positives and negatives.

EXERCISE 8

Beginning Level   Choose one of the following:

A. Write a continuous scene with two sequences, one horizontal and one vertical, in which Character A tries to learn a secret from Character B's past. The horizontal scene should be fast, the lines should be short, and emotion should run high. The conflict should build to a point at which Character B finally makes a confession, a surprise revelation, and the scene becomes vertical.

   B.   Write a continuous scene in three parts: moderate, slow, and fast. What does
        the protagonist want? Make sure long speeches are built from the least
        important to the most important. Use only one idea per speech. Make the
        mood different in each.

Intermediate Level   Choose one of the following:

   C.   Write a continuous scene in four parts, each with a different rhythm, about a
        character who breaks the rules. Listen to four different kinds of music. Write
        one section slow, lyrical, and gently flowing like a brook. Then write a harsh,
        staccato, fast, jumpy sequence, like white water rushing through a canyon
        around turns and over rocks. Next write a moderate part, with deep lows and
        high highs, like a river in the mountains flowing over a rocky falls into a deep
        pool. End with a light, fast sequence, like water bouncing and skipping down
        a hill. The reader should be able to clearly recognize the changes among the
        four parts.
   D.   Write a continuous scene with a horizontal conflict section and then a vertical
        section. Character A wants information Character B has not shared about an
        event. Character B refuses to divulge it. Character A uses various tactics to
        drag it out of Character B. Build the scene so that the rhythm begins slowly,
        increases to a faster and faster rhythm, reaches an emotional explosion, and
        then slows down for a deep vertical exploration. Start the scene on a positive
        note and end it on a negative one.

Advanced Level   Choose one of the following:

   E.   Write a comic romantic scene with three or four characters. Vary the rhythm
        within the scene to include a section with short speeches and a lot of physical
        activity, a slow love scene, and a moderate section. Look at one of Molière's
        plays for ideas. What sound effects, music, or props may be helpful?
   F.   Write three short scenes in which Character A is lying, cheating, and stealing;
        Character B is trying to catch her; and Character C believes Character A and
        supports her. The first scene should begin on a negative note and end on a
        negative note. The second should begin on a positive note and end with a
        negative value. The third scene should begin on a negative note and end on
        a positive one.

Summary

A play is developed though a series of scenes that vary in rhythm, length, and
mood. Rhythm provides the variety needed to hold audience attention and conveys a sense of progression. It also has the effect of maintaining a balance between
advancing the action and deepening the characters. A playwright needs to plan the
rhythm of a scene, alternating among fast, slow, and moderate.

What determines the rhythm has to do with both the emotional content and the lengths of the lines and speeches. A series of very short speeches will suggest a fast rhythm. Longer speeches or monologues with serious intentions will make the rhythm of a scene moderate or slow. A scene with considerable conflict, a variety of tactics, and a mixture of short and long speeches—abrupt and angry exchanges and apologies and further explanations—may bring a series of highs and lows or a staccato rhythm. A love scene needs to be slow to be believable. Expressing deep emotion, such as love or grief, cannot be done quickly. Words are less important than the responses and feelings they generate.

Horizontal action is concerned with moving the story from Point A to Point B. It occurs in a scene that advances the action. It's horizontal movement because it covers ground and takes us to a new point in the story. Vertical action occurs when the playwright slows the story down in order to explore its depth—what the characters are thinking or feeling or their back stories. Vertical scenes tell us something important about the story or about the characters that we didn't know before.

CHAPTER

6 Plot

The term *plot* is defined as the selection and arrangement of incidents in the story. It is the plan of the action, from the initial inciting action to the final resolution. *To plot* means to choose. Determining the structure of the plot means making choices of what to include and what to exclude. As the playwright imagines a character, he must select from the significant events in the character's life. In this chapter, we will explore the elements of plot; kinds of plots; the proper balance of a beginning, middle, and end; obstacles; the essential scene; common plot problems and advice for the playwright; and subtext.

Arranging the Incidents

The selection and arrangement of incidents in the story may not be completely clear to a writer until the first draft of a play has been completed. Regardless, she must begin with some kind of plan for the action, from start to finish, even if that changes during the process of writing.

The world wants a terrific story. Who are these characters? What do they want? Who is the protagonist? What are the forces against her? If the story isn't terrific, it doesn't matter how beautifully it has been written. The dialogue may be clever, the format perfect, and every comma in its place, but if the story is banal or flawed, the audience will not care about it. If you have a great idea and can't tell it well, no one will care no matter how profound it is. However, if it is a dynamite story that drives to a first-act climax, accelerates to a powerful second-act climax, and has a resolution of enthralling beauty, people will care. They will be engaged.

Stories are metaphors for life. Stories are like life lifted to a poetic level. They must rise above the specific. An understanding of the artform, the craft, is needed to tell a story well. As you imagine a character, you must select meaningful and significant events from the character's life and figure out how to arrange them into a strategic sequence to express and arouse emotions—to mean something.

There is no magic formula for organizing the actions into a carefully designed order that best fits the playwright's purpose. In today's theatre, the pattern does not necessarily mean telling the story in a straightforward manner. Theatre is eclectic and it uses forms, images, techniques, and patterns from all areas of life and history. There are many plays not written in chronological order that save the main revelation for the end, even if the event happened long ago. In *Equus,* by Peter Shaffer, a psychiatrist seeks to help a boy who blinded six horses. The psychiatrist's personal story and struggle moves forward in chronological order, while that of his patient, Alan Strang, is told in flashbacks. What caused Alan to blind the horses is not revealed until the final scene. A similar approach is used in *How I Learned to Drive,* by Paula Vogel, and *Agnes of God,* by John Pielmeier. The playwright's job is to craft the events in a play into the specific order best suited for the needs of the story, and only the playwright can decide what that is. For instance, in one play, X could happen and then Y and then Z. The same story with the same characters could be developed in another play with a different approach, and the order might be Z and then Y and then X.

Forming the Plot

There is no single approach to play construction. A great deal of individuality is found in play structures. Yet no playwright should conclude he has absolute freedom. The standard diagram of *plot* shows preparation, rising action, climax, falling action, and denouement. *Preparation* establishes the situations and indicates the coming problem. The *rising action,* starting with the point of attack, consists of discoveries and complications. The *climax* is the major confrontation scene and the highest point of tension. The *falling action* is the *denouement* or the resolution of the problems or conflicts. It's the cleaning up after the axe has cut off the head.

A play doesn't rigidly march forward to an insistent drummer or move in a straight line toward its goal. Playwrights often deliberately relax the tensions in order to be able to start up again. They use both vertical and horizontal movement. Some plays start at the beginning of the story. Others begin just before the climax. The point of attack may vary.

Plot is the expression of the playwright's philosophical tenets, just as character and thought are. In *Equus,* author Peter Shaffer created a psychiatrist who has led a dull, conservative life. He has a great affinity for the heroes of Greek legends, but he has never had the kind of passion in his life that he desires. He sees in Alan a boy who lives a passionate existence, and he struggles with the philosophical question of whether it is right for him to take that away from Alan. In *How I Learned to Drive,* author Paula Vogel did not want to focus on the graphic details of sexual abuse, or on the heroine as victim. She wanted to tell a story about a woman who was hurt by the ones who loved her and how that made her strong.

Every event means change. If you go into a building and the streets are dry and later come out and see puddles of water, you know something happened. It rained. However, meaningful change must happen *to* someone. A *story event* is a meaningful change in the life of a character expressed by the writer in terms of values—right or wrong, good or evil, just or unjust. Moreover, a play must illuminate one central dramatic event. The full-length play may have a dozen complications. The one-act will have perhaps only three to six. The ten-minute play will likely have only one. All need to have one central action.

The plot shows the play's thoughts. The playwright uses the plot to lead the audience to conclusions. The plot selects and emphasizes points, thereby stressing the play's meaning and it leads to the ultimate climax, which helps the playwright draw the audience's attention to the play's subject and theme. In David Auburn's play *Proof*, Catherine is introduced in the opening scene talking to her dead father—a brilliant mathematician who went insane. This scene sets up the main question: Since she inherited some of his genius, did she also inherit his insanity? In the second scene, we meet Hal, one of the father's former students, who has been looking through the materials in the mathematician's office. Catherine becomes suspicious and questions him about stealing one of her father's notebooks. Hal denies it and convinces us and Catherine that he is innocent. But when she picks up his jacket to give to him as he's leaving, a notebook falls on to the floor. We are shocked. The audience gasps. The playwright has led us to one conclusion and then given us the unexpected. When this kind of twist really works, it is thrilling. Later, after Hal and Catherine have spent the night together and she has grown to trust him, she gives him the key to a drawer in her father's desk. He finds a notebook with an amazing original proof. The author leads us to believe it was written by her father, but at the end of the first act, Catherine announces that she wrote the proof. It is another unexpected but well-prepared twist and further develops the notion that she inherited her father's genius.

A play is a series of meetings between people. To plot means to plan those meetings, arranging them to be happy or disastrous encounters and making them significant. Plot brings characters to life and illustrates their thoughts by showing them in action. Plot provides actions and reactions that reveal the characters under pressure and give us, the audience, an understanding of what they do and why. The total of the protagonist's and the antagonist's behaviors illustrates the play's theme.

The human who must cope with the unexpected crisis will have to face his or her own psyche while dealing with the situation. Each new challenge illuminates new aspects of personality. Plot provides these constant changes through conflict. Without conflict, there is no dramatic action. Plot creates, interacts with, and results from character. It develops suspense about whether the central character will achieve his goal—to live or die, find the truth, get the girl.

Kinds of Plots

A plot can be considered a series of actions that may be explained by a stimulus/response diagram. A *stimulus* causes a *response*, which itself becomes a stimulus, which causes a response, and so on. For example, Person A insults Person B, B responds by slapping A, A responds by hiding behind a chair, B grabs the chair away, and so forth. Plot provides surprise, sudden turns, new events, and unexpected twists. Character A lunges at B, pulling him to the floor. Character B suddenly stops all resistance and lies passively on the floor. The new event strikes Character A by surprise, and new aspects of the person may be seen as a result.

A play can be seen as a series of scenes building toward a final confrontation. Drama requires rising action; that is, increases in suspense and tensions. Each new event hurls the play forward.

Each of the following sections describes a specific kind of plot and how best to use it.

Action Plot.   In the action plot, the focus is on what happens next, with a lot of suspense and some surprises. The plot has the protagonist on a mission to solve a problem, discover a murderer, or get revenge. *Rumors, The Count of Monte Cristo,* and *The Desperate Hours* all fall within this category. *Rumors* is one of Neil Simon's active farces. *The Count of Monte Cristo,* by Charles Fletcher, is an action melodrama in which the Count seeks revenge for the injustice he has suffered. *The Desperate Hours,* by Joseph Hayes, is about several criminals who break into a home and hold a family hostage.

Thriller Plot.   Most thrillers are really puzzles that must be solved by the characters. Audiences experience intense identification with the main characters of thrillers. Audiences of puzzle stories demand constant novelty—old solutions will not do.

Deathtrap, by Ira Levin, is an ingeniously constructed play blending thrills and laughter. The play focuses on Sidney Bruhl, a successful writer of Broadway thrillers, who is suffering a "dry spell" and a shortage of funds. When he receives a script from a student in his seminar, Sidney immediately recognizes its great potential. Sidney's plan, which he devises with his wife's help, is to offer to collaborate with the student, an idea which the younger man quickly accepts. Thereafter, the suspense mounts as the plot twists and turns and continues to provide sudden shocks until the very last moment.

Wait Until Dark, by Frederick Knott, is a thriller about a blind woman who has a doll that some drug dealers want. The last scene, in which one of the drug dealers tries to kill her, is a very heart-in-your-throat, suspenseful, and scary scene. The tension continues to mount as the main character is isolated from help. These plays generally take place in a short space of time, such as a weekend.

Victim Plot.   The victim plot features a sympathetic protagonist who undergoes a series of misfortunes through no fault of her own. This is basically a plot of suffering, as shown in plays such as *Wings,* by Arthur Kopit, and *Whose Life Is It Anyway?* by Brian Clark. *Wings* explores the world through the perception of a woman who has had a stroke. *Whose Life Is It Anyway?* is about a sculptor who is paralyzed and wants to be allowed to die. Both plays show victims, often struggling with private anguish, in search of remedies.

Tragic Plot.   In the tragic plot, there is a sympathetic protagonist who takes a stand for what she believes. These protagonists cause their own downfalls but also take responsibility for their actions and for what they have caused. These heroes suffer misfortune because of errors in judgment or refusals to compromise. On finally learning of the error and recognizing her faults, the protagonist makes the morally right choice. Death may be inevitable, but the protagonist saves her soul. The tragic plot is shown in *Oedipus the King* and *Antigone,* both by Sophocles, and in *A Man for All Seasons,* by Robert Bolt.

Dilemma Plot.   The dilemma plot concerns divided interests or loyalties. The trick is to make the choices really difficult and to keep the reader from knowing in advance what your character's decision will be. In a dilemma plot, the ending comes when the central character makes up her mind about something important and difficult. In *Antigone,* the title character must decide whether to follow her uncle's decree or to bury her brother and be put to death. In *A Doll's House,* by Henrik Ibsen, Nora must make up her mind to stay with a husband she no longer loves or to go out on her own alone without her children.

Victory Plot.   The victory plot gives us a situation in which the protagonist wins or loses. The sympathetic central character faces a difficult problem. His attempts to resolve it fail and make the situation more desperate. The character then faces the major crisis—his last chance to win. The successful resolution must be brought about by the central character's own courage, ingenuity, and other qualities.

In *Rain,* by John Colton, which was adapted from a story by W. Somerset Maugham, the central character, Sadie Thompson, is a raucous trollop who is forced by quarantine to stay over at Pago Pago on her way home from Honolulu. There she is confronted by the fire-and-brimstone missionary, Mr. Davidson, who threatens to make trouble for the governor unless he deports her to the mainland, where a prison sentence awaits her. Sadie first tries to appeal to the governor and to Dr. Macphail. When these attempts fail, she gives in to Mr. Davidson and allows him to save her soul. She becomes a changed woman until Davidson has sex with her and then hangs himself in remorse. The next day, Sadie is dressed and made up in her old manner, and her raucous laughter rings out again. She has won. Note that the ending we are led to expect—Sadie reformed and going off to jail to repent for her sins—would be disappointing. The conflict that begins the story is only a sham, a work of misdirection. What we are waiting for is the surprise ending.

Most victory plots are built around some kind of conflict or competition about which the outcome is in doubt. The beginning of the story sets forth the terms of the competition; the middle is the contest itself; the ending is the outcome. If all stories followed this formula, however, they would be unbearably predictable. In practice, what usually happens is that the author uses the conflict structure to *misdirect* the reader. The real meaning of the story turns out to be something altogether different. Victory plots can be seen in such musicals as *The Full Monty,* by Terrence McNally, *Damn Yankees,* by George Abbott and Douglas Wallop, and

Hairspray, by Mark O'Donnell, Thomas Meeham, Marc Shaiman, and Scott Wittman.

Punitive Plot.   The antihero, hero/villain, or unsympathetic protagonist whose quest is not admirable is the focus of the punitive plot. As the antihero sets forth an immoral scheme, we can admire his rise above the fools around him. But when this character succeeds in victimizing truly good people as well, we feel shock and outrage. In the end, we feel a sense of vindication when the antihero reaches his ultimate downfall. This protagonist deserves his misfortune and suffering. We may admire the character's intellect or strength or audacity, but we are glad he gets it in the end. Iago in Shakespeare's *Othello* fits this description. Other plays in this category include *Amadeus,* by Peter Shaffer, *Killer Joe,* by Tracey Letts, *Les Liaisons Dangereuses,* by Christopher Hampton, *Hedda Gabler,* by Henrik Ibsen, *The Little Foxes,* by Lillian Hellman, *Tartuffe,* by Moliére, and *Richard III,* by Shakespeare.

Revelation Plot.   The revelation plot means the exposure of something previously hidden. In this plot, there is rising tension because each new event narrows down the choices and because we know that we are coming closer to the revelation of the truth and an understanding of the meaning. Martin McDonaugh's *The Beauty Queen of Leenane,* for example, tells the darkly comic tale of Maureen Folan, a plain and lonely woman in her forties, and Mag, her manipulative aging mother, whose interference in Maureen's chance of a loving relationship sets in motion a train of events that leads inexorably toward the play's terrifying end. Misled to believe that the mother is the villain, we have a revelation about Maureen and a surprising new understanding in the final scene.

Admiration Plot.   The admiration plot shows us a sympathetic hero who may suffer the loss of fortune or job or some other material matter, but he gains in the area of reputation and honor because of his integrity. The sympathetic protagonist suffers but overcomes the obstacles through his determination, strength of character and morally right action. Finally, he experiences a change for the better. *Mister Roberts,* by Thomas Heggan and Joshua Logan, *The Normal Heart,* by Larry Kramer, and *The Miracle Worker,* by William Gibson, provide us with admirable heroes and heroines.

Education Plot.   The education plot provides us with a sympathetic protagonist whose life, beliefs, attitudes, and insights are changed for the better through education. The protagonist starts out as inadequate and grows up. This inadequacy may be because of ignorance or naiveté, as in *Born Yesterday,* by Garcin Kanin, *Orphans,* by Lyle Kessler, *My Fair Lady,* by Lerner and Loewe, and *Educating Rita,* by Willy Russell. Or it may be more sophisticated, with the protagonist going through a series of disillusioning experiences that make him or her cynical or fatalistic, as in *All the King's Men,* by Robert Penn Warren, and *Death and the Maiden,* by Ariel Dorfman.

Born Yesterday, *performed at Idaho State University. Directed by Ron Hansen, Set and Lighting Design by J. David Blatt, Costume Design by Sonja Nelson.*

Maturing Plot.   The protagonist causes his or her own misery because of a mistaken view but eventually sees the light. He or she may be a slacker—shiftless and unfocused—or wrongheaded and stubborn. Some means must be devised to change the character's thoughts and beliefs. This often involves a coming-of-age story. We long for the protagonist to choose the right course of action, and we are satisfied in the end when she does. *Butterflies Are Free*, by Leonard Gershe, *Extremities*, by William Mastrosimone, *A Doll's House*, by Henrik Ibsen, *Ah, Wilderness!* by Eugene O'Neill, and *Da*, by Hugh Leonard, all provide us with maturing protagonists.

Reform Plot.   The reform plot shows us a protagonist who knows he is doing wrong but is too weak to do the right thing. As this character is faced with exposure, he must then choose an alternative course of action. Once we see through the character's mask, we feel indignation and anger. We want him to stop deceiving others and do what is right. These protagonists eventually face the truth and reform their ways. *All My Sons*, by Arthur Miller, *Fences*, by Auqust Wilson, and *Homesteaders*, by Nina Shengold, show us men who deceive but who face the truth in the end.

Testing Plot.   The testing plot puts the sympathetic protagonist into a position whereby she is pressured to compromise or surrender her moral principles. The character has to choose between keeping her principles or accepting the bribe offered—whether it means her life, reputation, money, or power. The play focuses on the question of whether or not the protagonist will give in. By refusing to compromise, the protagonist places herself and perhaps others in danger. The character may even risk death. However, giving in will mean losing her self-respect and our respect, as well. Plays such as *Kit Marlowe,* by David Grimm, *A Man for All Seasons,* by Robert Bolt, and *Becket,* by Jean Anovith, show us characters who face such tests and confirm that our faith in them is justified.

Degeneration/Regeneration Plot.   The degeneration plot shows a good person, one we can admire for his principles and actions. That character is then subjected to a crucial loss that results in complete disillusionment. He eventually reaches the bottom and must choose between trying to pick up the threads of his life and starting over or just giving up. If the character chooses to start over, we have the regeneration plot. This is the plot of the typical Hollywood biography. On stage, we see elements of this in Tennessee Williams's *Sweet Bird of Youth* and *Night of the Iguana,* and Neil Simon's *The Gingerbread Lady.*

Disillusionment Plot.   The disillusionment plot is the opposite of the education plot: We begin with a sympathetic protagonist who, after being subjected to some kind of loss, threat, or trial, loses faith completely. These plays show such characters left at the bottom—suspended, lost, incapable of dealing with reality, and unable to start over. We see figures such as these in Eugene O'Neill's *The Iceman Cometh,* Maxim Gorky's *Lower Depths,* Gerhart Hauptmann's *The Weavers,* and August Strindberg's *Miss Julie.*

Pivotal Plot.   This plot shows us generally estranged family members forced into interpersonal conflict at an emotionally sensitive event, such as a wedding or a funeral. The action occurs in a limited space that forces the characters to deal with each other. The time of the conflict is telescoped into a single day or a weekend, and the intensity of emotions demands that the characters resolve their discord quickly. These characters are the most vulnerable, dimensional, and human because their conflicts are like those experienced by ordinary audience members. Lorraine Hansberry's *A Raisin in the Sun,* Tennessee Williams's *The Glass Menagerie,* and Robert Harling's *Steel Magnolias* are examples.

These plot forms are not rigid little boxes into which every play must be crammed; rather, they are in a sense ideal categories. In actual practice, these forms are mixed in all kinds of ways. A play may be partly one of resolution, partly one of solution, and partly one of admiration. When you understand the simple forms, you can mix and combine them to make more sophisticated ones. There is no end to the plays that can be written, because the possible combinations of old forms will never be exhausted and because good writers keep on inventing new forms.

Balancing the Beginning, Middle, and End

A proper balance of beginning, middle, and end is essential. The beginning needs to grab our attention, develop our interest. It needs to be as neat and effective as you can make it. Start in the middle of an ongoing action. Jump into a conflict. Exposition and other elements can follow.

A play that has little or no beginning seldom brings the audience around to care about the action and the characters. There's just not enough information about the past and the present, about the inciting incident, or about the characters. No sense of urgency has been established. The solution is to start with a conflict and then work to make us care about the characters.

A play with too much beginning seems to start and start and start but never go anywhere. There is a feeling of wheels spinning. In this case, the playwright needs to consider cutting away everything that precedes the beginning of the action—that is, everything that comes before the first point of conflict.

The beginning must do the following:

1. Hook the audience's interest.
2. Imply forthcoming events of interest via foreshadowing.
3. Establish the inciting incident that starts the whole problem.
4. Indicate the mood of the play, and the genre—comedy, tragedy, or drama.
5. Establish the significant characters either by bringing them on stage or by implying their presence.
6. Establish essential relationships between the characters.
7. Indicate significant information about the time and place.
8. Start the action.

Missing from this list is *exposition*. It is better to get the action going first and then bring in essential background details, as needed. The inciting incident is usually not a part of the play but rather an event that has taken place before the play begins. In Euripides' *Medea*, the inciting incident is Jason's betrayal of his wife, Medea, by having an adulterous relationship with Kreon's daughter. In Edward Albee's *The Goat or Who is Silvia?* the inciting incident is Martin's affair with a goat. Both incidents occur before the plays begin. Both plays begin when the protagonists decide to take action.

The middle is the heart of the play and contains the movements of the plot and the character developments. It is the longest of the three parts. It goes up and down like a seesaw, reversing directions as characters respond to new conflicts. It is active with changes, complications, and "dragons" that the protagonist must slay. The protagonist works to achieve her goal while the antagonist puts up obstacles. There are complications and discoveries, victories and defeats, twists and reversals. Hopes are dashed and then given new life. Through it all, the play's basic line of conflict is increased. The complication is an obstacle, twist, reversal, discovery, or crisis—any new force that changes the direction of the play's action. A play with many and frequent complications will be one that generates excitement. A complication may come from inside the character or the external world.

The end of a play should not be used to deliver a message. If a play contains a message, it has to be integral to the overall action. Be very careful about the "author's spokesman's curtain speech." The playwright's meaning should be implied, not told. The end should answer the final questions. This doesn't mean that it only fulfills expectations. The complex play may lead us to expect one ending but then provide an unexpected twist that gives us a different but still very satisfying ending. This may also lead the playwright to end the play with a new question for the audience to ponder. For example, what happens to Nora after the end of Ibsen's *A Doll's House?*

Avoid the O. Henry trick ending that comes out of nowhere and is not really satisfactory. This gimmick is out of fashion and unpopular because it depends on awkward contrivances. O. Henry wrote hundreds of such stories. An example is his story of the widowed bakery owner who begins to have romantic feelings about a shabby man who comes in every day to buy a loaf of stale bread. Impulsively, she cuts a loaf open and conceals a pat of butter in it to surprise him. He later comes back in a rage because he is an architect who uses stale bread to erase pencil lines from his drawings, and she has just ruined six months' work. Any play, especially a mystery, may make this error if the ending isn't carefully prepared. We want to be surprised, but the surprise must be realistic and acceptable, completely within the scope of the characters, and motivated.

Also avoid the cliff-hanger. It may work in a kind of spoof to have every scene until the last one end with a cliff-hanger, but the final scene must not leave us hanging. A play needs a satisfactory resolution. You cannot have a play that centers on a man on a ledge about to jump and not let us know if he jumps or not.

Finally, don't end the play with the central question unanswered—letting the audience members make up their own mind. You need to make the decision and write the ending. Otherwise, it will not satisfy an audience.

Obstacles

An *obstacle* is something that stands in the protagonist's way. There is a major obstacle in the play and an obstacle in every act, every scene, and every beat. The antagonist blocks what the protagonist is pursuing, creating unpredictability, which excites the audience to participate mentally. Action requires obstacles to sustain attention. Obstacles challenge the protagonist to intensify his commitment and strengthen his will to succeed.

Ask the question, What character is stopping the protagonist in each scene? Not all obstacles have to be negative. Young lovers might have different attitudes and beliefs about sex before marriage. Character A may desire to have sex, but Character B may want to wait until marriage. If each character refuses to compromise, there is a strong obstacle and suspense. The audience wants to know what will happen. What will each character do to win? How far will he or she go? Will refusing to change result in a broken relationship?

The Essential Scene

No matter what the plot, each play must build to an essential scene—a major confrontation between the protagonist and the antagonist that decides whether the protagonist will win or lose. This is the scene that the audience expects. This is the scene they look forward to, wondering what the clash will be like and what the possibilities are.

In Ibsen's *Hedda Gabler*, the essential scene is between Hedda and Lovborg. She lies to him about the manuscript, gives him a dueling pistol, and orders him to use it. Everything after that scene shows the effects. In the last act, Judge Brack returns with the news that Lovborg is dead and that Hedda's pistol was found on him. Hedda also learns that Lovborg didn't die beautifully. Judge Brack's knowledge gives him power over Hedda. She realizes, "Everything I touch becomes ludicrous and despicable!—Its like a curse" (p. 424). In the end, she takes the remaining pistol and shoots herself. In Pielmeier's *Agnes of God*, the essential scene is the one in which we learn the truth about Agnes and the baby. In *Hairspray*, by O'Donnell, Meehan, Shalman, and Wittman, it is the scene in which Tracy Turnblad wins the contest.

Common Plot Problems

1. *The story is confusing.* CAUSE: Too many characters, too many scenes, no clear central action. The author has not found a way to focus the narrative on the central character or has not decided who the central character is. SOLUTION: Rewrite, focusing on the central character and his objective and the antagonist responsible for the obstacles. Increase the stakes—what the central character has to lose in each scene.

2. *Whose story is it?* The protagonist is passive, undermotivated, and not truly causing the action to unfold. CAUSE: This is a character problem, often the result of having a victim-type protagonist that bad things happen to, a passive protagonist who witnesses the plot events but doesn't participate, or a bumbling protagonist who acts stupidly without learning from her mistakes. SOLUTION: The central character doesn't have to be likeable or without faults, but she does have to be motivated to act and those actions should drive the plot. Make a list of the major plot events, and note the protagonist's contribution to each one. Does each action contribute to a change?

3. *The story line doesn't go anywhere.* The central character's goal isn't clear. CAUSE: The author started writing the story without any clear idea of its direction. SOLUTION: Give the central character a stronger motivation and make things more difficult. Make the central character's goal clear and more important, and strengthen the antagonist. Keep us uncertain about who will win in the end. Rewrite without looking at the old version.

4. *The plot structure looks complete, but the story seems pointless.* The play doesn't really have anything to say. CAUSE: The author has not carefully thought out what the theme is—what the play adds up to or shows. He has forgotten that we must care about the chief characters and what happens to them. Even when the plot is important, the characters are more important. SOLUTION: Go back to characters and build from there. Make the stakes higher. Make the characters' goals more important. Make the antagonist stronger. Show the main character's passion and a great struggle. Then the overall meaning will be clear.

5. *The ending isn't satisfying.* CAUSE: The author didn't plan ahead for the ending, hoping something would turn up, and in despair tacked on a weak, irrelevant, or illogical ending. The ending may also be disappointing because it is obvious and expected and the author failed to make the obstacles strong enough to make the outcome a question. SOLUTION: It is useless to treat the ending by itself; any tacked-on ending will seem tacked-on. Go back to the opening situation and work through the entire play, focusing on the central action.

6. *The story doesn't work because of structural weaknesses.* CAUSE: There may be any of several problems here. The protagonist is hidden and the audience can't tell whose story it is. There are scenes with supporting characters that have nothing to do with the major action. The protagonist doesn't have much to do with the main plot, or this person would never do what the plot requires him to do. The climaxes are rushed and the scenes not fully developed. SOLUTION: Such problems may derive from a misunderstanding of the purpose of structure. It's not a prison, chaining you to a formula; rather, it's a map to guide you. Learning structure can teach you when to modify it and when to branch out on your own. What is the major plot question? Focus all events that lead to the answer on the actions of the protagonist.

7. *The author avoids conflict in the writing.* Conflict is the fuel that powers the plot and forces the characters into action. Without it, you might have a nice slice-of-life portrait or a great character sketch, but you won't really have a dramatic play. CAUSE: Conflict in real life is often unpleasant, and some writers avoid it in their plotting as they avoid it in their lives. But just as we need discipline to grow, characters need adversity to change. And drama is about change. SOLUTION: You must provide conflict for your characters so that they will be forced to change. Linking conflict to character change will revitalize your story and avoid the problems of serial conflict or incoherent conflict, in which the conflict has nothing to do with who this character is or what she needs.

8. *There is a cast of thousands.* Secondary characters are distinguished from major characters because they make things happen in the plot, but their own conflicts and issues are not part of the story. Every secondary character with a personal story dilutes the impact of the major character's journey. CAUSE: Tracking secondary characters' lives and loves is a waste of time and confuses the audience in a protagonist-centered plot. SOLUTION: Avoid long speeches by secondary characters that dwell on their problems, not the protagonist's.

9. *The play moves too slowly.* There are too many cause-and-effect types of events happening in the play, or the scenes are too long, providing too much information. CAUSE: The author is trying to include too much in the story. SOLUTION: Selection is the key. What events are essential? What are the turning points? Can you raise the stakes and strengthen the major conflict? Are all the events of the plot related causally—that is, does the hiding of the gun in Act One set up the escape of the imprisoned protagonist in Act Two? Make sure every scene has at least one event that affects the main plot. Do some major editing.

10. *The plot has too many coincidences and isn't believable.* CAUSE: Drama is about cause and effect, and there's no cause and effect when the central elements of the plot happen by coincidence. Look at the chain of events. What would not likely happen unless you, the author, made it happen? How likely is it that your lawyer protagonist would just happen to get the stolen car case of the man he believes was responsible for the hit-and-run killing of his daughter? Not very. SOLUTION: Get rid of coincidence. Make events happen because of characters' decisions and actions. The lawyer doesn't just happen to get the case; he goes after it, determined to avenge his daughter's death. Now the conflict is not an accident but the result of the lawyer's need for vengeance. One primary purpose of the plot is to force the protagonist to change, usually by recognizing and overcoming some internal conflict. Know your character, and you will figure out your plot.

11. *The middle of the play drags.* The purpose of the middle scenes isn't clear. CAUSE: These scenes don't show a rising conflict, in which the protagonist is tested up to or beyond the limits of her ability. They don't develop the internal and external conflicts that influence the protagonist's actions. They don't set up the great crisis, climax, and resolution that will bring the play to an end. SOLUTION: Make the stakes higher. Challenge the protagonist more. What events can make her internal conflict impossible to ignore any longer? How can that internal conflict impede her progress toward the goal? Make the antagonist stronger and the obstacles bigger.

12. *The beginning is boring and takes too long.* CAUSE: You have too much exposition in the setup, and this will cause you to lose most of your audience. This is the age of television and film, when audiences don't like to wait and expect the visual picture to change every twenty seconds. SOLUTION: Start where the protagonist's problem starts, or just before that, and feed in the back story later. Start the conflict immediately. Don't tell too much too soon about the character's past.

EXERCISE 9

Beginning Level   Choose one of the following:

   A. Using the action plot, write a three-person scene with a beginning, middle, and end that builds to a climax. Have the protagonist on a mission to solve a problem, discover a secret, or get revenge. Lead the protagonist and the audience to expect one thing, and then provide a twist that hits both with a surprise, as David Auburn does in *Proof.*

B. Using the pivotal plot, write a four-person comic scene with a beginning, middle, and end that builds to an unexpected climax. Show estranged family members forced into interpersonal conflict at an event such as a wedding or a funeral. The action should occur in a limited space that forces the characters to deal with each other. Lead Character A and the audience to expect one thing, and then provide a surprising but logical twist at the end.

Intermediate Level   Choose one of the following:

C. Use the education plot and write a short scene that builds to an unexpected climax. Lead the audience to expect one thing, and then provide a twist that presents them with something different. Provide a sympathetic protagonist whose life, beliefs, attitudes, and insights change the teacher.

D. Write a scene in which Character A experiences a terrifying event. Perhaps he is confronted by an abusive father or spouse. Perhaps he comes home because of the illness and imminent death of a parent, but his estranged sister there is bipolar and in an altered reality. Perhaps the character's new roommate is psychotic and wears his clothes, takes on his identity, and uses his checkbook. Thrust your protagonist into an extreme situation. The antagonist is morally indifferent, creates a climate of fear, and is willing to kill.

Advanced Level   Choose one of the following:

E. Write a comedic scene in which adults act like children because of leaping to a wrong conclusion—a basic misunderstanding dealt with irrationally. The characters can get away with anything that isn't immoral. Because of the exaggeration of the story, the unreality of the misunderstanding cannot exist forever, so the time is frenetic and intense.

F. Write a scene with a revelation plot that exposes something previously hidden between two people once very close but now alienated. In this plot, the tension should rise because each new event narrows down the choices and because we know that we are coming closer to the revelation of the truth. Use exposition as a weapon.

Other Tips

1. *Write about something you care about, something that touches your heart.* There must be conflict. Conflict is essential to drama. Drama is the art of the showdown. Force must be opposed by force, person by person (or group), desire by desire. Let there be emotions. People need to care in your play. People feel strongly, whether it is love or hate, happiness or despair. If you are able to make them emotional, then your characters will more likely be active and do something. A play that succeeds on an intellectual level but doesn't engage us emotionally may be admired but it will not be loved.

2. *Limit the number of characters.* The usual play has from three to five characters. Three is a good number to start with, especially for a short play. Most theatres look for small-cast shows. Very few theatres today can afford to produce large-cast shows, unless they are musicals. Avoid utilitarian characters who make minor announcements and deliver packages or telegrams. All the characters must be essential to the basic action.

3. *Keep all your characters on stage as long as you can.* Too often, a scene developing a potentially exciting situation is deflated by the exit of a prime character. Another problem experienced by the beginning writer is to build up to a conflict in four or five pages and then end the scene once the first point of conflict has been reached. When this happens, the writer isn't developing conflict but rather running away from it. Begin the scene at the point where the conflict begins, and then take the conflict as far as it will go.

4. *Try to write with no breaks, scene shifts, or time lapses.* Why? The energy, the story, the audience's interest drops with every break. Start the plot as soon as possible. Jump into the conflict with the first line, if possible. Let the exposition, foreshadowing, mood, and character come later. Let the other elements emerge as we need to know about them. The protagonist is the main character whose conscious will is driving her to attain a goal. The protagonist may be an antihero. She may be self-destructive and not sympathetic, but we must be able to understand her. Good or bad, the protagonist initiates the action.

5. *Understand the purpose of a one-act play versus that of a full-length play.* A one-act play illuminates one dramatic event, in contrast to a full-length play, which is built on a series of dramatic events. Shakespeare's *Macbeth*, for example, has many events: the witches' prophecy, plans to kill Duncan, the assassination, shifting blame for the murder on the princes, and so on. A one-act play might be built upon only one of those events. A full-length play will unfold a number of dramatic events like a tapestry. A one-act may look at a single moment of that tapestry, and if the correct moment is shown, the audience will be able to imagine the whole.

Subtext

When a character seems to have one motivation or action or goal but in reality has another, there is *subtext*—what lies under the text that is not spoken directly but is made apparent to the audience. A scene or play may be well constructed, the characters polarized, and the action clear, but if there is no subtext, it will offer no mystery, no surprise, no sudden discovery. This happens when characters say exactly what they mean. It may be clear, but it's deadly. The author needs to withhold some information. He needs to make the motivation seem to be one thing but reveal that hidden behind it is another. What did happen in that house years ago? Why is there such an undercurrent of rage and resentment between the two of them?

Conceive of every action as having different levels of meaning. The first is the most apparent: John wants a drink. The second is the hidden meaning: He wants to throw the drink into Peter's face. The third meaning is that John really wants to humiliate Peter. The fourth meaning is that John wants to break his friendship with Peter because it costs more than he's willing to give. The fifth meaning is that John has had an affair with Peter's wife and can't face him anymore. All these revelations will only become apparent later in the scene or play, but they provide the actor with a depth of subtext during the initial action. Audiences go to the theatre because of the subtext—the deeper meaning—because they want mystery, suspense, and surprise. They want to be engaged emotionally. A work with no subtext may read well, but it won't play well.

Summary

The *plot* is the selection and arrangement of incidents in the story. It is the plan of the action, from the initial inciting action to the final resolution. *To plot* means to choose what to include and what to exclude. In imagining a character and her whole life, the playwright must choose significant items from the events in the character's life. *Structure* is a series of selected events composed into a strategic sequence to express and arouse emotions—to mean something. An event means change. However, in a play, meaningful change must happen to someone. A story event is a meaningful change in the life of a character expressed by the writer in terms of values.

Among the various kinds of plots are (1) action, (2) thriller, (3) victim, (4) tragic, (5) dilemma, (6) victory, (7) punitive, (8) revelation, (9) admiration, (10) education, (11) maturing, (12) reform, (13) testing, (14) degeneration/regeneration, (15) disillusionment, and (16) pivotal.

A proper balance of beginning, middle, and end is essential. The beginning needs to hook the audience's interest; imply the forthcoming events via foreshadowing; clarify the inciting incident that has caused the whole problem that will be dramatized; indicate the mood, genre, and style of the play; establish the significant characters and their relationships; and establish the time and place. Most important, the beginning needs to begin the action. The middle is the heart of the play and the longest of the three parts. Here, the protagonist works to achieve his or her goal while the antagonist puts up obstacles. There are discoveries and complications, victories and defeats, twists and reversals. Through it all, the play's basic line of conflict is increased, building to a major climax. The resolution ties up any loose ends and answers any questions left after the climax.

An *obstacle* is something that stands in the protagonist's way. Every obstacle complicates the story. By blocking what the protagonist is pursuing, the antagonist creates unpredictability. Obstacles challenge the protagonist to intensify his commitment and strengthen his will to succeed. Action requires obstacles to sustain attention.

No matter what the plot, each play must build to an essential scene—a major confrontation between the protagonist and the antagonist that determines whether the protagonist will win or lose. This is the scene that an audience expects and looks forward to.

Among the common plot problems are the following: (1) The story is confusing, with too many characters, too many diverse scenes, and no clear central action. (2) The protagonist is passive or undermotivated and not truly involved in causing the plot to unfold. (3) The story line doesn't go anywhere. (4) The story seems pointless and doesn't really have anything to say. (5) The ending isn't satisfying. (6) The story doesn't work because of structural weaknesses—scenes that have nothing to do with the major action or a protagonist who has little to do with the main plot. (7) The author avoids conflict in the writing. (8) There is too much focus on secondary characters and their personal stories, which dilutes the impact of the major character's journey. (9) The play moves too slowly because the scenes are too long or include too much. (10) The plot has too many coincidences and isn't believable. (11) The middle of the play drags and doesn't show a rising conflict in which the protagonist is tested to the limits. (12) The beginning of the play is boring and takes too long.

Other tips are as follows: (1) Write about something that touches your heart. The characters in your play need to care and feel strongly. There must be conflict with high stakes. Drama is the art of the showdown; force must be opposed by force, person by person. (2) Most theatres look for small-cast shows, so limit the number of characters. Avoid utilitarian walk-on characters. (3) Keep the characters on stage as long as you can. (4) Try to write with no breaks, scene shifts, or time lapses. Jump into the conflict and the action quickly, and let the exposition, mood, and character come later. Develop a sympathetic protagonist whose conscious will is driving her toward a goal. Provide an antagonist as strong as the central character and equally as uncompromising. (5) Understand the purpose of a one-act play versus that of a full-length play.

Subtext refers to the hidden motivations and deeper meanings that lie under the text are are not spoken directly but made apparent to the audience. Subtext is what gives the audience mystery, surprise, and sudden discovery. It is what keeps the audience mentally and emotionally engaged. It is why they go to the theatre.

CHAPTER

7 Structure

In this chapter, we will explore masculine or linear construction, which follows a traditional narrative approach from ignition of the action; what distinguishes a beat, scene, sequence, and an act; building to a major climax and resolution; dealing with exposition; foreshadowing; positive and negative story values; concepts of unity; and feminine or nonlinear construction (often circular and episodic), which uses techniques such as flashbacks, direct address, shifts in time and perspective, and the use of theme as the unifying glue.

Masculine Structure

Greek philosopher and critic Aristotle first outlined his views on effective dramatic writing in *The Poetics* about 350 B.C. He examined Greek tragedy, analyzing what elements were essential, what approaches were more effective than others, and what effects it had on the audience. Western civilization adopted Aristotle's *masculine* or *linear* framework of storytelling.

Until the twentieth century, most plays were written and produced by men and for a predominantly male audience. Apart from the obvious anatomical differences, there are chemical and character distinctions to the sexes. More important are the typical roles assigned to men and women by society. For the past 2,500 years, dramatic writing has primarily followed the masculine or linear approach. Only within the last century has a feminine approach to playwriting emerged, powerfully redefining the structure of drama.

Note that the use of a masculine or feminine structure is not necessarily connected to the dramatist's gender. Nor do these structures imply that only male playwrights only write linear, masculine scripts and that female playwrights only write circular, feminine scripts. In fact, it is rare to find a play that is rigidly one structure or the other, just as it is rare to find a human being who is unwaveringly feminine or masculine. However, most dramatists generally identify strongly with a masculine or a feminine approach to play construction at any point in time, regardless of gender. Playwrights Nicky Silver, Tennessee Williams, and Arthur Miller have all used a feminine structure for some plays, and Beth Henley has used a masculine structure.

The Linear Approach

The masculine or Aristotelian structure centers on Aristotle's unity of action and a linear plot. In this basic order of events, one event follows another in chronological order, and this chain of events has a beginning, middle, and end. There is a unity to the events—in other words, no event is arbitrarily thrown in without reason. Events are chosen by the playwright to accelerate the forward momentum of the plot.

When does the play begin? The plot, like any chain, has a beginning, but it does not necessarily begin when the lights come up. Every Aristotelian play begins in a state of balance that identifies which part of our chaotic world it's going to show. It is a balance because, peaceful or painful, it will go on without change forever. It is Oedipus's home of Thebes before the plague in Sophocles' *Oedipus the King*. It is the quiet Kansas town of William Inge's *Picnic* before Hal shows up. It is the raging world of the wild child Helen upsetting life at the Keller home before the arrival of Anne Sullivan in *The Miracle Worker*, by William Gibson.

Ignition

The spark that lights the fuse of an explosive is the first link of that chain. This is the "no turning back" action that alters that balance. The ignition that propels Oedipus forward is his decision to find the cause of the plague and eliminate it. Annie Sullivan's decision to take on Helen Keller starts the action of *The Miracle Worker*. The action in Shakespeare's *Hamlet* starts when Hamlet sees the ghost and swears revenge. The mere arrival of Blanche Dubois in Tennessee Williams's *A Streetcar Named Desire* is the ignition for that play, just as Hal's entrance ignites the flame, upsetting the world of women in Inge's *Picnic*. Their intrusion on a balanced world has the same impact as the outlaw bursting through the bank's front door.

In some plays, the inciting action happened long ago. When the curtain rises, we are already in the midst of the conflict, and we find out the *antecedent action* through *exposition*—the information you need in order to know what's going on. In Molière's *Tartuffe*, for example, the father has upset the balance of his family by bringing home a hypocritical religious zealot, causing the family to rebel. Molière's play begins in frenzy, with the fuse already burning.

After the fuse has been ignited, the play builds through a series of *beats* to a *scene* and through a sequence of scenes to an *act*. The term *sequence* indicates that the scenes are tied together by cause and effect. Each scene and act builds eventually to a *climax* and *resolution*. The masculine structure, which evolved from Aristotle's outline for play composition, unifies all the script's actions to fuel the ultimate climactic event. Following the climax comes the resolution, and after the resolution, a new balance is established. Again, the masculine script is linear. It has a clear beginning, middle, and end. Each point on that line can be identified by its function.

Scenes

A change in a character's life equals an event or *scene*. What values are at stake at the beginning of the scene? Is it positive or negative? Two brothers who share a one-bedroom apartment are seen getting dressed. They are in a good mood and teasing one another. While hunting for a shirt, John finds his girlfriend Sarah's scarf in brother Mark's closet. They get into a conflict about Mark's history with women, trust, and loyalty. John decides to kick Mark out of the apartment. The value of the scene has changed from positive to negative. The scene ends with unresolved conflict.

This alienation scene can be divided into five *beats:*

1. *Teasing.* Mark teases John about his taste in clothes. John teases Mark about his superficiality. Mark notes that John has no sense of humor. John decides to wear one of Mark's shirts. In Mark's closet, John find's his girlfriend's scarf—a gift he gave her.

2. *Accusation.* John confronts Mark, who tries to lie his way out of the situation. It turns ugly. Mark disparages John's masculinity. John brings up Mark's previous despicable treatment of women.

3. *Threats.* Mark threatens to take Sarah away from John. John threatens to tell her about Mark's previous indiscretions. Mark threatens to tell their father about one of John's secrets.

4. *Pleading.* John pleads with Mark not to tell his father. Mark apologizes. One chance remark, however, and John turns angry and withdraws.

5. *Crisis.* John rejects his apology, gets into a physical fight with Mark, and gives Mark an ultimatum: Take your stuff and get out, or I'll throw your stuff into the street.

Beats

A change in human behavior is a *beat*. A beat contains a character's objective, what he or she wants. There is an *external stimulus* that arouses an inner *need* (see Figure 7.1). The character reviews the *alternatives* and makes a *choice*. Once a choice has been made, the character has an *intention* of what to do and a *strategy* of how to do it. That is the *objective*. When the character acts on that objective, that is the *response*. The action must be stage worthy—one that is visible to and can be read by the audience. The response then becomes the stimulus for the other character.

What kind of stimulus involves "hitting below the belt?" In Edward Albee's *Who's Afraid of Virginia Woolf?* Martha hits below the belt when she tells the truth about George's novel—that it is a thinly disguised account of his killing of his

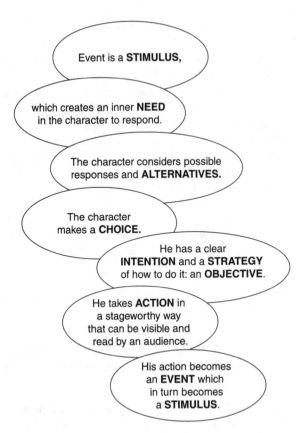

FIGURE 7.1   The Stimulus/Response Model

parents. In Tennessee Williams's *Cat on a Hot Tin Roof,* Maggie hits below the belt when she brings up Skipper. A character that is losing may bring up a taboo subject in any scene. It is always a sore subject—whatever weakness the other person has—that is sure to hurt.

The character's goal or need provides the motivation for her action—what the character says or does. The objective may lead to a series of actions. If Character B blocks Character A from getting what she wants, Character A will then change tactics. Each character anticipates, adjusts ahead, and adapts to new information. But when the other character responds in a way that is unexpected, a gap opens between expectation and reality, requiring the character to adjust and adapt her response to the reality.

We have a series of beats, or changes in human behavior, composed in a certain order, with the last beat bringing about the greatest change. In creating the scene and the moment-to-moment actions of a character, the playwright should ask, What does the character want? What strong choices does he make? Like the actor, the playwright should think of strong verbs when developing each beat. Strong verbs can reveal what the character is thinking and feeling, rather than what he or she is saying. Compare the following strong active verbs with their weaker passive counterparts:

Active Verbs	*Passive Verbs*
To defy	To tell
To hurt	To get angry
To needle	To suggest
To trick	To learn the truth
To force his hand	To ask
To embarrass	To laugh
To "baby"	To feel sorry for
To intimidate	To hint

The beats should get beneath the surface of the dialogue and express the dynamics that motivate the characters. The playwright must, therefore, have a deep insight into the psychology of human motives. As noted in Chapter 12 on dialogue, characters do not say exactly what they mean. Each has a public side and a private side. The public side may appear to be sympathetic while the private side is seeking to demean and destroy the other character's self-esteem. Thus, the playwright must focus on the *subtext,* what the character is not saying. This is most easily done if the playwright has a clear vision of the intention of the character. The playwright should select beats with a sense of progression, growing from weakest to strongest. This series of beats forms a scene with a climax.

Acts

Thus far, we have beats, a scene composed of a series of beats, and a series of scenes that make up a sequence. A sequence of scenes makes up an *act.* A full-length play today is generally made up of two acts. The five-act form was used from Roman times into the eighteenth century. In the nineteenth century, the four-act form became standard. By the beginning of the twentieth century, plays were written in three acts. By the 1970s, the two-act became the standard. Today, a growing number of plays have basically one act and run for about ninety minutes, without an intermission. However, even within the two-act or one-act form, there are generally three major actions.

A *story* is a series of actions that bring about major changes and culminate in an irreversible climax. Classical structure requires a closed ending. All questions raised in the audience's mind must be answered and all emotions must be satisfied. There is a single protagonist who is active. The main conflict is external, with the protagonist in a struggle with other characters. The protagonist goes through major irreversible changes. In one way or another, the story makes us wait for the other shoe to drop. We are waiting for the resolution of a conflict, the solution to a puzzle, or the explanation of a mystery, and it is this anticipation, as much as anything else, that makes us continue to be interested.

The Resolution

The rising action creates conflict and stress not only for the characters but also for the audience. After identifying with the characters and emerging from the climax, the audience wants to survey the ruins or celebrate in the victory. This postclimax event is the *resolution,* sometimes called the *denouement,* which is a French word for unraveling the complication.

After a hurricane, television cameras in helicopters pan over the ruins. They take in the entirety of the locale: houses, cars, and businesses in ruins; power lines down; bridges washed out; devastation for miles around. After a climactic event, it is human nature to want to see the outcome. After a new house is built, the owners are given time for a room-by-room inspection. There is the media discussion on television after a presidential debate. There are interviews with actors after they win Oscars. These are all forms of closure. Without closure, we feel uncomfortable. If a close relative dies, a friend moves out of town without saying good-bye, or we are forced to leave a competitive event before the end, we experience the pain of an unresolved, incomplete situation. People relish release and even like to heighten the sensation through delayed gratification. Sex is perhaps the most primal example: an intense build-up of stress until an explosive release.

This ultimate release of conflict or stress in a play, as in life, is the *climax.* Drama thrives on conflict. The intensifying stresses and releases within the plot build up pressure like a covered pot boiling rapidly and spouting bursts of steam until it finally explodes. The play's opposing forces pressurize to the point that an ultimate, final victory is imperative for only one. That event is the climax.

A climax can be defined by a number of criteria. It can be a climax of action, such as Stanley Kowalski's rape of Blanche Dubois in Williams's *A Streetcar Named Desire.* In fact, Stanley defines the dramatic climax: "We've had this date with each other from the beginning" (Act 3, scene 4). There can also be the climax of an idea, such as Thomas More's assertion in Robert Bolt's *A Man for All Seasons* that he must obey God's law or Eliza's assertion that she is independent of Professor Higgins's control in George Bernard Shaw's *Pygmalion.* In classically based tragedy, it is a climax of recognition—reversal and discovery. Oedipus learns that he is the unclean cause of the plague—he killed his father and married his mother. Regardless of type, the sequence of stresses and releases within the play builds to the final showdown: the climax

A *plot,* then, is a series of imaginary events planned to create anticipation in a story of conflict. The ending may take the form of a resolution, a revelation, a decision, an explanation, or a solution. It establishes a new balance, either the restoration of the initial one or a change to one that is better or worse. After the climax of Williams's *Streetcar,* Blanche is taken away to an asylum, and the balance is restored. In Albee's *Who's Afraid of Virginia Woolf?* George and Martha have killed the illusions, and although it is unendurably painful, there is hope for a new beginning. Everything in the script after the climax is the resolution. Some scripts give false climaxes to lure you into believing that you are free and clear, only to jolt you with a more powerful moment. At the end of the film *Fatal Attraction,* the Glenn Close character is supposedly dead in the bathtub but suddenly rises up out of the water.

Exposition

The best exposition is unnoticeable: information that is brought in only because it is essential and tied to the characters and action. In numerous comedies of manners from the seventeenth century well into the twentieth century, exposition was obvious, with servants discussing the situation, the main characters, and the events going on. In *The Real Inspector Hound,* a satire of British murder/mysteries, Tom Stoppard pokes fun at the obvious exposition of these drawing-room plays when the maid answers the phone, "Hello, the drawing room of Lady Muldoon's country residence one morning in early Spring" (pp. 10–11).

Addressing the audience directly with the exposition is expedient and has been practiced since the early Greeks. For example, the prologue to Aeschylus' *Agamemnon* begins with the watchman telling us of the situation. Contemporary plays require more subtlety. In David Grimm's historical play *Kit Marlowe,* Thomas sets the scene by complaining: "And yet, Christ forsake it, look at me! Five hours of a sore backside on a testy nag, riding through the rain and mud to a destination I wish didn't exist" (Act 1, p. 10). He goes on to say, "When I knock at his door—when I find it—a young boy—what—fifteen—with sleep in his eyes, sends me away. 'Try down by the river,' he says. 'He's swimming.' Swimming—I ask you!" (Act 1, p. 10).

In Martin McDonagh's *Beauty Queen of Leenane,* we learn on the first page that Maureen has been out in the rain. Mag, who has a "urine infection," had to get her own porridge, and she's scared of having to deal with hot water. Maureen is annoyed that Mag can't tidy up the house and wants to be waited on. Mag complains of her bad back. Maureen complains that she isn't appreciated. The information comes from the interaction of the characters. As they rail at one another, we are sucked into the play and interested in the characters, and we're not really aware that this is exposition.

Exposition is one of those "dragons" that a playwright must overcome. Exposition is background information intended primarily for the audience. It tells the audience who the characters are, where they live, their current relationships, and how the past influences them. Because exposition is information, it typically does not propel the play forward in the present and to a sense of future. In today's theatre, it is best to jump into the conflict immediately and then bring in the exposition a bit at a time, only when needed in the present. Let it be part of the action, dragged forth reluctantly by one character insisting on answers. Make it a part of the conflict, with one character resisting the telling, the other insisting. Have the antagonist use relevant background information as a weapon against the protagonist.

Foreshadowing

Foreshadowing is an important tool for playwrights. It awakens audience interest by telling them of an event to come and guiding their attention toward it. It can give characters motivation and depth. Foreshadowing needs to be subtle. The term *foreshadow* means to give a hint or suggestion beforehand. Thus, the playwright introduces a problem by a brief reference, a prop, a phone call, a letter, or some other device. This arouses audience anticipation. If a knife is used to chop vegetables in the first scene, it may be the murder weapon later when the husband kills his wife. When a man is cleaning a gun early in the play, it suggests that the gun will be used later. A phone call from an alcoholic relative will lead us to expect to meet her later.

If foreshadowing gives us an idea that there is something in the dark at the top of the stairs, it also creates anticipation, expectation, and mystery. Once we are led to expect something, we anticipate the fulfillment. We want to be led up those stairs. We wait until the light is turned on. The tension creates suspense.

Story Values

Values are those qualities of human experience that can be positive and negative at different times—qualities such as courage and cowardice, love and hate, interest and apathy. Changes in characters' lives are achieved through conflict. Coincidence isn't enough. Motivated change through conflict is necessary. A scene may begin on a positive note and end on a negative note or in the opposite way. A scene may also start and end on a positive note or the reverse. The playwright needs to be conscious of the positive and negative values and to make sure there is variety in how scenes begin and end.

The Unities

The traditional idea of the *unities* was that the play should have one central action that takes place in one setting within one day. This began with Aristotle's analysis and interpretation of the Greek tragedies. Artistotle stressed that unity of *action* was essential. Much later, the unities of *time* and *place* became required.

In today's theatre, the unities of time and place are frequently disregarded for full-length plays, especially musicals. Only the unity of one central action is still standard. However, the rising costs of sets and costumes have also brought limits to changes of locale and time. Many professional theatres cannot afford to produce multiset, nonmusical comedies and dramas. Changes in time also usually call for costume changes, another financial concern.

Action

The action is brought to life by the protagonist's desire—her passionate need—to achieve a certain goal. The desire is an emotional quality. The protagonist is one who feels even more than she thinks. This character will move nonstop to her objective. A protagonist must have a passionate need to right the wrong, to punish the guilty, to recover the lost child, to make the marriage work, or to get revenge. The protagonist's goal must be made clear relatively early in the play and have a sense of urgency. While full-length plays have more events and complications than short plays, there must still be one central action. Today's theatre is streamlined. Every word, line, and event must advance the plot.

Time

The concept of the unity of time dates back to Aristotle's *The Poetics* and his explanation that a tragedy should deal with events within one revolution of the sun, or essentially one day. Although this later became a prescription for generations, playwrights today are free to manipulate time as they wish. The brevity of the one-act or ten-minute play limits changes in time. Jumps in time cannot depend on scenic devices or elaborate lighting techniques to communicate the change. One-acts, however, still may be composed with jumps in time, but plays that call for lighting changes or sound effects to indicate time changes and do not require costume or set changes are more acceptable.

Place

Today, plays are not limited to single places. We can create multiple locales and have the technology to change from one to another quickly for musicals. However, for a nonmusical play, if the action moves from place to place, it must do so without elaborate stage devices to indicate the changes. In general, no set changes should be required. Some kind of unit set—usually, one that is simplified, abstract, nonrealistic—with minor changes combined with lighting must be the answer. A simultaneous staging technique or a unit set still boils down to one set.

The Play in Today's Theatre

The "straight" play in today's theatre—that is, a contemporary comedy or drama that is not a musical—typically has only a few characters and is an examination of a single dramatic incident. Most full-length plays are divided in two acts. The usual running time is two hours, including a fifteen-minute intermission, although in today's theatre, the ninety-minute play with no intermission has also become popular. Most of these plays have a single or unit set.

Most one-acts run thirty to forty-five minutes. Usually, a bill of one-acts includes two or three plays. It is especially important for a short play to stay within one time and one place. It isn't practical to change sets within a short play, particularly if any degree of realism is required. There are, of course, short plays with a series of locales and time changes, but these are generally produced without any attempt to physicalize the changes. In a play such as *Fun*, by Howard Korder, for example, two young men go to many different places, but the changes are accomplished solely by the actors and lighting. There are no set or costume changes.

In the 1990s, ten-minute play festivals developed. The popularity of the ten-minute play has become a national phenomenon. The Kennedy Center American College Theatre Festival selects ten of these for each national festival. There are also eight regional festivals across the United States, each of which presents ten plays. Other ten-minute play contests are held in many cities. In Miami, for example, City Shorts produces a series of these plays each summer. Generally, there is one locale, one time, and one continuous scene, with no time breaks and no costume changes. The casts are small.

EXERCISE 10 _____

Beginning Level   Choose one of the following:

  A. Write a linear scene using the stimulus/response model. In the scene, Character A and Character B should each try to win Character C to his or her side. Character A should use various tactics and may exaggerate or even lie. Character B must be very quick and inventive to show the true side of Character A.

  B. Write a linear scene in which the protagonist uses the tactics listed earlier under "Active Verbs." Focus the conflict on a desire, a goal, a secret, or a third character.

Intermediate Level   Choose one of the following:

  C. Write a scene that jumps into the conflict immediately between two characters that know each other well. Have Character A use information that he knows as a weapon to discredit, criticize, expose, demean, degrade, or inflame Character B. Let the exposition be dragged forth reluctantly from Character B. Allow Character B to finally reveal some new information that pulls the rug out from under Character A.

D.   Write a scene with different moods and five physical actions. Label each beat with a verb according to the type of behavior: *to joke, plead, bargain, demand, seduce, defy, bribe,* and so on. Write the verb in pencil in the margin at the start of each beat. Usually, a beat is short. It changes every time the leading character in the scene changes his or her objective.

Advanced Level   Choose one of the following:

E.   Write a five-page scene with three characters, in which the first part clarifies Character A's expectations and ideal scenario and the second part brings him or her face to face with a very different reality. Label each beat with a verb according to the type of behavior: *to bargain, demand, seduce, ignore, flatter, threaten, deny, refuse, ridicule,* and the like.

F.   Write a conflict scene resolved by the protagonist's decision between two difficult choices or a conflict resolved by a revelation from another character. Label each beat with a verb that describes the behavior: *to joke, plead, bargain, demand, seduce, ignore, flatter,* and so on. Put the verb on the page at the beginning of each beat.

Feminine Structure

In the twentieth century, women emerged as a force on an equal par with men, gaining new power in all areas of life in the United States. With this power came new forms of expression, such that uniquely feminine artistic structures now prevail in Western civilization. This is not to say that these forms didn't exist before. Certainly, women were expressing themselves in distinctly feminine ways before the twentieth century. However, because the selections for play production were being made overwhelmingly by men, these forms were either suppressed or lost over time.

Other than the obvious anatomical differences, there are hundreds of other contrasting qualities to the sexes. Science has uncovered a variety of gender-specific differences. For example, women's wide-field vision is more accurate, yet men's night vision is stronger. Due to hip placement, men can run faster, yet women have more endurance. Females have better manual dexterity; males are better at spatial relationships. Males have more muscle mass, whereas females have more fat reserves: strength versus stamina. One could theorize that these differences evolved for species survival: Females were built to bear and protect children and males to feed and secure the genetic line. Fortunately, civilization and technology have made the physical restrictions that limit lifestyle choices obsolete.

Our gender differences are most apparent in our sexual responses. Modern research has shown that men radiate that energy from their sexual organ, whereas women express themselves sexually through their entire bodies. Most relevant to playwriting is this: Men are focused primarily on the climax, whereas women are focused on the overall sensation. A man can have a rewarding experience with nothing but a climax, and a woman can have a rewarding experience without a climax. Each sex may also experience the energy of the opposite sex, since both qualities are present in varying degrees in both. However, each sex generally reacts with gender-specific responses.

The differences in our evolutionary development and our sexual responses help explain how playwriting evolved as having a chain of events targeted toward achieving a purging climax. The male playwrights and audiences of Aristotle's time up to the twentieth century were naturally more moved by making a linear progression to a final goal. Yet a *nonlinear* structure can also provide a full, satisfying theatrical experience.

Nonlinear Approaches

According to Judith Michaelson (1988) in her article "Woman Playwrights and Their Stony Road," "only seven percent of the plays written in this country are by women, and those that are produced generally cluster at the bottom rungs of the theater ladder" (p. 47) somewhere off-off-Broadway. Throughout history, women playwrights have faced discrimination, and they were largely ignored until the twentieth century. Today, however, more and more women are telling stories. Is there a woman's aesthetic, or is true art genderless? Are women creating their own artforms?

There is no agreement to these questions, even among women. For some, art is art no matter who writes it. Others see a difference between a male and a female aesthetic, and they consider *linear* writing as male and *nonlinear* writing as female. "We tend to write in a circular fashion," says playwright Kathleen Betsko (quoted in Michaelson, 1988, p. 47), basing her opinion on talking to thirty women playwrights and reading hundreds of plays by women. She notes that women live a very fragmented life doing a large variety of tasks—making beds, dropping the kids at school, cooking dinner, handling part-time or full-time jobs—and tend to write shorter scenes and share the dialogue more generously among all the characters. As a result, there are often several leading characters as opposed to a single protagonist and antagonist. Betsko also notes that women playwrights "have a lot of problems structurally because we are trying to force our perceptions and our vision into predominantly male forms" (p. 47).

The underlying foundation of the male form is a play made with rising conflict until it reaches a climax and then tapers off. Women's work, according to Betsko, has a lot of small climaxes: "Women tend to want to return to where they began at the beginning of the play" (p. 47). Mexican playwright Sabina Bergman notes, "I am in search of structures closer to the feminine, that is circular dramatic structures" (quoted in Michaelson, 1988, p. 47).

In the same article, Canadian playwright Margaret Hollingsworth also notes a difference between men and women regarding the use of conflict. She says, "This word *conflict*. Plays have to have *conflict*. I hate that word! It's a male model of how to write a play, and it's been very damaging to our work. What a play needs is push and pull, it needs energy and tension, something that drives it forward, but that is not necessarily conflict" (p. 47).

If you were traveling by car from New York to Miami, you could do it two ways. One way would be to get on Interstate 95 and drive south until you hit the city. This should take about two days, but you would only see a lot of highway. Or you could start heading south on a road that isn't a major interstate expressway, stop at a few towns you have never seen, visit some natural landmarks, and maybe take a tour of a southern mansion in Georgia. You would get to Miami eventually, but you would also see countless sights on the way.

In the first method, the masculine script emphasizes the goal in the shortest time and the least expensive way possible. In the second method, the feminine script emphasizes the experience. Some people may employ bits of both. The emphasis depends on priority.

Circular Structure

While the masculine script emphasizes singular or parallel plot lines climaxed by a powerful event, the feminine script emphasizes the process of exploring a basic thematic idea through a succession of varied but equally weighted scene variations. What follows are the structural elements of the feminine script.

For the scene variations to have continuity, they need a unifying focus. That unity is generally provided by a theme. Johann Sebastian Bach perfected a popular form of music in the eighteenth century called the *fugue.* A fugue is a composition with many voices, each treated with equal importance, each exploring a given theme. That theme is usually a short melody line that is stated by any one voice at the fugue's beginning. The first thing you hear in a fugue is the identifying subject—the melody line. Then you hear the answer, which is another voice interpreting that subject, and then you hear others still, added onto those first two voices. The fugue ends when the subject has been fully expanded and the contrasting voices rejoin in unison.

The unifying force of the feminine script, like the fugue, is the subject. The *subject* is the concept or thematic idea the playwright wishes to explore. It can be an observation about human behavior, a debate on social structure, an exploration of an emotion, or even the celebration of life's joy. The subject of a feminine script says, "This is what we're talking about here," just as the subject of the fugue says, "This is the sound we're going to play with."

Unlike the ignition of a linear script, the subject of a circular script doesn't have to be stated at the script's opening or in the title, although it often is. In fact, if the subject is considered difficult to swallow, it might even be best left until the end. To construct a house, you have to begin with the foundation and build to the roof. To construct a jigsaw puzzle, you can begin with any two pieces that match. Constructing a house requires a linear progression. Constructing a puzzle requires relationships between varying pieces and can be constructed in any sequence. The feminine script is like a jigsaw puzzle.

The scenes within the circular script are the topic variations. Each topic variation examines an angle or point of view on the thematic subject. When the variations are pieced together in complementary relationship to each other, the entire picture is created. The circular script's variations do not utilize Aristotle's tidy unities. Instead, the script layers variation upon variation through diverse scenes and devices. Since topic variations don't have to follow the logic of time or unified action, the notes played and instruments used can be unlimited—constricted only by necessary thematic consistency. For example, in Paula Vogel's *How I Learned to Drive*, the subject is sexual abuse, inflicted on Li'l Bit by her uncle who also taught her to drive. The play begins in the parking lot. The scenes within the play are also titled to suggest driving lessons, but they are metaphors, as well:

> *Sample Scene Titles*
> Safety First—You and Driver Education
> Idling in Neutral Gear
> Shifting Forward from First to Second Gear
> Vehicle Failure
> Defensive Driving

Vogel wanted to explore the conflicting effects of love that hurts. A linear exploration of a specific plot would have been too logical and realistic, drawing attention to the details of abuse rather than the dysfunctional family and how Li'l Bit was able to survive and overcome it. Instead, Vogel focuses the audience on the subject through the title and adds flashbacks until the whole picture is complete.

Mother Courage, by Bertolt Brecht, is an episodic and circular play. The play explores what happens to a mother and her children as she pulls her wagon along with the troops in a war. The scenes show the devastating effects of the war. It would be possible to eliminate some of them or to change their order without destroying the play. The play is concise and powerful without needing to justify a coincidental relationship between the characters or to weave an intricate plot line for unity. A similar structure is used for all of Brecht's epic theatre plays.

Since the circular script does not rely on chronology, one way to recognize this structure is to determine if you could transpose the order of the scenes without losing the integrity of the story. Obviously, the playwright orders the scenes for artistic reasons, and they shouldn't be altered. But in the overall understanding of the play, cause-and-effect sequence is less crucial than the thematic relationship and counterpoint. The feminine script encircles a theme with topic variations that complete a full picture.

In linear writing, the endpoint is the resolution. In circular writing, the ending is complete when the circle has been closed; the closing point is the completion. Rather than provide a climactic showdown, the circular script ends with a satisfying totality, similar to the feeling you have when you finish viewing a museum collection. There is a sense of fulfillment, saturation, and entirety. All the parts have merged into one experience.

As with any circle, it is impossible to pinpoint the end. You cannot point to the completion scene in a circular script as easily as you can identify the climax of a linear script or spot the last piece of the jigsaw puzzle. However, at the circular script's finish, that satisfying fulfillment is felt. When the playwright or fugue composer has explored as many variations as he or she needs or senses to complete the work, the play or composition is over. If the playwright or artist is successful, then completion will be achieved. If he or she falls short, then the audience will be left frustrated, confused, or unsatisfied.

By the end of *How I Learned to Drive,* you feel an enormous satisfaction. Vogel provides a concise exploration of another way to experience the world through the attention paid to the subtle details of a dysfunctional family and to Li'l Bit's survival of the abuse from an uncle who loved her and gave her life lessons in driving.

Note the following comparison and contrast of the masculine and feminine viewpoints using specific concepts. The masculine structure can be broken down easily into distinct steps. Feminine script elements have fewer rules and more options. The effectiveness of the masculine script can be measured by the successful, unified completion of its steps—no loose ends, an exciting climax, and a character journey. The effectiveness of the feminine script is measured by the satisfying wholeness felt at the final curtain. If the subject has not been fully explored, then the script will have fallen short. If it has made a strong impression and created a full experience, then it will have achieved its goal.

Comparison of Structures

Masculine/Linear	Feminine/Circular/Episodic
Action and event	Topic variation
Protagonist and antagonist	Ensemble
Climax and resolution	Completion
Architect	Sculptor
Building blocks	Jigsaw puzzle
Novel	Short-story collection
Narrative storyteller	Storytellers/Different stories
Travel	Tour
Five-course meal	Buffet
Having sex	Making love
Goal	Process

Very often, male critics have adjudicated scripts as being ineffective because they have looked only for the familiar elements of linear progression. It is up to the performers and directors to show that our world is not limited to one viewpoint. But doing so requires a clear understanding of the tools. Actors who project a linear build on a circular constructions weaken the collage of topic variations. Actors who place equal weight on all events of linear construction, as though they were topic variations, rob the thrusting momentum of events that build to the climax.

Episodic Structure

The *episodic* structure develops a play through a series of separate scenes that are generally complete in themselves. The episodic structure may be circular or a combination of chronological elements—scenes arranged in climactic order, from least important to the most important, and an ending that takes us back to the beginning. Aristotle wrote in *The Poetics* that he did not have a high opinion of episodic structure: "But of simple plots and actions, the episodic are the worst. I call the plot episodic, in which it is neither probably nor necessary that the episodes follow each other."

However, a play may have an episodic plot that does follow a linear cause-and-effect structure. There are many successful plays with episodic plots. The key is for the playwright to set up the rules of the play. Whatever those rules are, the playwright must be consistent with them. A play with a major plot and a subplot may also be developed with alternating scenes that come together in the final act. A subplot may be the opposite of the main plot and used primarily as comic relief. A subplot may provide a comparison or a parallel to the main plot, highlighting the overall theme. A subplot may take the form of a counterplot, a plot which progresses in contrast to the main action.

Most expressionistic plays have an episodic structure. The scenes are separate stories involving the protagonist, in which the hero's problems become worse and worse with each episode. Expressionist plays—such as Eugene O'Neill's *The Emperor Jones* and *The Hairy Ape*, Georg Kaiser's *From Morn to Midnight*, and Elmer Rice's *The Adding Machine*—illustrate progressively worse circumstances for the protagonist, finally ending in death. These plays also call for a separate set for each scene, many costumes, special effects, and generally large casts.

Because each scene is an entity unto itself, it is possible with some episodic plays to omit a scene completely or to change the order of scenes without destroying the play. Ibsen's romantic drama *Peer Gynt* is seldom produced in its entirety. Many scenes in the second part are often omitted to shorten the playing time. The same is true of Brecht's epic theatre plays, such as *Mother Courage, The Caucasian Chalk Circle*, and *The Good Woman of Setzuan*. These plays are episodic. Each may have an overall linear framework, but within it are scenes that are variations on a theme. The plays are not realistic, and many theatrical devices are used.

In the contemporary American theatre, there are successful writers who continue to use an episodic or cinematic structure. Wendy Wasserstein is the well-known author of *The Heidi Chronicles*, which has won the Pulitzer Prize, the Tony, and the New York Drama Critics Award for best play. Wasserstein said in an interview in *The Playwright's Art*, "All of my plays have episodic structures; they all break down into around eight scenes. For me they're fun to write because basically I know that within ten pages I'm out of the scene—so I'm not stuck there. In some ways you can move the action forward in that way, and also in a way you can make the action and the storytelling elliptical" (1994, p. 264).

Most plays follow a defined chronology or sequence of events, without which the story would make no sense. When there are cause-and-effect relationships between the events in a play (and there almost always are), then there is a chronology that cannot logically be changed. If the telling of a story is linear, the structure of the play follows chronology. The first events described are the ones that happened earliest, the lasts events described are the ones that happened last, and everything that happens in between is described in order. A play with flashbacks and foreshadowing (events described out of sequence) can have a much more complex chronology. Many literary devices are available to bend time. No device is necessary, however, to describe a well-ordered, linear sequence of events: It is what happens automatically, unless an effort is made to the contrary.

Some contemporary writers use a nonlinear structure. We are familiar with the use of flashbacks and foreshadowing even within conventional plays. Williams's *The Glass Menagerie* is told in flashback by the narrator Tom. There are also flashbacks in Arthur Miller's *Death of a Salesman*. Both plays employ a mixture of styles: realism and expressionism. The world in each play is seen through the eyes of the central character, one of the main aspects of an expressionistic play. Each play also has a bit of a dream quality. The set for each play is suggestive and expressive, rather than totally realistic. However, the acting style used in both plays is realistic.

Nicky Silver, a playwright who came of age in the 1990s, uses a nonlinear structure. His themes include topics from cannibalism to incest, from unattractiveness and AIDS to eating disorders, maternal obsession, and suicide. Many, if not all, of these issues tie into his portrait of the contemporary American family. Among his major plays are *Fat Men in Skirts, Pterodactyls, Raised in Captivity, Fit to Be Tied, The Food Chain, Free Will and Wanton Lust,* and *The Altruists.*

In *Fat Men in Skirts*, Silver introduces us to three character types that we encounter in only slightly varied versions in his other plays. These include a young man; his domineering, middle-class mother; and a loopy young woman who is a bit confused and often unfocused. After surviving a plane crash, Phyllis and her son Bishop are stranded on a desert island for five years. During these years, Bishop changes from a stuttering little boy into a feral savage who eventually rapes his mother. Phyllis evolves from a glib, callused sophisticate to a helpless, addled shell. Left to fend for themselves, the characters dine on the dead bodies of those who perished in the crash. Back in civilization, we see Howard, Phyllis's husband and a famous movie director, continuing life with his dizzy mistress, Pam.

Again, Silver's style is nonlinear. He uses direct address, shifts in time and perspective, and the overlapping of settings to show the parallels between environments and situations. Characters frequently move into a spotlight and talk directly to the audience.

Fat Men in Skirts is typical of Silver's nonlinear approach. The first act opens with a monologue by Phyllis and a scene with her and Bishop on the beach. The next scene flashes back to Phyllis's wedding night, returns to the beach, goes to Phyllis's recounting of a dream in the present, then to a scene with Pam and Howard back in civilization, a monologue by Bishop about Katherine Hepburn, a flashback to the struggle over the naming of Bishop, a monologue by Pam about her relationship with Howard, a scene in the present with Bishop eating a baby and verbally taking charge, a scene of conflict between Pam and Howard, a monologue by Bishop about monkeys, and so on.

Getting Out, by Marsha Norman, probes into the past and present of a young woman attempting to find her way after release from prison. Arlene returns to a rundown apartment in Louisville, intent on starting her life over. Rebellious, disruptive, and abused as a young girl, she has found strength in religion and wants to put her youth as "Arlie" behind her. As Arlene struggles to find her way in the present, flashbacks of her past as Arlie shed light on what she must overcome. Her two personalities are represented by two actors, who sometimes appear on stage simultaneously. The unit setting focuses on the living room of her apartment, but it is surrounded by the prison of her past, with areas representing a jail cell, a catwalk, and a principal's office. There are shifts in time and place from the present to the past, and sometimes both are reflected at the same time.

Getting Out, *performed at University of Alaska Anchorage. Directed by Leroy Clark, Set and Lighting Design by Frank Bebey, Costume Design by Lois Aden.*

In Harold Pinter's *Betrayal*, George S. Kaufman and Moss Hart's *Merrily We Roll Along*, and Stephen Sondheim's musical version of *Merrily We Roll Along*, the scenes play in reverse chronological order. That is, the last scene in the story is presented first and the beginning event that happened years earlier is presented last. *Rashomon*, by Fay and Michael Kanin, based on the movie by Akira Kurosawa, is the tale of a rape and murder told through the eyes of four different individuals involved with the crime. Each version tells a different story, but eventually, we learn the truth behind these crimes and see a stunning perception of people's diverse altering of perceptions.

EXERCISE 11

Beginning Level   Choose one of the following:

A. Select an organic object, such as a twig, a piece of natural wood, a leaf, a vegetable, a fruit, a flower, or a weed. Write a conflict scene that in your mind is shaped like the object. Follow the structure of the organic object and shape the scene like it. Bring the object to class with the scene.

B. Write a dream scene in which your characters, objects, locales, and events are free from the restrictions of reality. Dreams do not obey linear thought or structure. Do not worry about interpreting the dream. Follow the dream of one character: the behaviors and events, what is said, the images. Let it flow. Is it a daydream, a nightmare, a quest dream, or a problem-solving dream? Who is good and who is evil? What does the person like? Hate? What does he or she fear? Want? Love? How do age, race, occupation, religion, family, lifestyle, needs, and desires affect the character in the dream?

Intermediate Level   Choose one of the following:

C. Write a nonlinear scene with a specific theme. It can be an observation about human behavior, a debate on social structure, an exploration of an emotion, or even the celebration of life's joy. To construct this jigsaw puzzle scene, use flashbacks, direct address, shifts in time and perspective, dream sequences, or fantasy sequences.

D. Rewrite one of your previous scenes, turning one character into a talking mechanical object. Find an object that best describes or identifies the character. Think of the object as animated—as if it were somehow alive in this technological age—and rewrite the scene. For example, in the musical *Beauty and the Beast*, there are talking pieces of furniture.

Advanced Level   Choose one of the following:

E. Write an expressionistic scene about a theme. The setting, costumes, and props should be seen through the eyes of the protagonist and may be distorted and exaggerated. The other characters should be types identified by the protagonist's perception of them. In this world, there are transformations. Characters and objects may change into other things. Masks, direct address, fantasy scenes, dream scenes, shifts in time and perspective, and the overlapping of scenes in different simultaneous settings may be used.

F.   Write three short scenes about an event that happened. Each scene should portray the same event as seen through the eyes of a different character involved. Masks, direct address, fantasy scenes, dream scenes, shifts in time and perspective, and the overlapping of scenes in different simultaneous settings may be used.

Summary

The masculine or Aristotelian structure centers on Aristotle's unity of action and a linear plot. In this basic order of events, one event follows another in chronological order, and this chain of events has a beginning, middle, and end. The play has a rising action that builds to a climax and is followed by a resolution.

A change in the character's life equals an event or *scene.* A scene may begin or end with a positive or negative value. A scene that begins in a positive way may end in unresolved conflict. A scene that begins with conflict may end with a resolution. The playwright must vary the values that begin or end scenes.

A scene is developed from smaller units, or *beats.* A change in human behavior is a beat. A beat contains a character's objective or intention. The need provides the motivation for the action—what the character says or does. The objective may lead to a series of actions. Each character pursues an objective that is often the opposite of what actually happens. A gap opens between expectation and reality.

A play is composed of individual beats that are put together in a series to create a scene. A series of causally connected scenes makes up a sequence. A series of sequences makes up an *act.* A series of acts makes up a *story,* which brings about a major change that is irreversible.

Resolution, something called *denouement,* shows what happens after the climax. It answers any lingering questions related to the protagonist.

Exposition sets forth the necessary background information. It tells the audience the given circumstances: who the characters are, where they live, what their current relationships are and why, and how past actions influence the present. Exposition does not propel the play forward. The playwright must use exposition cautiously, bringing it into the dialogue only when needed in the present conflict.

Foreshadowing is an important tool that playwrights can use to awaken audience interest by telling them of an event to come.

Values are those qualities of human experience that can be positive and negative at various times—qualities such as courage and cowardice, love and hate, interest and apathy. Changes in characters' lives are achieved through conflict. Coincidence isn't enough. Motivated change through conflict is necessary.

The traditional idea of the *unities* was that the play should have one central action that takes place in one setting within one day. In today's theatre, while the unities of time and place are frequently disregarded, the unity of one central action is still standard. The rising costs of sets and costumes have also brought limits to changes of locale and time.

While the masculine script emphasizes singular or parallel plot lines that climax in a powerful event, the feminine script emphasizes the process of exploring a basic thematic idea through a succession of varied but equally weighted scene variations. These scene variations have continuity and a unifying focus that is generally provided by a theme.

A play follows a defined sequence of events, without which the story would make no sense. If the telling of a story is *linear*, then the structure follows chronology. If the telling of a story is *nonlinear*, then there is no chronology. Plays with events described out of sequence can have a much more complex structure. These plays are *episodic* in structure. The telling of a story may go along many paths, each with its own implicit chronology. Some plays have a circular approach, coming back at the end to the same or a similar situation as the one in the first scene. Among the nonlinear techniques are the use of flashbacks, foreshadowing, direct address, shifts in time and perspective, and the overlapping of settings to show the parallels between environments and situations.

8 Physical Characteristics

A person's external characteristics are determined by his or her physical attributes, social aspects, and psychological profile. *Physical attributes* influence how a person sees himself or herself and how others see him or her. Physical and mental defects—real or imagined—shape behavior. *Social aspects*—education, economic status, religion, environment—affect behavior, as well. Finally, someone's *psychological profile* is the product of the physiological and sociological and includes fears, insecurities, phobias, complexes, inhibitions, feelings of guilt and desire, and fantasies. These three areas determine the posture, the movement, the speech, and the other daily actions of a character.

Development of Physical Character

As you begin to think about a character, consider the physical dimension that is important to that character. Think of the different world Fred Astaire would have faced with a clubfoot. What would have happened to Marilyn Monroe had she been flat chested? What if Barbara Streisand had been given Hank Aaron's pitching arm and he had been given her voice? In each case, the choices of profession and personality would have been different.

Society shapes us by reactions to our appearance, size, sex, build, skin color, scars, deformities, abnormalities, posture, bearing, and voice. In William Inge's play *Picnic*, Madge is a golden girl, pretty and popular. Her looks have given her a certain importance in the town. Her sister Millie, who is plain and wears glasses, has cultivated her intelligence. Madge envies Millie for her intelligence, and Millie envies Madge for her looks and sophistication. In a more extreme case, in Shakespeare's *Richard III*, King Richard III is deformed and hunchbacked. This permeates how he sees the world and the world sees him. In Gibson's *The Miracle Worker*, Helen Keller is blind and deaf. In Williams's *The Glass Menagerie*, Laura has only a slight limp, but it is magnified in her mind and affects her self-image and actions.

Appearance

Studies have shown that babies respond more to a person who is attractive and whose features are symmetrical than one who is less attractive with less symmetrical features. Attractive men and women are often hired over less attractive people with better qualifications. Studies have also shown that taller men are hired more quickly than short men. They also receive more raises and promotions and generally make more money overall. People flock to attractive people, and ignore average people. For example, if an attractive man or woman drops several folders or packages, people passing by will stop to assist him or her, whereas the average people who drop something will be ignored, as people walk around and avoid them.

Society's standards of physical beauty affect our self-confidence. When society dictates that being attractive means having ears close to the head and a small nose, having ears that stick out and a big nose can make life miserable for you. If you are fatter, thinner, scarred, or in any way different from the norm, your peers will attack you where you're vulnerable. Whether a perceived flaw is large or small, it can take on proportions that far exceed its real dimensions. It often becomes magnified in the mind, and the person with the flaw behaves in a way to reduce calling attention to it. Someone who feels flawed may avoid mirrors, wear his hair in a certain way or dress to disguise the flaw, or avoid contact with the people who pick on him. Such a person may become withdrawn, a loner, or a class clown.

Physical flaws often affect the vulnerability of a character. Society's prejudices and intolerances are made excruciatingly clear.

Posture and Movement

Characterization is conveyed by the posture and movement of the actor. In actor training, the first thing the actor must focus on is the body—his or her instrument. Actors explore exercises in relaxing, sitting, standing, centering the body, moving, gesturing, and exploring space. Actors are trained to control their bodies and to use them to take on characteristics appropriate for the characters they are playing. Playwrights should be aware of the physicality of their characters—their movement and sense of self and how their bodies have shaped them. The audience is strongly influenced by the physical portrayal.

In Edmond Rostand's *Cyrano de Bergerac*, the title character lets society convince him that the length of his nose is so ludicrous that no woman will be interested in the man behind it. Accordingly, Cyrano does not dare woo Roxanne for himself. He does not realize until it is too late that she could not care less about his obsession. His problem is not his nose; it is how he feels about his nose. Any disfigurement, deformity, or problem with one's appearance generally leads to low self-esteem, a degree of psychological withdrawal from society, and difficulty in relationships.

Modern theatrical training provides actors with makeup skills to change their appearance. Highlights and shadows on the face can make the nose appear crooked, create wrinkles, and make the face seem round or angular. Crepe hair can add a mustache or a beard or turn the eyebrows bushy. A wealth of makeup products can create disfiguring scars, along with cuts and bruises, and it can make the nose bigger or longer. A head can be made bald, or by using wigs and hair extensions, it can be given any kind of hairstyle imaginable.

Michael Hood as Cyrano de Bergerac in the University of Alaska Anchorage production. Directed by John Rindo, Set and Lighting Design by Frank Bebey, Costume Design by Fran Lautenberger.

As a playwright, develop in your mind a clear image of each character. People hold their tension and their energy in different ways. After a while, the body's contour and stance reflects this. One of the first things an actor must learn is proper posture and how to center his or her body in order to be grounded and move gracefully. However, some dramatic characters are not healthy and beautiful. They are warped, wounded, and bent out of shape. Actors, therefore, have to learn how to use their bodies to develop these characters.

Body Types

There are five types of bodies (see Figure 8.1). The first body is the normal one. The second body leads with the head; the back and shoulders are bent forward, the arms are bent at the elbows, and the legs are weak. The energy center is in the front stomach area, as though the character is protective, but this stance reflects low energy and is not stable. The high-level energy version of this body reflects an overdevelopment of the upper body—arms and shoulders—so that the figure takes on the aspects of a gorilla.

The third body is the military stance, with the shoulders thrust back, the arms clasped behind, and all the tension and anger concentrated between the shoulder blades. This is the most negative and aggressive posture. The softer area of the front—stomach and chest—is made hard. This body is grounded, but because it is rigid, movement tends to be awkward or mechanical, not graceful.

The fourth body leads with the stomach, and that's where the energy is. The back is swayed and blocks the aggressive energy of the rear of the body. The stance

FIGURE 8.1   These sketches of Margery and Gilbert from *Shakespeare's Journey*, by Leroy Clark, were designed by Marilyn Skow and Marina Pariji. They show two different body types: the normal lower-class tavern wench (first body) and the portly gentleman who leads with his stomach (fourth body).

is heavy but jolly, and sentimental, not aggressive. This body is the easygoing, "Aw, what the heck" personality. This character is talkative, outgoing, and hides the pain.

The fifth body is all angles, characterized by a twisted view of the real world and a greatly reduced ability to carry out daily tasks. All the major joints are disassociated, and the head is cocked sideways. The right hand doesn't know what the left hand is doing. This body is unstable, poorly grounded, and lacks grace in movement.

You, as the playwright, need to take a walk mentally with each of your characters. Stand in their shoes. What contour, kind of body, and kind of energy is part of each character? How do they stand, move, gesture? How does the body reflect the personality?

Voice

In creating a character, the playwright must be able to hear her voice. The voice conveys a great deal about who the person is, where she came from, and what she does. While it is not appropriate to make fun of someone with a speech impediment or to seek a vocal quality that may be harmful to an actor's voice, the playwright may create a character with a special voice. If a character is supposed to sing well, this should be clear from the dialogue and from the character's behavior. If a character must be strong and masculine, both physically and vocally, this should be clear in the dialogue and actions. A character with an accent should be written in the rhythm of that dialect.

Certain roles have become associated with distinct voices. Judy Holliday created Billie Dawn in Garcin Kanin's *Born Yesterday* with a high, nasal, "dumb-blond" voice. Actresses in subsequent productions have cultivated a similar voice. We learn about a character not only from the description provided by the playwright but also from what the character says and what other characters say about her. In Eugene O'Neill's *The Long Voyage Home,* the character Olson says, "I mean all the time to go back home at the end of a voyage. But I come ashore, I take one drink, I take many drinks, I get drunk, I spend all money, I have to ship away for another voyage. So dis time I say to myself: Don't drink one drink, Ollie, or, sure, you don't get home. And I want to go home dis time" (p. 73). Speeches such as this give us a clear understanding of the character's state of mind and the life he or she she has led that brought about this life-changing moment.

Physical Activity

We also learn about a character by his activity or stage business as well as his actions. Consider the corporate executive swinging a golf club in his office, or the woman who drinks from a bottle of gin, or the man who is knitting. A character's major decisions are also shown as actions, such as Proctor's refusal to sign the confession that he is a witch in Arthur Miller's *The Crucible,* Thomas More's refusal to go against the church in Robert Bolt's *A Man for All Seasons,* and Nora's walking out on her husband in Ibsen's *A Doll's House.*

Physical character is important in many plays. In Tennessee Williams's *Cat on a Hot Tin Roof,* Brick hops around on crutches after injuring his ankle. In Inge's *Picnic,* Hal must be masculine, muscular, athletic, and attractive. The actor must assume a twisted posture to play John Merrick in *Elephant Man,* by Bernard Pomerance, and this affects his every movement. *Extremities,* by William Mastrosimone, explores attempted rape and torture. In each of these plays, the character's physical actions are extremely important.

In the 1964 movie *Tom Jones,* there is a wonderful comic scene in which actors Joyce Redmond and Albert Finney are sitting at a table in an inn, eating. Not a word is spoken, but through their eyes, their facial expressions, and their manner of eating, they convey their attraction to one another, their carnal desire and lust. Finally they rush off to bed to have sex. In Eric Bogosian's *Suburbia,* the slacker characters get angry at a shopkeeper and throw Chinese food. Physical actions and props can be very useful in creating a scene.

EXERCISE 12 _____

Beginning Level   Choose one of the following:

A. Write a scene in which there is a physical obstacle within the locale. This obstacle must be something that will affect the characters in the scene, such as a disabled woman in a wheelchair in her home seeking to escape a drug addict trying to rob her, a character that has been kidnapped and tied up by another, or two people trying to move a large object but being unable to. Maybe the characters are trying to open a box, defuse a bomb, or unblock a cave in.

B. Write two half-page, single-spaced monologues. In one, have Character A describe how Character B looks, and in the other, have Character B describe how Character A looks. What is the conflict between the characters? Who is she talking to? What does she want? Focus only on important details. Each monologue should tell us not only about the character being described but also about the character speaking. Think of the times you have told someone about a person you saw at school or at work. You describe the person's appearance and what she did that was outrageous and memorable. Why did you tell the story? Did you color the image to make that person more comic or eccentric?

Intermediate Level   Choose one of the following:

C. Create a dream scene. What objects are visible? Perhaps it is in an open field, a room of refrigerators, a shop of old appliances, or a room with many easels and paintings. What if a character is locked in a cellar of an old house with the ghosts from the past? Describe the locale and then write a dream scene. In dreams, characters, objects, and actions are free from the restrictions of reality.

Dreams do not obey linear thought or structure. Do not worry about interpreting the dream. What are the actions, the sounds, the images, the costumes?

D. Write a climactic scene for your play with three characters. The action should result from the direct conflict between the protagonist and the forces of opposition, whether internal or external. The protagonist—a character who is a prime mover—should take action. There are clearly defined consequences. Are any physical actions important to the scene?

Advanced Level Choose one of the following:

E. Write a conflict scene between two characters that builds to an important physical action. The action may be comic or serious—perhaps a food fight, a pillow fight, a sword fight, destroying an object, or creating an object.

F. Write a scene in which Character A makes an important discovery. Character A suspects that Character B has done something and so questions him or her and pulls out the evidence—some letters, an e-mail, a bill, a record of phone calls. Character A has made assumptions. Character B resists, using a variety of tactics. He or she denies, lies, shames, verbally attacks, and finally pulls the rug out, making Character A realize that his or her assumptions and expectations were false. Character B provides new information that enlightens Character A.

Summary

Consider the physical aspects that are important to a character. Society shapes us based on our appearance, size, sex, skin color, scars, deformities, abnormalities, posture, bearing, voice, etc. Some men are tall, dark, and handsome. Others are short and pudgy. Some women are slender and beautiful. Some are thin and stringy. Whatever their appearance, others react either positively or negatively. Studies have shown that people are more attracted to the so-called beautiful people. You need to determine what external features of your character are important and how they affect the character's self-perception as well as those of others.

Physical characterization is conveyed by the posture and movement of the actor and by the costumes and makeup he or she wears.

There are five body types: The normal posture is centered. The second body leads with the head; shoulders are bent forward, the arms are bent at the elbows, the legs are weak, and the energy center is in the stomach area as though the character is protective. The stance may reflect low energy and instability; in the high-level energy version, there is over-development of the upper body so that the figure takes on the aspects of a gorilla. The third body is the military stance with the shoulders thrust back, the arms clasped behind, and all the tension and anger balled up between the shoulder blades. This is the most negative and aggressive posture, and because it is rigid, it causes movement to be awkward or mechanical, not graceful. The fourth body leads with the stomach and that's where the energy is. The back is swayed and blocks the aggressive energy of the rear of the body. The stance is heavy, jolly and sentimental, indicating an easy-going personality. The character is talkative, outgoing, and hides the pain. The fifth body is all angles. All the major joints are disassociated and the head is cocked sideways. The right hand doesn't know what the left hand is doing. This body is unstable, poorly grounded, and lacks grace in movement.

The playwright must hear the character's voice in his head. The way the character talks should not only reflect his age, health, and origin, but also his personality.

The playwright needs to select physical activity appropriate to the character and develop stage business with props that helps to clarify and emphasize the important physical elements.

CHAPTER

9 Sociological Characteristics

Characterization refers to the externals—the surface or appearance of the character. The external characteristics of a character that are determined by physical attributes influence that character's self-view and behavior, as well as how others see him or her. Social aspects—education, economic status, religion, and environment—affect the character's behavior as well. These two areas determine the posture, the movement, the speech, and the kinds of responses the character makes in his or her life's choices. These two areas lead to the character's psychological development (see Chapter 10).

As the writer, you must slip into the character's shoes, just like the actor does. You must seek to determine the character's superobjective or goal in the play. You must consider the objectives and intentions in each scene. You must explore what the character does to achieve his goal. You must determine the characters' relationships to each other and their lifestyles, educational backgrounds, occupations, social statuses, social adjustments, manners, and attitudes toward sex and religion and politics, plus the role each one plays. Conflict upsets the equilibrium of each individual character. It results in emotional turmoil—determination to reach a new goal, fear of failure, laughter and eagerness while planning, anger and tears when frustrated by obstacles. The three basic emotions are anger, fear, and love.

Development of Character

Each character sees the world differently. Why do people—even those who live together or attend the same event—have different stories? Our stories don't come out of nowhere. First, we observe and take in information and experience the world. Second, we interpret what we experience and give it meaning. Third, we draw conclusions. By age seven, we are all programmed so that our observations and experiences are interpretations that are somewhat predisposed according to conclusions we have already drawn.

Observations

We all have different stories about the world because we all take in different information and process it in our own unique ways. In difficult conversations, too often we only trade conclusions back and forth, without exploring the information and interpretations that lead us to see the world as we do.

There are two reasons we all have different information about the world. First, as we proceed through life and experience situations, the information available is overwhelming. We simply can't absorb all of the sights, sounds, facts, and feelings involved in even a single encounter. Inevitably, we notice some things and ignore others. And so the second reason is that what we choose to notice and ignore will be different for each of us. We each have access to similar information but different sets of perceptions and thus different memories.

We notice things, people, places, and events depending on our interests. When I was about eleven, my father took me to see stock car races. I enjoyed the excitement, the hot dog and the Coke, and getting to be with my dad. I got to sit in one of the winning cars, but I didn't know one car from another. For my father, a mechanic who rebuilt cars and outfitted them for racing, his interest was in which cars performed the best and what problems the others had. In a sense, my father and I experienced and remembered completely different events. My dad assumed that what he paid attention to was what was significant about the experience, but for me, just being with him was the most significant aspect. Each person assumes he has the facts and that others have the same facts.

What we notice also has to do with who we are and what we care about. Some of us pay more attention to what we feel, what we know, what we like, or what we are afraid of. Some of us are artists, others are scientists, and others work in business providing goods and services. Some of us want to prove we're right; others want to avoid conflict or smooth it over. Some of us see ourselves as victims and others as heroes, observers, or survivors. Some of us see only what a person is wearing. Others pay attention to the sad eyes or the kind manner. We may go through a whole conversation—or even an entire relationship—without ever realizing that we all pay attention to different things, that our views are based on different information. Therefore, we all live in different worlds.

We know ourselves better than anyone else can, so in addition to choosing different information, we each have access to different information. Others have access to information about themselves that we don't. They know the pressures and restrictions they are under; we don't. They know their secrets, hopes, dreams, and fears; we don't. We act as if we have access to all the important information there is to know about them, but we don't. Their internal experiences are far more complex than we imagine. What influences each character to perceive as he or she does? How is that character's information different? Imagine that everyone around you is as complex and as internally conflicted as you. Is this a jarring thought?

Interpretations

As noted earlier, the second reason people and characters have different stories about the world is that even when they have the same information, they interpret it differently and give it different meaning. One sees a cup as half full of coffee;

another sees a piece of antique china she would love to see at auction. One's thirsty; the other's a poet.

Two important elements in how characters interpret what they see are past experiences and the implicit rules they have learned about how things should and should not be. The past influences what we do in the present and what is meaningful to us. Sometimes, it is only in the context of someone's past experience that we can make any kind of sense out of what she is saying or doing. Whether we like a particular sport, whether we spank our kids, whether we can stay within our budget for food—each is influenced by what we have observed in our own family and learned throughout our life. Often, we aren't even aware of how these experiences affect our interpretation of the world. We simply believe that's the way things are.

Our past experiences often develop into rules or habits by which we live our lives. Whether we are aware of them or not, we all follow such rules. They tell us how the world works. As such, rules have a significant influence on the stories we tell when we find ourselves in difficult situations.

We get into trouble when our rules collide. Our implicit rules often take the form of things people should or shouldn't do: You should spend money on books but not on magazines. You should never criticize a student in front of others. You should never leave the toilet seat up, drink out of the milk container, or use the "F" word. You should go to church and change your sheets once a week.

Morals, being both relative and taught, fall into this category, as well. The list is endless. Creon, in Sophocles' *Antigone*, lives by one set of rules, Antigone by another. What is moral for one is considered immoral by the other.

Conclusions

When a character tells his own story about the world, it often reflects his own self-interest. The character looks for information to support his view and gives that information the most favorable interpretation. Then he feels even more certain that his view is right.

This tendency to develop unconsciously biased perceptions is very human and can be used to develop your characters. When you have two characters, both of whom believe they are right—especially when they have something important at stake—then you have conflict. Character A is thinking "How can he think that?" and says, "That's the most selfish, shallow, ridiculous thing I've ever heard!" Character B is thinking "How can she be so irrational?" and says, "It's the best possible solution."

Explore the way in which each of your characters views the world differently, interprets the information differently, makes different assumptions, and reaches different conclusions. These affect both characterization and deep character.

Each character's profession, job, hobby, hometown, and educational level provides him with a distinct vocabulary. Every character has a certain body of knowledge and a vocabulary related to what he does. Those involved in the theatre learn a vocabulary that outsiders would have a difficult time understanding. *Blocking, strike, tech-dress, combat, SM, TD, AD, walk a flat, wagon, French scene, stile, Fresnel, Leko*—these are just a few of the terms that have special meanings in the theatre. Similarly, the medical profession uses many terms not readily understood by the average person.

Observe the people around you in your daily life. Watch what they do and how they speak. Take notes in your journal. When you sit down to write, ask yourself these questions: What is the biggest decision this character has made? What were the consequences? What happens when she doesn't understand something? How does what this character knows show up in her speech? Is it easy for the character to explain or difficult? Is this speech the character's first effort at trying to articulate her feelings—words never said before?

While characterization and character are closely related concepts, there are important differences. *Characterization* refers to the externals, the surface, the appearance of the character—all the objective things that you can observe. Deep *character* is shown by a character's action in a crisis, when he is pushed to the extreme. It is created by the choices the character makes under pressure, such as the man who risks his life for freedom or the woman with desperate financial problems who embezzles a million dollars.

Social Development

Characters are formed not only by their physical development but also by their environment. Children are shaped by the economic and social status of their parents or guardians as well as their education, profession, religion, values, and attitudes. Children's own attitudes and values will shape how they respond to the society in which they live and their behavior will determine how that society will respond to them.

Consider how events experienced during childhood have affected the character's interaction in society. What is the character's social class? What was the economic status of her parents? What kind of neighborhood did she grow up in? What kind of schools did the character attend? What were her parents' attitudes about work, sex, money, politics? Was the character given a lot of freedom, or did she suffer harsh discipline? Character is forged by the society in which a person lives. The boy who grew up in the country in Kansas has lived a different life than the boy who grew up in Chicago. The girl who was gang raped at twelve has a different life than the one who is a virgin at twenty-five. What was important in the character's development? How has that affected the character's motivations?

The events experienced during childhood help create the person's or character's automatic responses to similar events throughout life. For example, suppose a girl grew up in the projects in the Bronx and was chewed by rats as a kid, causing her fingers to have some ugly scars. That event might have caused her to be afraid to sleep or fearful that other kids would make fun of her hands. She might become hysterical every time she sees a rat. How might that event influence the character's goals? Every character must have a *need* and an *objective*. Perhaps this girl decides to become a pianist to make her hands beautiful. She is driven to practice daily to become a professional.

In the film *Erin Brockovich,* for example, Erin needs a job and goes to a law office with the objective to get one. Her dress, manner, vocabulary, and behavior are all in contrast to the head of the firm, which shows a difference in their social backgrounds. The lawyer tries to get rid of her, but she refuses to take no for an answer. She has somehow learned to be aggressive, outspoken, and strong enough to overcome her background. In *Getting Out,* a drama by Marsha Norman, Arlene gets out of prison, determined to change her life and go straight, no matter what obstacles she must face. In *Orpheus Descending,* by Tennessee Williams, Carol Cutrere is an outcast, and although she acts outrageously, she really wants to be loved. How these characters react in social situations sheds light on who they are and where they came from.

Just as an actor or playwright seeks to develop the profile of a character by examining his physicality, so must certain areas be explored to determine the character's social profile. The following areas should be explored to discover the current social life of a character and the influences on him: relationship with parents and peers, current family life, education, religious upbringing and current practices, cultural and recreational activities, job or business, political activities, friends and lovers, organizational memberships, and social role (father, son, daughter, mother, sister, boss, employee, activist, feminist, environmentalist, thief, mistress, terrorist, arsonist, convict, etc.).

Our attitudes and mannerisms color everything we do. It is likely they have been created to conceal how vulnerable we are to the world's opinions and how deeply those opinions have wounded us. To deal with this, we often create personalities far removed from our true essence. In creating a character, try to find both the naked and private character underneath and the layers added to hide that vulnerable self.

Life Script

What is a *life script?* It is a character's history, the major events that determine the character's outlook and future responses. What are the major events in the character's past life: a life-changing event, such as the birth or death of a sibling, a divorce, a move from one environment to another; a catastrophic event, such as a bombing, hurricane, or earthquake; a traumatic event, such as a murder, a rape, or a car accident? How have these events affected the character's outlook?

The character's history reflects his expectations—often unmet. Writing your character's history should help you uncover the early decisions your character made unconsciously as to how life should be lived. Early in life, a central emotional position is established, which becomes the automatic position to which that individual will tend to return for the rest of his days. The easiest approach to creating this profile is to list the ten major events in the character's life (see later in this section).

Your character acts not according to what things are really like but according to her life script. It gives rise to mental images of what the character perceives things to be. How the character sees the world creates the action. Is your character waiting for Santa Claus or rigor mortis? How does the character's life script dictate her actions in the scene? How does the character's childhood shape her point of view in the scene? What were the good times? The bad times? Although the playwright must provide some back story, it must be injected into the play in small bits, which are exposed one at a time when there is a need to know in the present.

Create a life script for every main character. Not all of the profile is needed in the play itself, but the work involved in developing it will be helpful in creating the character, to know what motivates her (see Figure 9.1). Henrik Ibsen was a master of exposition. In Ibsen's *Ghosts*, Mrs. Alving wants to tell her son, who has been away in Paris since he was a child, the truth about his father. Interrupted, she is not able to tell him until the last act. Similarly, in Ibsen's *A Doll's House*, Nora doesn't confess her secret until the middle of the last act. Ibsen brings in bits and pieces of information about the past only when they are needed in the present. Moreover, the characters

FIGURE 9.1   The costumes designed by Betty Monroe, Wichita State University, for *Shakespeare's Journey* show the Dark Lady's high status as a member of the court and Beulah's lower-middle-class status in *Orpheus Descending*. The costume designer helps bring a character's profile to life by showing the status, style, and physical character.

use these bits of information as weapons to get what they want. The final revelations are generally earth shaking and connected with an epiphany—a new insight.

Some characters do not change within the course of a play. Shakespeare's Hamlet, Arthur Miller's Willy Loman in *Death of a Salesman,* Harpagon in Moliere's *The Miser,* Organ in Moliere's *Tartuffe,* and Stanley in Tenessee Williams's *Streetcar* are essentially no different at the end of the play than they were at the beginning. Other characters grow and change, such as Nora in Henrik Ibsen's *A Doll's House,* Liza in G. B. Shaw's *Pygmalion,* and Rita in Willy Russell's *Educating Rita.* Some characters change not only psychologically but physically, as well. Liza and Rita undergo quite amazing physical and psychological changes, as does Adam in Neil LaBute's *The Shape of Things.*

For as a life script example, look at the following profile of ten major events in the life of James Dean:

1. He is born to parents on a farm in rural Indiana.
2. His family moves to Los Angeles when he is five.
3. His mother dies when he is nine.
4. His father ships him back to Indiana to live with his aunt and uncle.
5. At age eighteen, he moves back in with his father in Los Angeles.
6. He moves to New York and is accepted by the Actors Studio.
7. He lands a supporting role in a Broadway production.
8. He is offered a leading role in a major film and moves back to Los Angeles.
9. He falls in love with a girl who marries another man.
10. He buys a Porsche.

As you are developing your leading characters, decide what the ten most important events in their lives are.

One of the qualities for a playwright to strive for is an acceptance of all characters, no matter what their sins or woes. Too often playwrights editorialize and present an attitude that labels a character good or bad. The great playwrights such as Shakespeare, Lope de Vega, and even modern American writers such as O'Neill, Miller, Williams, and Albee seem to be able to create characters without passing judgment upon them. They are able to show the character, even those whose behavior or actions are despicable, with understanding and insight that doesn't label or editorialize in a negative way. Characters are shown with their good points and faults, and we are left to make up our own minds.

EXERCISE 13 _____

Beginning Level   Choose one of the following:

  A. Make a list of the ten most important events in the life of a character. These are the major events that have shaped that person. Pick one event in the growing up of your character that clarifies the social aspects. Suppose your character suffered a traumatic event as a child. How would that affect the character now, ten years later? Imagine a scene in which the character uses that event to gain sympathy from someone else. What does the character want? He or she must have a need and an objective. Write a five-page conflict scene in which Character A uses that event to gain sympathy from Character B.

B. Write a scene in which Character B is asked by Character A about an event in his past that he is reluctant to talk about. What is the locale, the characters' relationship, the climax of the scene? Each character should have his or her own manner of speaking. Experienced playwrights often collect interesting vocabulary and phrases, keeping a notebook of snatches of conversation they overhear. In your dialogue, focus on vocabulary. People use the vocabulary of their professions, of what they know, and of their social class. Focus on vocal patterns, rhythms, emphasis. In Williams's *Cat on a Hot Tin Roof*, Brick doesn't want to talk about Skipper, but Big Daddy pushes him to tell the truth. In *The Homesteaders* by Nina Shengold, Neal and Jack are reluctant to talk about their past because they avoided the draft by moving to Canada.

Intermediate Level

C. Write a scene in which Character A makes a decision based on feelings about an event which happened to him as a child. In the scene, Character A should be asked by Character B about an incident in the past that he is reluctant to talk about. What secret is Character A afraid to reveal? What is the relationship of the two characters? Is it positive or negative? What is the climax of the scene? Each character should have his or her own way of speaking. Where is the scene set—in a public or private place? How does the locale affect the situation?

Advanced Level   Choose one of the following:

D. People may make a decision based on their feelings about an event which happened to them as children. Write a scene in which a character's past affects her present actions. This could potentially be a very bad decision for someone whose life is destroyed, not because of what she did, but because someone else acted in a negative way due to a past personal event. Consider the following: (1) a lawyer interviews a witness negative to her client because of an unrelated incident in the witness' past, (2) a race car driver has a run in with the mechanic who worked on his father's race car the day his father died, or (3) a businessperson has to fly to Bermuda and questions the pilot about the small, private plane because of an incident when she was ten.

E. Write a conflict scene in which two people who experienced the same event have very different perceptions of the event because of what they each chose to notice. As they each try to convince a third person of the truth, how are their different perceptions and thus different memories revealed?

Summary

By age seven, an individual is programmed so that his or her observations, experiences, and interpretations are somewhat predisposed according to conclusions he or she has already drawn. A character is formed not only by his DNA, which determines physical development, but also by the environment, which influences the social development. Children are shaped by the economic and social status of their parents or guardians as well as their education, profession, religion, values, and attitudes. Children's own attitudes and values will shape how they respond to the society in which they live, and their behavior will determine how that society will respond to them.

What events determine a character's outlook and attitude toward life? Early in life a central emotional position is established, and it becomes the position to which that individual will tend to return automatically for the rest of his days. Each character is influenced by the major events in his life, usually involving major changes, such as a move, a divorce, a birth, a death, an accident. Writing a character's history should help you uncover when your character made that decision consciously or unconsciously, as to how to live his or her life. How the character sees the world creates the action of the play. The character makes a decision, acting according to his perceptions with certain expectations. He finds reality is different than expected. The character must then make another more important decision. That leads to another and another and so on. Each act is a bigger risk than the last, until finally the character must come face to face with his adversary in a major confrontation.

CHAPTER

10 Psychological Characteristics

The third dimension of character is the psychological, which is the product of the physiological and sociological. The physical attributes of a person shape his self-image, physical development, and social development. Thus, the person develops ways of thinking and behaving related to the physical. The little girl who is smart, pretty, and well coordinated is treated in a positive way, while the dyslexic, chubby, and uncoordinated girl is treated negatively. The first is confident, unafraid, and popular. The other develops a poor self-image, is afraid of being called on to read, and is the last to be chosen for a team.

The social aspects are equally important in shaping personality. The first little girl grows up in a college-educated, religious, comfortable middle-class family. She has a stay-at-home mother and a financially stable father, both of whom are very loving. She goes to a well-equipped, top suburban school. She is exposed to cultural events and given special music and ballet classes. Her parents are already planning for her college education. The second girl grows up living in a third-floor tenement apartment. Her mother is a single parent who works two minimum-wage jobs just to pay the bills. She goes to an old, ill-equipped, and poorly staffed inner-city school. She is exposed to drug dealers and addicts. Her only cultural experience is going to the movies. She gets no real support at home, and she hates school and can't wait to quit.

Each girl is programmed by her heredity and environment, but her supposedly inevitable outcome could be changed at any moment by other events in her life. A car accident could wipe out the first girl's family. A caring teacher might change the second girl's life.

Psychological Development

Within this area of character, we find fears, phobias, insecurities, complexes, inhibitions, feelings of guilt and desire, and fantasies. The psychological dimension also includes intelligence, aptitudes, special abilities, habits, sensitivities, talents, kinds of reasoning, and sources of anger. When the playwright creates a character, he seeks to understand what the character wants and does—and why. The playwright must develop a psychological profile for the character so that the audience can understand why the character says and does what he does.

Study human nature in the everyday world around you. Continue to write notes and observations in your journal. Make character sketches of the people you meet. I once knew a woman who was the wonderful wife of a minister and the mother of three children. She was the last person in the world I would have expected to get an abortion, but she did. What in her psychological makeup caused this or led to this? Your friend wants a divorce. Why? Why did your character become a doctor or drop out of school or end up to jail? What in his psychological makeup led him to that point?

Let's follow the story of Ray. He grew up in a poor family. Until he was twelve, he and his parents lived behind his father's garage in three tiny rooms with no running water, no bathroom, and no doors—just curtains. Ray wet the bed almost every night. He took a bath once a week in a round metal tub in the middle of the kitchen floor. Most of the time, he smelled like urine. His mother made shirts for him that looked like drapes. He was an only child—small, introverted, and shy. His father hated sports, so Ray never learned any. He was not popular on the playground. At twelve, he moved into an unfinished house, still without doors but with water and a bathroom. He started smoking at thirteen and drinking at sixteen. Like his father, he had a vocabulary filled with excessive profanity and obscenities. He worked for his father in the garage during the summers when he was fourteen and fifteen. His father was a severe alcoholic, who drank a fifth of whiskey a day and sometimes went into violent rages. At sixteen, Ray was working in the shipping department of a shoe factory, loading and unloading trucks. Neither of his parents went to high school. He had never been in a church. He was probably destined for a future at a minimum-wage job in a factory. However, everything changed for him when he went from a large-city high school to a small rural academy during his sophomore year. He excelled academically, and he had a teacher who took a special interest in him. Sexually abused repeatedly by an uncle at age fourteen and fifteen, Ray channeled his terrible guilt and fear of being found out into his studies.

Ray's early life programmed him psychologically. He was afraid of being laughed at and would go to great lengths to excel, to win, to succeed, and to avoid new and uncomfortable situations. He learned how to tiptoe around his father and not make waves. He learned how to hide the inner demons and present the public persona of a super intelligent and studious student who was also a talented actor and writer. He became editor of the yearbook, was elected senior class president voted "Most Likely to Succeed," and was accepted into the nearby university. Yet inside, he was still afraid of failing, afraid of being laughed at, afraid of sex. However, with his drive to succeed and control his life, Ray earned a Ph.D. and became a successful teacher.

The profession of your character also affects how he acts. While both are in their sixties, the characters of James Tyrone (an actor) in Eugene O'Neill's *Long Day's Journey into Night* and Willy Loman (a salesman) in Arthur Miller's *Death of a Salesman* have been affected by their different professions. James has a strong voice, erect bearing, and strong gestures. He has a strong sense of self. Willy dresses quietly, talks to himself, and slouches. He's losing his grip on reality and no longer measures up to his former image in the eyes of others. However, in his own mind, he is still the great salesman of his youth; he clings to the past. He once believed that having the gift of gab, getting a shoeshine, and making friends were the keys to success. Now, he has to beg for money.

What does your character know? Suppose she is a pianist, a drummer, a nurse, or a pharmacist. What terms of that profession does she use in everyday speech? How does the profession affect her? Does the character love or hate her job? Someone's occupation and work history influence her outlook on life, perceptions, vocabulary, and behavior. What happens to a young man who is fired from a job? What happens to a man who has worked twenty years for a company and is then laid off? You've read their stories in the newspapers. The young man wants revenge and sets his former place of work on fire. He takes his gun to the post office and kills his former supervisor and co-workers.

Ask people about their jobs. Make a list of the terms, words, and operations appropriate to each job. Imagine two characters from different professions in a non-job situation. For example, two people from different educational and class backgrounds go to work. One is a store manager, and the other is a carpenter. Put these two people in prison together, strand them in a forest after their plane has crashed, or trap them in an underground parking garage after a tornado or earthquake. Each character has a different physical and sociological makeup. One has succeeded because of strength and endurance and the other because of brains. Each has fears, psychological scars, and a life script that influences how he will react under pressure. Depending on the situation, one of the characters will take control. Will brains or brawn be more effective in a prison? In a forest? Underground?

Characters must be dynamic, not passive. Avoid characters that are static, wishy-washy, and don't know what they want. Your character's psychological profile should be alive with passion and strong emotions: lust, anger, greed, ambition, love, hate, revenge, malice. Do you have a character that is determined to find out the truth? Do you have a character that is trying to hide the truth or hide from it? What tactics does the character employ? What will bring the confrontation to a climax? What will be different in the relationship, once the truth is known?

Most characters have habitual emotional responses to stress and conflict. When they are under pressure and their frustration or tolerance level has been reached, they may revert to their habitual defense mechanisms. Doc, in William Inge's *Come Back, Little Sheba*, is a reformed alcoholic who goes back to drinking. Mary, in Eugene O'Neill's *A Long Day's Journey into Night*, begins taking morphine again. Oscar, in Lillian Hellman's *The Little Foxes*, tries to be nice for a while, but his sadistic nature returns and he takes pleasure in hurting his wife. Bishop kills his antagonists and eats them in Nicky Silver's *Fat Men in Skirts*. Under stress, Honey gets sick and vomits in Edward Albee's *Who's Afraid of Virginia Woolf?* In Shakespeare's *Richard III*, the title character's twisted body is mirrored in his twisted actions (see Figure 10.1). A man of ambition, intellect, and unlimited faith in force, he is tyrannical, disposes of all who oppose him, and eventually becomes a child killer.

FIGURE 10.1 Costume sketch from *Richard III*, performed at Wichita State University. Directed by Joyce Cavarozzi, Set and Lighting Design by Brad Reissig, and Costume Design by Betty Monroe.

Playwrights endow some characters with individual idiosyncrasies that make them come alive as unique and vibrant characters. In *And Miss Reardon Drinks a Little,* by Paul Zindel, Catherine snacks on raw meat hidden in a candy box, Fleur steals toilet paper and towels from the school where she teaches, and her husband, Bob, doesn't use the bathroom in their apartment. When Beatrice gets dressed up in Paul Zindel's *The Effect of Gamma Rays on Man-in-the-Moon Marigolds,* she always wears feathers. Captain Queeg takes out steel balls and rolls them in his hand in Herman Wouk's *The Caine Mutiny Court Martial.*

Some characters are created with special abilities that require the actors playing them to already have or learn those same abilities. In *Suburbia,* by Eric Bogosian, the character of Buff arrives on Rollerblades. Terrence McNally's *Master Class* calls for actors who can sing opera. Artie, in John Guare's *The House of Blue Leaves,* is supposed to play the piano and sing. The actors playing Annie and Helen in William Gibson's *The Miracle Worker* must know the sign language alphabet for the deaf. Each Vietnam veteran in *Tracers,* written by the original cast of Vietnam veterans, must know how to handle a rifle.

What if one of your characters had a knife collection? What if one of them was a sculptor? A baker? A computer repairman? A butcher? What if one of them smuggled items into the country for extra cash? What if one of your characters had a phobia about telephones? What if one were colorblind? What if one was allergic to rye flour, peanuts, or wasps? You may be writing a conventional love story of boy meets girl, but by adding layers and specific details to the individual characters, your play can become original and your characters unique.

The Johari Window

In a psychology class years ago, I learned about the four different aspects of each person, which can be presented in the *Johari window* (see Figure 10.2). This model describing the process of human interaction was named after its inventors, Joseph Luft and Harry Ingram. As you are developing each character, consider the four following questions:

1. What is the character's public persona? Each of us has a *public self*—that information about ourselves that we readily share with others.
2. What is known to the public that the character is blind to? Each of us has a *blind self.* We cannot see ourselves. We may have a particular walk, gesture, or habit that stands out to others but that we are unaware of.

PUBLIC SELF	SECRET SELF
Known to Self and to Others	Known to Self but not to Others
BLIND SELF	UNCONSCIOUS SELF
Known to Others Unknown to Self	Unknown to Self and to Others

FIGURE 10.2   The Johari Window

3. What is the character's *secret self*? What is it that she doesn't want anyone to know? All people have secrets: things in their past they're ashamed of or secret fears or desires.
4. What is your character's *unconscious self*? What desires, wants, or fears have become buried in her subconscious?

Take two of your characters from a previous exercise, and make a list of answers for each of the above questions for each character. What knowledge does Character A have that Character B does not have and vice versa? It will soon be apparent that much of what goes on inside one character's head is not known by the other.

Defense Mechanisms

It is easier to see another person's blind spots than it is to see our own. Our *defense mechanisms* can blind us to our inconsistencies and leave others wondering why we don't act more responsibly. In spousal abuse, for example, an abusive individual may believe that violence against family members is wrong. But the inhibiting effect of this value can be neutralized by a defense mechanism permitting violence to occur. The abusive individual may rationalize, "When I drink, I lose control, so it's not my fault." Similarly, wherever people organize for a purpose, their group leaders may talk about the value of working together in unity yet behave in ways that polarize and alienate their members.

Even in our own relationships with ourselves, defenses and blind spots are there. Some people who advocate health continue to have unhealthy habits. Some doctors still smoke. Values are guides for action. When we are inconsistent with our own values, an internal tension arises as a signal something is wrong. We are motivated to reduce that tension to maintain a sense of self-consistency. This if often done by employing defense mechanisms. Life maps are formed early, and core beliefs are more persistent than peripheral behavior patterns. People often use defense mechanisms to justify conduct after the fact. This temporarily props up their self-esteem but ensures that the self-defeating behavior will continue.

Here are some defense mechanisms that can create blind spots and serve a good purpose in terms of creating conflict:

1. *Denial:* This primitive defense protects a character from painful reality by having him refuse to acknowledge it. When faced with a well-documented event, the character thinks "That just wasn't me" or "That simply did not occur." Painful memories can be excluded from awareness rather than remembered, but if they are brought up, they are often denied. In this context, people deny being prejudiced. They deny having a dependency on alcohol or drugs or any action that isn't acceptable to their picture of who they are. People may also see others not as they are but as they want them to be.

In Anton Chekhov's *The Cherry Orchard*, the Ranevskys live in denial about their economic plight and lose their home. In Molière's *Tartuffe*, Organ is blind to the true character of the hypocrite Tartuffe, and when others attempt to tell him the truth, he refuses to listen. Roy Cohn, in Tony Kuchner's *Angels in America*, denies that he is a homosexual and he has AIDS. In his mind, homosexuals are weak and have no power. He tells his doctor that he has power, that he is a heterosexual who has sex with men, and that he has cancer, not AIDS. In Ariel Dorfman's *Death and the Maiden*, Dr. Miranda denies that he raped and tortured Paulina.

2. *Repression:* Repressed material is really forgotten. A character may have been so traumatized by an event that she blocks out all conscious awareness of it. A character may also forget what she doesn't want to remember. In this context, an individual may not remember being sexually abused, seeing her father kill someone, or being in a car accident.

John Pielmeier explores Dr. Livingstone's search for the truth, which Sister Agnes has repressed, in *Agnes of God*. While searching for the answers to the questions of who fathered the baby, and who killed the baby, Livingstone forces Agnes, the Mother Superior, and herself to face some harsh realities. Halle, in Sam Shepard's *Buried Child*, seems to have repressed all knowledge of the dead baby, and Tilden has no recollection of his son Lenny.

3. *Projection of blame:* One person's responsibility for a behavior is sometimes shifted to someone else, so that the abuser is now the victim. "She hit me first" is rather obvious. Blame can also be transferred to bad luck, alcohol, job stress, or a boss or subordinate. A rapist may blame his victim for being a slut or for the crimes of other women.

In Tracy Letts's *Killer Joe*, a father and son team up in a plan to murder the mother. She stole the son's drugs. She is a hateful person. The father divorced her years ago. She makes everyone miserable. The world would be better off without her. The father and son blame her for their problems and see her death as a solution.

4. *Displacement:* Here, feelings are shifted or displaced from the original source of frustration to another source. The character in conflict with her boss may displace her anger to her husband, who in turn may take it out on a child, who may then take it out on a sibling or a pet. A robber may blame his behavior on his boss or his parents or society in general for treating him with no respect and making him feel powerless.

In Kenneth Lonergan's *This Is Our Youth*, Warren is a slacker who gets stoned all the time. His father is abusive and beats him. Both blame their behavior on the fact that Warren's sister was murdered.

5. *Undoing:* Often people try to undo what they have done. Atonement, apologizing, and asking for forgiveness are typical responses, but real repentance is a 180-degree change that seldom happens. Thus, the abusive husband apologizes, buys his wife gifts, and swears he won't do it again. The wife wants to believe him, so she stays.

In *This Is Our Youth,* Warren is kicked out by his abusive father, so he steals $15,000 from his father's briefcase. Near the end of the play, Warren decides to give the money back. He calls his father and tries to patch things up. Playing poker with his friends, Stanley in Tennessee Williams's *A Streetcar named Desire* gets angry because Mitch goes off to talk to Blanche. He throws the radio out the window and strikes his wife, Stella. Blanche takes Stella upstairs to another apartment, but when Stanley gets on his knees and calls to his wife, Stella forgives him.

6. *Rationalization:* The character may devise seemingly logical explanations to reinterpret her weakness as admirable qualities. The loser with a million schemes, the politician who took a few uncredited gifts, the contractor who uses poor-grade materials, and the manufacturer who ships defective parts can all come up with a reason that doing so was necessary.

Meg, in Beth Henley's *Crimes of the Heart,* has a reason for sticking her finger in every chocolate in Lenny's box of candy, and Babe has a reason for shooting her husband. Babe didn't like his looks, and Meg is hunting for one with nuts. In their minds, their reasons justify their actions. In *The Visit,* by Friedrich Durrenmatt, Clara states that she will pay a huge sum of money to the town if someone will kill Anton Schill, her lover of long ago who cast her out. The people refuse, but soon the hypocrites are buying things on credit. Schill is eventually murdered, and the townspeople rationalize that what they did was for the good of the town.

7. *Labeling:* Once a character has been labeled, she doesn't have to consider the truth in what the other characters are saying. Once a character has been lumped into a category—she is the girl next door, a loose woman, a career woman, a murderer, a beauty queen, a liar, an alcoholic, or a drug addict—she is no longer an individual.

In *The Heiress,* by Ruth Goetz and Augusta Goetz, Catherine is labeled by her father as a pathetic ugly duckling without any charm. When a suitor woos her but doesn't show up on the night of their planned elopement, she takes this as confirmation that what her father said is true.

Although not a complete list, these are some of the common defense mechanisms that people use unconsciously to reduce anxiety. All defense mechanisms involve some degree of self-deception and distortion of reality. Consider the ways in which your characters are deluded and suspicious, conjuring up in their minds all sorts of possibilities. Each character looks for signs that prove his theory right, and regardless of whether the signs are truly there, the character will interpret what he sees as proof of what he believes.

Unrealistic Expectations

Because of their past experiences, people develop unrealistic expectations. These lead people to choices and behaviors that are often destructive. To provide a protagonist, antagonist, or supporting character with one or more of these unrealistic beliefs can be helpful in polarizing the characters. Doing so can be great fun, too, but you must have a rational character to provide contrast and balance. Unrealistic beliefs that make a character upset include the following:

1. *"I must be loved (or approved of) by other human beings for what I do and what I am."* Meg, in Henley's *Crimes of the Heart*, has held on to the view "I must be loved or approved of by men." Blanche, in Williams's *Streetcar* has also lived according to this view. The more rational approach is to realize that loving others is the only thing a person can control. They cannot make others love them. Given the many natural conflicts among humans, it is more realistic to expect disapproval now and then.

2. *"I should be perfectly competent, intelligent, and successful in all possible respects. In short, I must be perfect."* Naturally, no one is perfect. Shelly Levene is a former top salesman having a streak of bad luck in David Mamet's *Glengarry Glen Ross*. He refuses to acknowledge that all human beings have limitations or that he is an average human being. He makes excuses, blames others, and acts defensive. Suckered into a scheme by one of his colleagues, he robs the office. Only at the end, after he has been caught, is he forced to admit that he is responsible for his own mistakes.

3. *"It is horrible, catastrophic, and awful when things are not the way I want them to be."* This is the view held by cousin Chick in Henley's *Crimes*. She is appalled at the whole family because she's afraid of how their actions will reflect on her. It is catastrophic that Babe has shot her husband. It is disgraceful that Lenny buys her children cheap presents. It is awful that Meg has had all those men and earned a trashy reputation. It is horrible that their mother hung herself and her cat. While her relatives have suffered much, their suffering has only been a nuisance, a minor inconvenience for Chick. Yet she goes on and on about them, as if they signaled the end of the world.

4. *"Certain acts are wicked, awful, or bad. Individuals who do these bad things should be severely punished."* This is the philosophy of Sister Mary Ignatius in Christopher Durang's wacky comedy by the same name. She believes that homosexuality, adultery, abortion, and almost everything else are all bad, and when her students are guilty of any of these things, she believes they should be severely punished. This power of public criticism is also seen in Lillian Hellman's *The Children's Hour*.

5. *"Life should be fair and just; there should be equality."* This is the theme of many plays dealing with injustice, prejudice, and discrimination. However, in reality, fairness is arbitrarily defined by each person. In most cases, someone eventually seizes the power to require that her concept be accepted by others. Laws often originate this way and remain in effect until there is a change in power. From Babe's point of view in Henley's *Crimes of the Heart*, life should be fair and her African American, sixteen-year-old lover should have equality. When her husband treats him badly, she seizes power and shoots her husband.

6. *"The past must continually affect my current feelings."* This is the view held by every character who is a victim. As Paula Vogel stated in reference to *How I Learned to Drive,* on *the News Hour with Jim Lehrer,* that this is the typical role of the victim, and in her play, she wanted to show a more rational approach. Li'l Bit learns from her past experiences, but they do not determine her current emotion and behavior. She doesn't dwell on being abused as a child but rather celebrates her strengths as she encounters each new moment of her life as an adult.

7. *"Other people cause my misery."* The black man and white woman in LeRoi Jones's *The Dutchman* each blame the other's race as the cause of their problems. In Simon Gray's *Butley,* the university lecturer of the title rails against the petty university politics and unease caused by student dissent. In fact, however, other people cannot really cause a person to feel bad. He or she can choose to be happy or not.

8. *"I need someone or something stronger than myself on which to rely."* Again, this is Blanche DuBois's *modus operendi* in Williams's *Streetcar,* and it fails her. Stanley, on the other hand, takes a rational view. He is willing to take risks, even if they don't pay off. He knows the results are seldom as bad as feared, and he knows he has to take charge of himself.

9. *"My happiness can come by passively waiting."* Skeeter, in Jack Kirkland's *Tobacco Road,* and Lenny, in Henley's *Crimes of the Heart,* are both unwilling to work hard for what they want. Skeeter is lazy and prefers to steal rather than work. Lenny has a shrunken ovary and is afraid no man will want her. She eventually decides to risk it and learns that people are happier when active and focusing positive attention on another person. Skeeter never learns anything.

10. *"I have no control over my emotions."* Many of the plays mentioned already have characters who exhibit this philosophy. Meg and Lenny in Beth Henley's *Crimes of the Heart* act impulsively and without control. Evy in Neil Simon's *The Gingerbread Lady,* Stanley in Williams's *Streetcar,* and Uncle Peck in Paula Vogel's *How I Learned to Drive* are others who don't seem to be able to control themselves.

Characters who exhibit unrealistic expectations are hard for reasonable people to deal with. They wouldn't have such feelings if they were rational. Moreover, they are often not consciously aware of the forces within them. Rational people often recognize certain idiosyncrasies and try to avoid upsetting them. You may have heard relatives say things such as: "Don't tell Charlotte the dress didn't fit. She'll think you don't love her." "Don't say anything to Tom. He's hated Charlie since high school when Charlie was valedictorian. He blames Charlie for taking away his scholarship. Of course, it never was his, but you can't reason with Tom."

EXERCISE 14 _____

Beginning Level   Choose one of the following:

  A. Using the Johari window as a model of human interaction, write a conflict scene between two or three characters. Character A digs into one of Character B's secrets, perhaps exposing it to a third character, while Character B exposes Character A's blind self. What knowledge does each character have that the other does not have? Make it apparent that much of what goes on inside one character's head is not known by the other person.

B. Write a scene about a situation or event in which one character acts in a reprehensible way, lies about it, and then is confronted by another character who has learned the truth. Select at least two or three defense mechanisms that the guilty character uses to try to deflect the other character. Make sure the other character is connected to the guilty one in an important way such as being her parent, spouse, boss, sibling, or teacher.

Intermediate Level   Choose one of the following:

C. Write a scene in which Character A confronts Character B about something Character B has done. Character A demands to know why Character B avoids A's question, but A slowly gets at the truth. In what ways are the characters polar opposites? What is the climax? What is different in the relationship at the end of the scene?

D. Write a scene with three archetypal characters in which Character A deliberately lies to Character B about a past action that he has done. What is he hiding or afraid of? Who is he protecting? When Character B is out of the room, Character A tells the truth to Character C. Why? What does A want from C? What if Character B learns the truth?

Advanced Level   Choose one of the following:

E. Write a scene about two characters who hate each other on the surface but underneath really love each other. For each character mix two or three archetypes: Boss, Best Friend, Rebel, Intellectual, Warrior, Seductive Charmer, Innocent, Adventurer, Nurturer.

F. Write a scene with three characters of different status. At the climax of the scene, the status of two of the characters is reversed by a revelation from the third character. For example, a Boss may be in conflict with his Rebel-Intellectual son, blaming him for an event. The son's Charmer friend reveals that the Boss actually caused the problem.

Character Is Action

All that can be known of a character comes from her actions and reactions. A character is the sum of her actions during a play. What a character does conveys who she is more clearly than anything else. In Shakespeare's *Othello*, Iago is a smooth talker who appears to be Othello's friend, yet his actions show him to be a villain. Action is the clearest indicator of character.

Characters are constructed of playable emotions. They have wants and needs that drive them to make choices. They care about things. Strong and contrasting emotions build strong characters. In Henrik Ibsen's *A Doll's House*, for example,

Nora is characterized as a doll, an empty-headed plaything, but we soon see that she is a very strong woman who is willing to do whatever she feels she has to do. Strong emotions are caused by putting characters in situations of extremes and forcing them to make crucial, pivotal decisions.

"Show, don't tell" is one of the most important essentials of good playwriting. Themes come through not by having characters tell about them but by making what happens in a play illustrate the themes. Consider one character who says "I'm angry" and another who says "Go to hell" and in a fit of rage dumps over a table. The first one tells; the second one shows. In Neil Simon's *Barefoot in the Park*, the actions of the characters show us that for a marriage to survive, compromise is necessary. This is clear through what the characters say, do, and learn. No one has to tell us this. If the sum of the actions of the play equal the premise or theme you intend, the audience will observe the interactions of the characters, discover the story, and come to the conclusions you want.

Recently, as I was reading a student's first draft of a scene in my playwriting class, I discovered that he was *telling*, not showing, in the stage directions. For example, he was telling what the character was feeling or indicating that the character should move. What he didn't understand was that a specific action—such as a man throwing a beer can across the room—would show anger. If he had used stage directions that showed action, he wouldn't need to tell us the man was angry. He would have shown it.

Deep Character

Deep character is revealed by a character's action in extreme circumstances. It is created by the choices the character makes under pressure. For example, the woman who is sexually harassed by a boss and takes legal action, instead of just putting up with it, shows us a person of integrity and principles who is willing to take action for what she believes is right. In *A Man for All Seasons*, by Robert Bolt, we see Thomas More refusing to buckle under to the will of the king; he is a man who stands up for what he believes, even though it means his own death. The same is true for the title role in Jean Anouilh's *Becket*.

Not all characters are able to make such noble decisions. Blanche, in Tennessee Williams's *A Streetcar Named Desire*, is unable to face reality. She wants to see the world through rose-colored glasses. She actively lies, embellishes, and tries to hide. When Mitch rejects her and Stanley rapes her, she slides further into a world of fantasy. Willie Loman, in Arthur Miller's *Death of a Salesman*, also loses touch with reality and escapes into the past.

The choices the protagonist makes under pressure are usually in contrast to his characterization. The audience knows people are not who they seem. True character is formed by the choices the character makes under pressure. An individual brings certain qualities to his choices and must have the moral qualities that will convince him to act on those choices. Three-dimensional characters have complex motives and conflicting desires. They want something and go after it. They have worries, grievances, and fears. They have strong passions and ambitions, which make them alive. They have often committed great sins and endured terrible sufferings.

Looking at it subjectively, writing involves sitting at a desk and getting inside the mind of the character, walking in his shoes. Take a character to the limit:

1. What are the possibilities?
2. What is the worst possible thing that could happen? Make it happen.
3. What does the character fear most? Make it happen.
4. What is the dream? What steps does the character take to make it a reality? Or is it a pipe dream that she knows is impossible and so does nothing about.
5. Where is the passion in your character's life?
6. What reduces her to "a kid at Christmas?" Heart comes from the details.
7. What is at stake? What is the character risking? What will happen if she loses? The higher the stakes, the more there is to lose and the more dramatic the story.
8. What is the character's ideal scenario? What are her expectations?
9. How does the character deal with reality when it is different from her expectations?
10. What does the antagonist do to stop the protagonist from succeeding?

Contrasting Types

It is important to create characters that are not stereotypes. We do not need another sweet young girl next door, or another whore with a heart of gold, or another handsome hunk hero. *Stereotypes* are characters that are too familiar; they say and do what we have come to see as a general profile. The key to originality is real knowledge. If you don't have the knowledge, then you will have a cliché. There will be no surprises. Think of what makes each character unique, special, and different. What are his contradictions? When all the audience's expectations of a character are fulfilled, when there are no contradictions or surprises in the character, you have a stereotyped role.

The secret of a fresh, nonstereotyped characterization is to combine character traits that the audience wouldn't expect to find in the same character. You might create a professor who reads comic books, a tough detective who has a pet bird, or a grandmother who loves boxing. Contradictions can be found in everyone. They need to serve the purpose of the play and affect the character's emotions and behavior. In *Crimes of the Heart,* by Beth Henley, Meg has had many men; Lenny has had only one. Meg is selfish; Lenny is selfless but a complainer. Meg is popular; Lenny is not. Meg has had a nervous breakdown; Lenny has cared for her grandfather. These characters are complex.

One of the ways to develop a fresh character is to make a list of attributes for that character and then incorporate them within different scenes in the play. That's what Elia Kazan did when he was preparing to direct Arthur Miller's *After the Fall*. (Meyer & Meyer, 1965, p. 57–59). He wrote the following about Louise:

> Louise believes in certain rules of behavior, of right and wrong.
> She is dominated by the "ought to" and "should."
> Louise has been taught and believes if she conforms to those rules, she'll come thru O.K.
> Sin is absolute. She can't forget it.
> Quentin is soiled, disgusting [to her].

Kazan wrote the following about Quentin:

> Quentin has patronized her.
> Quentin has used her—as a mother.
> Quentin has used her—as a servant.
> Quentin has been totally selfish.
> Quentin has made her feel insignificant.
> Quentin never granted her individuality.
> Quentin has truly shared NOTHING with her!

Character Questionaire

In a similar way, the playwright can begin by answering the following questions for each character and then finding ways of showing the qualities that are most important:

Physical Traits
How old is the character?
How does the character feel about her appearance?
What does she usually wear?
What are her ethnic origins?
What is her self-image?
What is her favorite footwear?

Social Traits
What is the character's occupation?
What are the conditions at her job like?
How is the character regarded in the community?
Who was her favorite teacher?
How did she vote in the last election?
What insect does she hate the most?
Who is the person the character most admires?
What kind of car does she prefer?

What is her status?
What is her income?
What is her attitude toward work?
What was her attitude toward school?
What was the last book she read?
What does the character have in her pocket?
How often does she do her laundry?
What kind of music does she listen to?
When was the last time she was scared?
What does she like to do for fun?

Psychological Traits
What are the character's sexual practices and attitudes?
What is her dominant view of self?
What secret does she have?
What did she dream about last night?
What is her greatest ambition?
What is the character's dominant view of the world?
Who is most important to her?
What is her greatest fear?
What is her earliest childhood memory?
What is the dark side of her character?

EXERCISE 15

Beginning Level   Choose one of the following:

A.   Action is the clearest indicator of character. Write a scene in which a character makes a decision at the beginning of the scene with unexpected consequences. Give the character playable emotions. What are the wants and needs that drive the character to make the choice she does? Put the character in an extreme situation and force her to face a crucial, pivotal decision that causes extreme emotions.

B.   Write a scene that shows us a person of integrity and principles who is willing to take action for what he believes is right. Provide a devil's advocate who tries to persuade the character not to take action.

Intermediate Level   Choose one of the following:

C.   Write a scene in which there are two contrasting characters who exhibit contradictions. The secret of fresh, nonstereotyped characterizations is to combine character traits that the audience wouldn't expect to find in the same character, such as a smoker who worries about eating healthy foods, a tough detective who doesn't like bad language, or a grandmother who loves boxing. The contradictions need to serve the purpose of the scene and affect the character's emotions and behavior.

D. Write a scene in which a character has committed a sin or a bad deed of some kind. Take a character to the limit. What is the worst possible thing that could happen? Make it happen. What does the character fear most? Make it happen.

Advanced Level   Choose one of the following:

E. Develop a character with an unrealistic belief system. In many cases, if one of the rationalizations discussed is applicable, so are three or four others. Begin with a female character of low esteem who bases her self-worth on the opinions of others. When she isn't perfect and is put down by others, she thinks those people who say bad things to her should be severely punished. She blames others for her misery. She finally assaults someone, verbally or physically.

F. Write a scene with two characters in which appearance, movement, clothing, or physical activity is the cause of conflict. Reveal to your audience how each character combs his hair, gestures, dresses, and goes about his stage business. Imagine your character's physical life. Healthy? Athletic? What does the character wear and do to hide his flaws? In the scene focus on the conflicts. Do not give us any description of the characters before the scene. Let us learn about each character from his or her behavior. For example, imagine how a teenager rebels against his parents in terms of dress, hair, piercings, tattoos, smoking, or drinking. Imagine a wife who comes home and finds her husband wearing her clothes.

Summary

The third dimension of character is the psychological: the product of the physiological and sociological. Within this area, we find fears, insecurities, phobias, complexes, inhibitions, feelings of guilt and desire, and fantasies. The psychological dimension also includes intelligence, aptitudes, special abilities, habits, sensitivities, talents, kinds of reasoning, and sources of anger. The psychological profile should make clear why the character does and says things.

When we are inconsistent with our own values, an internal tension arises as a signal something is wrong. We are often motivated to reduce that tension and maintain a sense of self-consistency by employing defense mechanisms. Life maps are formed early, and core beliefs are persistent. People often use defense mechanisms such as denial, repression, projection of blame, displacement, undoing, rationalization, and labeling.

Because of their past experiences, people develop unrealistic expectations and beliefs, which lead them to choices and behaviors that are often destructive. When reality hits, conflict is bound to occur.

All that can be known of a character comes from his actions and reactions. A character is the sum of his actions during a play, including what he says (verbal action) and does (physical actions) and the decisions he makes (mental actions). Characters are constructed of playable emotions. They have wants and needs that drive them to make choices. They care about things.

Deep character is revealed by a character's actions in extreme circumstances, as determined by those choices she makes under pressure. Deep character is shown by putting characters in extreme situations and forcing them to make crucial, pivotal decisions.

The secret of a fresh, nonstereotyped characterization is to combine character traits that the audience wouldn't expect to find in the same character. Create contradictions. Use polar opposites. Characters need to have different backgrounds, attitudes, beliefs, and goals so they have disagreements over issues.

CHAPTER

11 Orchestrating the Characters

We might compare orchestrating the characters in a play to baking bread: If you don't have the right ingredients in the proper portions, the results will not be good. Imagine what might happen if you add too much water, leave out the yeast, or substitute corn flakes for flour.

Audience members make up their minds about who a character is and whether he or she is likeable in the first four minutes the character is on stage. Playwrights need to be very careful that the first impression is the one they intend to be conveyed. With the bread, if the first taste is bitter or too sweet or disgusting, that will determine the outlook toward the entire loaf. Similarly, each character must be clear and vivid in the first four minutes of his or her first scene so the audience will know how the author wants them to respond.

In this chapter, we will discuss six important concepts related to orchestrating characters:

1. Using significant events in the back story of the character to tell the story in the present
2. Selecting a polarized mix of characters with different personalities and goals
3. Making sure the protagonist and antagonist are evenly matched
4. Bonding the characters in a crucible so their motivation to continue in conflict is greater than their desire to quit and run away
5. Using the entrance of another character to heighten the conflict or suspense
6. Applying techniques to get to know your characters

The Back Story

A character profile is needed to develop a back story, and frequently, the writer doesn't know the answers until he sits down and begins to make specific decisions about the characters. The *back story* is not just the biography of the character. Rather, it comprises, previous significant events in the life of the character that can be pulled out and used to tell the story in the present.

In Henrik Ibsen's *Ghosts*, the back story about Mrs. Alving's husband is essential to the plot of the play, but we learn that story only gradually, in bits and

137

pieces. Following her parents' wishes in the days of arranged marriages, Mrs. Alving weds a man she doesn't love. She loves another—Manders. She discovers after her wedding that her husband is a womanizing drunk. Cooped up in a drab, provincial town with a dull, petty, routine job, he finds nothing to stimulate his mind or feed his spirit. He thus drinks to excess and has numerous affairs with other women. He has even seduced the maid and is actually Regina's father. Mrs. Alving goes to Manders for help, but he tells her to do her duty and stay with her husband. So she does her duty, sends her son away to Paris, and never lets him know the truth about his father until near the end of the play. Then, Oswald reveals that he is suffering from syphilis, which he has inherited from his father. He begs his mother for euthanasia when his next attack occurs because the doctor has told him that it will result in dementia.

In Tennessee Williams's *Cat on a Hot Tin Roof*, Big Daddy finally pushes Brick to admit the truth. His best friend, Skipper, had revealed to Brick that he has homosexual feelings for him. Brick then turned his back on Skipper, and Skipper killed himself. Brick finally tells Big Daddy the truth—that everyone has been lying to him and that he is dying of cancer. These revelations provide major turning points both in the plays and in the characters' lives.

Good Orchestration

Good *orchestration*—selecting the right mix of characters, who have different beliefs and goals and will definitely clash—is essential. The characters need to be different. Look at the mother and daughter in Tennessee Williams's *The Glass Menagerie* and Martin McDonagh's *The Beauty Queen of Leenane*. In the first play, Amanda wants a "gentleman caller" for Laura. Laura is afraid and wants to play with her glass collection. In the second play, Maureen wants to go to America with a man. Her mother, Mag, wants to make sure her daughter doesn't leave her alone. The gay title character in Paul Rudnick's *Jeffrey* decides to give up sex because he is afraid of getting AIDS. He then falls for a man who is HIV positive. They are polar opposites in many ways, with far different wants, needs, and dreams, but it's a comedy and they both finally come together because each man loves the other.

The key to creating a good mix of characters is to put together people with polar or contrasting beliefs, personalities, and wants. The ideal cast is polarized. Imagine the characters sitting together at a dinner. If a bottle of wine were tipped over, how would they react differently? With polarized characters, no two would act the same. One would be all upset and appalled. One would deal with it in a practical, expedient manner and clean it up. One would ignore it. One would think it was funny and laugh. One would complain about how much the wine cost. One would go get another bottle. If you do have two characters that will respond in the same way, eliminate one of them.

The real unity of opposites is one in which compromise is impossible. This assures us that the characters will not make a truce in the middle or call it quits.

Any uncompromising character creates the expectancy of conflict or tension. In conflict, the true self is revealed. The conflict also shows who is loyal, who is a coward, and who is selfish. It tests the other characters in terms of their relationship with the protagonist.

In Sophocles' *Antigone,* the young woman, Antigone, and Creon, her uncle and king, are opposites for whom compromise is impossible. They are united by blood. They both share a love for Haemon. Yet Creon believes in duty to the state, and Antigone believes in duty to the individual. Neither will change or relent or back down. As a result, Creon walls up Antigone in a cave. His son, who loves her, commits suicide. When Creon learns of this tragic outcome, he sends men to recover Antigone, but it is too late. She has hung herself.

In *A Doll's House,* by Henrik Ibsen, Nora and Helmer are united by marriage, love, home, children, and society, yet they, too, are opposites. Neither one meets the other's standards of desired behavior. Helmer is not the kind of man Nora thought he was, and she is not the kind of wife that Helmer will tolerate. This knowledge only comes to them in the final scene, after a series of complications and reversals. Again, *compromise is impossible.* Nora walks out and slams the door on both Helmer and her children.

A play tells the story of how someone deals with danger. Until the protagonist decides to fight the injustice, rather than run away from it, there is no story. The character who is willing to take on the struggle and give it her all is the kind of uncompromising character that is needed. The character cannot be passive. We want characters who take action.

Archetypes

There are many male and female archetypes that may be helpful in terms of orchestration, analyzing the characters you already have, or layering different qualities in each character. Archetypes are the original or basic model for all characters of the same type. Some of the typical archetypes include:

The Boss

Male Version.   He is the father, the leader, the corporate executive, the platoon leader, the captain. He likes to take control. He is a problem solver. He likes new challenges. He expects people to do what he wants. He is decisive, committed, goal oriented, stubborn, and domineering, and he may appear to be cold and unfeeling. He is intelligent and competent. His way is the *right* way.

Female Version.   She is the mother, the career woman who climbs to the top. She is strong and tough and takes charge. She is a problem solver and doesn't mind bending the rules. She is decisive, goal oriented, and arrogant, and she can be cold, calculating, and ruthless. She expects others to do what she wants, and she will mow them down if they get in her way.

The Rebel

Male Version.   He never follows the rules and is unwilling to play the game expected of him. He is reckless, daring, cocky. He has a chip on his shoulder. He maintains his reputation as a "bad apple." He acts according to his own code of ethics. He is charismatic, cool, volatile, pessimistic, dangerous, and very attractive to others. He is always at odds with authority figures.

Female Version.   Like the male rebel, she is a free spirit—unconventional, spontaneous, and impulsive. She has a strong sense of individuality and is guided, even ruled by her emotions. She wants to be liked for who she is. She is sincere, positive in her approach to life, and imaginative. She is undisciplined, makes promises she can't keep, and hides her inner pain. (See Figure 11.1.)

The Best Friend

Male Version.   He is the pal, the guy with the shoulder to cry on, the guy you can depend on. He's calm during a crisis, finds solutions, and negotiates the peace. People trust him. He is a follower and has trouble asserting himself. He doesn't have a good self-image and puts himself down a lot.

Female Version.   She is the loyal friend, full of spirit, and reliable. She has guts and a good sense of humor. Everyone loves her. She lacks self confidence and plays down her attributes, covering her insecurity with a sarcastic wit. She is the eternal optimist, fun to be around, and the voice of reason.

The Intellectual

Male Version.   He is a logical, analytical, committed expert in some field. He takes his time, thinks things through, and is task oriented. He is open and honest but also blunt and inconsiderate. He is inflexible, used to getting his own way, and he's doesn't deal with other people or change very well. He is inhibited with women. He is either very sharp and organized or an absent-minded geek.

Female Version.   The female intellectual is more organized than the male. She is bright, efficient, and dependable but straight laced. She dresses very conservatively, but when she lets her hair down, she is a passionate woman. She is stubborn, opinionated, self-reliant, and a perfectionist. She is often inhibited on the romance level with men, but she considers herself an equal.

FIGURE 11.1   Costume sketch by Betty
Monroe for Carol Cutrere, the fast-driving,
hard-drinking rebel in Tennessee Williams's
Orpheus Descending, performed at Wichita
State University.

The Warrior

Male Version.   A hero, he is a man of high standards who is searching for justice
in a world where everything is viewed as right or wrong. Dark, dangerous, and
disciplined, he fights evil and is merciless to his enemies. He is tenacious, relentless, and noble but also a loner, stubborn, and sometimes unpopular. He chooses
friends carefully, but he is always loyal.

Female Version.   She is the crusader, the spunky street fighter. She is a problem
solver. She is an activist. She is goal oriented, confident, tough, and tenacious. She

fights evil, seeks justice and truth, and looks out for the underdog, the disenfranchised, and those afraid to stand up for themselves. She is trustworthy. She means what she says. She can be stubborn and rash.

The Seductive Charmer

Male Version.   He is the dashing, charismatic, smooth-talking man who makes people around him feel special. He is fun and gets by on his warm personality and great sense of humor. It is a mask, however, and he doesn't allow others to see the real man underneath. He makes others believe in fairy tales, but if the going gets tough, he gets going. He is creative, romantic, fun, and unreliable. He makes promises he can't keep.

Female Version.   A seductress, she uses the force of her looks and personality to get what she wants. She beguiles and seduces men by being manipulative, calculating, and provocative. She hides her distrust behind a protective and alluring cover. Strong, fiery, assertive, clever, and cynical, she is a chameleon, changing her persona as needed. She has the instincts of a man, but they are disguised by her femme fatale manner.

The Innocent

Male Version.   He has a heavy heart, filled with angst. He is a lonely, lost individual who suffers pain. He wants love and happiness but is incapable of reaching out to find it. He's a wanderer, an outcast, a loner. He has an artist's temperament. He is creative with the voice of a poet and a deep soul. He is vulnerable, idealistic, pessimistic.

Female Version.   She is sweet, naïve, trusting, vulnerable, and kind. She has considerable inner strength and resiliencey. She is adaptable, willing to risk it all for a chance at happiness, and doesn't complain. Frequently an orphan, she seeks a home and rushes into relationships but never finds the happy life. It is easier for her to give in than fight.

The Adventurer or Nurturer

Male Version.   This is the adventurer. He is athletic, thrives on action, and is not afraid of danger. He is a thrill seeker, who is impulsive and leaps before he looks. He is colorful, passionate, fearless, selfish, foolhardy, and unreliable. He doesn't like commitment and dances to his own tune. He always has a new goal to reach and an eye on the horizon.

Female Version.   This is the nurturer. The opposite of the adventurer, she takes care of everyone and always thinks of others first. She is wise, giving, caring, capable, conscientious, and reliable. She needs to be needed. She is in control and enjoys other people, but she can be too much at times—too idealistic, too much the martyr. She gives her love to others unconditionally.

Examples

In Tracy Letts's *Killer Joe,* Dottie is the Innocent, Joe is the Boss and Charmer, and Carla is the Seductress. In *The Music Man,* by Meredith Wilson, Harold Hill is the Charmer while Marian exhibits the characteristics of the Intellectual. In Lerner and Loewe's *My Fair Lady,* Henry Higgins is the Intellectual and Eliza Doolittle combines the Innocent with a bit of the Rebel. In *Streetcar,* Stanley embodies the Boss and the Rebel. Shaw's Major Barbara combines qualities of the Crusader and the Nurturer.

Characters are often created that exhibit the qualities of one major archetype but combine the characteristics of two or more others, making them more complex and original. Still others show an individual evolving from one archetype into another. For more information on archetypes, consult *The Complete Writer's Guide to Heroes and Heroines,* by Tami D. Cowden, Caro LaFever, and Sue Viders (2000).

Equal Opponents

The *protagonist* is the character who initiates and follows through with the central action of the play. Usually, the protagonist is the character the audience sympathizes with. In a few plays, the protagonist is an antihero, an unpleasant person who evokes little sympathy but captures our attention in another way. For example, the character of Jimmy Porter in John Osborne's *Look Back in Anger* is an aggressive, working-class man who often treats his wife and best friend badly. He is highly critical of the British establishment and of his wife's upper-crust family. He wants to be waited on hand and foot. He has an affair. In short, he is an unpleasant antihero. Yet we understand him and where he's coming from. We can even admire some of his good qualities. The important point is that the protagonist is the one who acts, who makes the action happen. Jimmy Porter acts and makes things happen.

The *antagonist* is the one who puts up the resistance. The antagonist doesn't have to be unsympathetic. Usually, if the protagonist is sympathetic, the antagonist is not, but in some plays, both are sympathetic. There can be no struggle or worthwhile conflict, no story unless the protagonist and the antagonist are evenly matched. Helen and Annie in William Gibson's *The Miracle Worker,* George and Martha in Edward Albee's *Who's Afraid of Virginia Woolf?* Beatrice and Benedict in Shakespeare's *Much Ado about Nothing*—all are evenly matched.

Raymond Hull (1983) in *How to Write a Play,* created this formula: M + G + O = C, or Main Character + his Goal + Opposition = Conflict. Good opposition requires that the antagonist counter each of the protagonist's actions with equal force and cunning. Good opposition doesn't require that your protagonist be completely good or that the antagonist be a villain. The antagonist may be as pure as the protagonist. The characters of Helen and Anne in William Gibson's *The Miracle Worker* are both sympathetic, as are both Beatrice and Benedict in Shakespeare's *Much Ado about Nothing*. The antagonist may be just as heroic as the protagonist. What is essential is for both characters to be well motivated, well rounded, fully fleshed out individuals, determined to have their own way.

A Crucible

Moses Malevinsky calls "the pot, or the furnace"—in which the drama is "boiled, baked, stewed or hibernated"—a *crucible* (quoted in Frey, 1987, p. 35). The crucible is the container that holds the characters together as things heat up—the bond that keeps them in conflict with one another. Characters in a crucible won't quit or walk away in the middle. They have to stay to the end. Characters are in the crucible if their motivation to continue in conflict is greater than their motivation to run away. You have failed to put the characters in the crucible if the audience asks "Why doesn't she just leave?"

Here are some examples of characters with a bond: A husband and wife will remain in conflict until separated by divorce or death. Marriage is their crucible. Lack of self-esteem, lack of money, and fear and ignorance may hold an abused wife in place. She may be in a bad marriage, but she may see no viable alternatives. A father and son in conflict will remain in conflict if they are bonded by love and duty. Love and family ties are their crucible. Two cellmates in prison who are in conflict will remain in conflict because there is no escape from their cell. A soldier in the army cannot get away from his platoon leader. The army provides his crucible, and he cannot leave without severe punishment.

When Another Character Enters

Recently, Phyllis went to Clearwater, Florida, to visit family. Many of her twelve siblings, now in their 70s, 80s, and 90s, are still alive, including one brother and nine sisters. Her entrance into that scene was so dramaturgically appropriate that it almost seemed scripted. First, there were the various rounds of reintroduction and catching up ("You've gained weight," "You look great!" "Your hair's different," "How was your flight?" and "How's Tom?"). Tom is her husband. Because Phyllis was a new character to the scene, this catching-up process was a legitimate and believable sharing of information. Woven throughout this was character work. Her sister, Aura, had already planned activities for everyone, and they all had to comment on those. And then, just as Phyllis began to sense something wrong, they said to her, "We have something we have to tell you." The something turned out to be that Dotty, one of the still-surviving sisters, had terminal cancer. And the rest of the trip dealt with the conflict and turmoil caused by that situation.

A new character in a scene brings new information and new conflict into play. Such a character can be viewed as an opportunity. If you need to put some life into the world of your play, you can introduce a new character or bring back someone from offstage, as long as that character brings a new twist to the conflict of the scene. An example of this is found in *The Caretaker,* by Harold Pinter. The main action concerns the bum, Davies, who is taken in by the kindly Aston and allowed to live with him in the attic of his crumbling homestead. Davies takes greater and greater advantage of the beneficent Aston, and the possibilities of the play seem limited—until Pinter introduces Mick, Aston's younger brother. Mick is clearly a schemer, along Davies's own lines. Davies throws in with Mick, betraying his own benefactor.

The play is far more complicated than this, but the point is that Pinter constantly reintroduces one or the other of these two brothers into the scene with Davies. And that rejuggling of the personnel in the room keeps the action moving. When your story gets boring or runs out of steam, open the door and bring in another character. Then watch what happens.

Although the "door" is sometimes the playwright's friend, it is not a good idea to bring in a new character every time it opens. Keeping the cast size small is important, for several reasons:

1. It is easier to fully develop a few characters.
2. A large cast tends to diffuse the story.
3. A large cast also ends up with characters that are functionary stereotypes.
4. Actors don't want to play the "waiter" or the "clerk" or the "third woman."
5. Producers don't want to to pay for a large cast. Such shows have very limited appeal to producers and are likely to be rejected because most theatre companies never have enough money.

Focus your attention on a clear storyline with six or fewer fully developed characters in a simple setting, and then use returning characters in various combinations. Even with four to six characters, there are many possible combinations.

Get to Know Your Characters

Although we may have an idea or an experience to write about for a scene or a play, we may have characters who are not fully fleshed out at the beginning. In *Shoptalk,* conversations about theatre, edited by Dennis Brown, Lanford Wilson says of his work that "the first thirty pages are always terrible" (p. 12). Only after he had written enough to begin to see the characters more fully and understand what their situation was did they start to be interesting and clear. As a result, he generally threw away the first thirty pages.

I have often found that I have to write several scenes before I begin to know the characters. I often end up writing dozens of scenes that do not end up in the final version but do give me insights into the characters' behavior. There are also other methods for discovering character, such as answering a character questionnaire or asking the typical questions that you would like answers to when you meet an exciting new person.

Frank Moher, a Canadian playwright and teacher on the web (Escript.com), explains that when you don't have a fully developed character already in mind at the beginning, you can answer a series of questions and see what emerges. One of the exciting things about this method is that through the accumulation of enough random details, you will eventually find yourself shaping a three-dimensional character. It is also important to have these details so that if you get stuck while writing, you can go back to the character's biography.

Character Analysis

The following list contains questions for another character questionnaire that I have revised for actors and directors over the years for character analysis work. Answer the relevant questions as precisely as possible. Don't just note that your character likes to drink beer. Note the brand and whether she prefers a can, a bottle, or a glass.

Your "stained glass" image of the character can be made up of a handful of pieces of colored glass, or it can be made of hundreds or thousand of pieces. Is your character a Coke bottle or a window from Chartres Cathedral? The more pieces, or the more detailed, the greater the depth of understanding and the clearer the image. When you write a play, you spend many hours with the characters. Make sure you are interested in them, like them, and want to spend this time with them.

I. What is the character's spine—his major goal in the play and in life?
   A. What does he want?
   B. What is he willing or able to do to reach that goal?
   C. How conscious is the character of his own motives?
II. What is the character's background?
   A. What influence did the character's family have on him?
      1. What were the character's relationships to his father, mother, brother, and sister?
      2. What type of discipline was he subjected to?
      3. What was the economic, religious, political, and social status of the family?
      4. Were there any special situations in the family, such as divorce, drinking, or illness?
   B. What is the character's level of intelligence?
   C. What is the character's educational background? How does this affect his language, attitudes, and interests?

    D. What effect does the political and sociological environment—war, occupation, pioneering, disillusionment, travel, temper of the times—have on him?

    E. What are the character's adjustments to his background and the forces that molded him?

       1. What are his social adjustments—manners, kinds of friends, membership in organizations, sex attitudes, attitudes toward others, role played in a group?

       2. What is his lifestyle in terms of a home, car, furnishings, clothes, and food?

       3. What are his hobbies and interests?

       4. What are his ideals, beliefs, heroes, and hates?

       5. What is his marital situation?

         a. Whom did he marry?

         b. How has he adjusted to marriage?

         c. What is his relationship to a spouse and children?

       6. What is the character's vocation and career?

         a. What kind of work does he do?

         b. How does he feel about that work?

       7. What is the character's general emotional state?

         a. How does he react to stress or conflict?

         b. How much pressure can he tolerate?

         c. How does he deal with or adjust to crisis?

III. What external features of the character are important?

    A. How does age affect him?

    B. What is his appearance (health, major facial expression, eyes, size and height, hair color and style, style and quality of clothing and attitude and treatment of it, posture)?

    C. What characterizes his movements?

       1. How does he walk (fast, slow, limp, meek)?

       2. How does he gesture (vigorous, weak, controlled, incomplete)?

       3. What props might be used to help establish character?

       4. What is his energy level?

    D. What is his voice like?

       1. Is it loud, fast, slow, deeply resonant, or high pitched?

       2. Is his articulation careless or precise?

       3. Is his pronunciation standard or colloquial?

    E. What is the character's rhythm (jerky or smooth, volatile or even, impulsive or deliberate, ponderous or light, broken or continuous)?

IV. How does the style of the production affect the character's portrayal?

    In the play *M. Butterfly*, by David Henry Hwang, the character of Song Liling appears to be a delicate Chinese opera star. She has a twenty-year affair with a French diplomat in Beijing, who then learns that his delicate Asian lover is a spy—

M. Butterfly, *performed at Wichita State University. Directed by Joyce Cavarozzi, Set and Lighting Design by J. David Blatt, Costume Design by Betty Monroe.*

and a man. The character's major goal in the play is to conceal her true identity from the diplomat and provide her government with classified information. She is very conscious of manipulating her lover because of his desire to see her as a submissive Asian woman. She has been trained to impersonate women. Her mother was a prostitute, and she learned from her how to deal with Western men. She is very intelligent. Her relationship with the diplomat gives her special status. She even fakes having a child. Eventually, Song removes all of his clothes and makeup and stands naked before the diplomat as a man. The external features are extremely important. The costumes, makeup, movement and gestures, and voice and manners must convince the diplomat and the audience that this character is a woman until the unmasking.

Stage Business

One of the useful tools in bringing a character to life is to involve her in actually doing an activity—for example, folding laundry, washing dishes, painting a chair, fixing a small appliance, cleaning out a drawer, cutting up vegetables for a stir fry, ironing, sewing on a button, or making a bed. Such physical activities require that the actor really iron, really cut up vegetables, or really sew on a button to bring realism to the scene. In *The Knack*, by Ann Jellicoe, for example, one man actually paints the walls of the room during the play.

The director sometimes adds such action to a scene to help the actor perform with a sense of truth. The playwright may find that adding an activity to a scene takes it to a more truthful level. This use of hand props and activity can be used by the playwright to highlight the action and to express emotion. Consider how a

The dead baby in Buried Child *was created by using a doll, rags, and mud. Performed at the University of Alaska Anchorage, Directed by Leroy Clark, Set and Lighting Design by Frank Bebey, Costume Design by Lois Aden.*

very neat man versus a very sloppy man might fold clothes. Consider how the neat man might go about refolding the clothes done by the sloppy man. Such activity might cause a conflict between the two that would escalate into the sloppy man angrily throwing the clothes all over the room or grabbing some scissors and cutting them up. Consider the possibilities of a woman character instructing her daughter-in-law in how to cut up vegetables. Consider a wimpy man forced to iron his own shirts by a verbally abusive wife, who finally reaches the end of his tolerance level and irons her hand. In McDonaugh's *The Beauty Queen of Leenane*, the daughter gets so angry at her mother that she drags her to the stove and plunges her hand into a frying pan.

As a director, I often insist that every actor bring a prop to rehearsal that his character would always have. One character might always have food in her purse—a banana, a candy bar, a roll. Maybe she steals a roll every day from the bakery on the corner. Maybe she never had enough to eat as a child and food gives her comfort, a feeling of security. Another character always carries a knife for protection. For the playwright, selecting such a prop may give new insights into the character. What props would your character use? See the list in Chapter 14.

Practicalities

The appeal of the characters and the practical realities of staging affect the selection of a play by a producer or a theatre. Assuming the play under consideration is a good play, several practical factors may affect its choice for production.

One of the first considerations is *cast size*. A director or producer will look at the cast list and very likely toss a script requiring more than ten actors—or six or four or whatever she sees as viable. Special skills for a role may also be a blessing or a killer. A producer will reject a play if she doesn't think it will be possible to find an actor capable of both sword fighting and singing beautifully; one who has training and excellent skills in modern, ballet, jazz, and tap dance; or one who can roller skate, play the piano, juggle, and of course, really act. On the other hand, if the producer has just the right actor, that may mean immediate selection of the script.

The design and technical elements may inspire either great interest or absolute rejection, as well. In terms of scenery, a play with one set is easier to produce than a multiset show. A play in which the set is a major element, such as the ice mountain in *K2* or the carousel in *Carousel*, by Rodgers and Hammerstein, may not be feasible in some small theatres or financially practical on a huge stage. However, a play with a challenging set may be so exciting for a particular designer that he will get the play accepted.

A third reason that a play may be accepted or rejected is the costume requirements. *The Mystery of Irma Vep*, by Charles Ludlum, only uses two actors. However, each actor plays four roles and must change from one costume to another for a total of forty-two quick changes. Doug Wright's *Quills* requires period eighteenth-century French costumes. Whether the costume designer is enthusiastic or hostile to a play may well seal its fate.

The fourth consideration centers on special props, such as the live animals in Tennessee Williams's *Rose Tattoo* and Sam Shepard's *Curse of the Starving Class,* the talking and singing plant in the musical *Little Shop of Horrors,* and the car in the musical *Grease,* by Jim Jacobs and Warren Casey. If the production company is excited about doing the play and knows they can borrow, rent, buy, or make the special prop, then the problem will be solved. If not, the play will be rejected. A play may also be specifically selected because the director or designers are excited and challenged by a particular concept.

Given these considerations, it is wise for the playwright to ask a few realistic questions when developing the characters and story for a play: Will the number of characters be acceptable or impractical? Does any character have such a specialized talent or requirement that it would limit (or enhance) the play's marketability? Will the set, costumes, or props be a limiting factor? Is anything about the play so unique or intriguing or special that it will really attract people to want to produce it?

EXERCISE 16 _____

Beginning Level   Choose one of the following:

A.   Write a scene in which your characters are in conflict yet bonded in a crucible they cannot leave. The cause of the conflict should be a third character not present. Character A wants something related to Character C but is met with resistance from Character B. Character A tries various tactics to achieve his objective, but Character B counters each one. For example, Bull wants to rape the new kid in prison, but his cellmate won't let him. Martha wants sole custody of her daughter, but her husband refuses. Rachel wants to put her mother-in-law in a nursing home, but her husband wants to keep her home.

B.   Write a scene in which your characters are in conflict and in a crucible. The scene should include the protagonist with an unfulfilled need. He seeks to accomplish what he wants but is met with opposition and resistance by the antagonist. The protagonist tries various tactics to achieve his goal, but the antagonist counters each one. Take the scene to the limit and break the bond between the two characters. Remember to keep their voices unique and distinct.

Intermediate Level   Choose one of the following:

C.   Write a scene in which Character A confronts Character B about an action Character B has done. Character A demands to know why Character B avoids A's question, but A slowly gets at the truth. In what ways are the characters polar opposites? What is the climax? What is different in their relationship at the end of the scene?

D.   Write a scene with three archetypal characters, in which Character A deliberately lies to Character B about a past action that she has done. What is

Character A hiding or afraid of? Who is she protecting? When Character B is out of the room, Character A tells the truth to Character C. Why? What does A want from C? What if Character B learns the truth?

Advanced Level   Choose one of the following:

E. Write a scene about two characters who on the surface act like they hate each other but underneath really love each other. For each character, mix two or three of the archetypes: Boss, Best Friend, Rebel, Intellectual, Warrior, Seductive Charmer, Innocent, Adventurer, or Nurturer.

F. Write a scene with three characters, each of a different status. At the climax of the scene, the status of two of the characters should be reversed by a revelation from the third character. For example, a Boss may be in conflict with his Rebel/Intellectual son, blaming him for an event. The son's Charmer friend reveals that the Boss actually caused the problem.

Summary

The *back story* is not just the biography of a character but the previous significant events in the life of the character that can be pulled out and used to tell the story in the present. Details should be brought in only when essential in the current action.

Selecting the right mix of characters, who have different personalities and goals, is essential. The key to creating a good mix of characters is to put together people with contrasting or polar beliefs, personalities, and wants. If the cast of characters is polarized, conflict will occur whenever they open their mouths. With polarized characters, no two will act the same. The most dynamic situations arise when the leading characters are in opposition and will not compromise. Audience members makes up their minds about whether a character is likeable in the first four minutes that the character is on stage. The playwright needs to be very careful that the first impression is the one she intends to be conveyed.

The protagonist is the character who initiates the central action of the play. The protagonist acts, or makes the action happen. The antagonist is the one who puts up the resistance and the obstacles. In a few plays, the protagonist is an anti-hero, an unpleasant character who evokes little sympathy. Usually, if the protagonist is sympathetic, then the antagonist is not, but in some plays, both are sympathetic. There can be no struggle or worthwhile conflict, no story, unless the protagonist and the antagonist are evenly matched and there is a real possibility that the protagonist may lose.

A *crucible* is the bond that keeps the characters in conflict with one another. Characters in a crucible won't quit or walk away in the middle. They have to stay to the end. Characters are in the crucible if their motivation to continue in conflict is greater than their motivation to run away from it. A crucible can be created by family, a marriage, a contract, or a certain environment—anything that forces the characters in conflict not to give up until one of them has won and the other has lost.

If a playwright needs to put some life into the world of the play, he can introduce a new character or bring back an offstage character. Doing so will bring new information and a new level to the overall conflict of the play.

Often, a playwright doesn't have all of the characters fully developed in her mind at the beginning. One approach to develop them is to answer a series of questions for each character and see what emerges. One of the exciting things about this method is that through the accumulation of enough random details, you will eventually be able to shape a three-dimensional character. It is also important to have these details so that if you get stuck while writing, you can go back to the character's biography.

CHAPTER
12 Dialogue

Another way to discover and explore the characters in your play is through voice. Unlike the fiction writer or poet, who may develop a personal voice or recognizable style as an author, the playwright deals in different voices. In fact, the author's voice should not intrude upon the play. The audience wants to know how the *characters* see and experience the world, and that needs to be reflected in both what the characters say and how they say it. Just as how characters behave and act reveals who they are, so, too, does how they speak. Voice is one of the most potent character-building tools of all.

In this chapter, we will explore the use of language, accents or dialects, sentence structure, rhythm, details, slang, profanity and obscenity, and poetic speech to create characters.

Use of Language

Every character, by the way he uses language, reveals something of his spirit, habits, capabilities, and prejudices. If a . . . character . . . speaks in . . . a way that . . . suggests he often likes to . . . pause and think before . . . speaking, . . . then we get the impression that that character is thoughtful or reflective or perhaps just a little slow. If a character . . . you know . . . constantly interrupts himself . . . well, I don't mean interrupts, but . . . well, yes, sort of changes his mind, you know . . . or tends to EXCLAIM and talk in sentences without a lot of commas where in the ordinary course of things you would expect commas—Then we understand that this individual is a bit hyper and his ideas come so fast they tumble over each other. This character probably doesn't have a very peaceful inner life.

Make use of sentence construction, grammar, vocabulary, and voice in building characters. One way to capture the rhythm of everyday speech is to observe and listen. Take a notebook and go to a public area, where you can overhear the conversations of others. Listen to how differently people actually talk and jot down snippets of their dialogue. Other good sources for natural speech are reality-based television shows, such as *Survivor* and *Fear Factor*. Consider how your choices of words, images, and sentence structures can help create the character.

Accents and Dialects

Everyday conversation isn't necessarily dramatic. In fact, it's often full of pauses, repetitions, vocalized "ahs," and curse words. In creating art for the stage, we generally need to be selective. We want to avoid language that is commonplace, awkward, wordy, poetic, archaic, or dated.

If an accent or dialect is needed, you must decide whether to write the dialect or present the dialogue in a normal manner, seeking to capture the appropriate rhythm but spelling the words correctly. Since written dialect is difficult to do and difficult to read, you may want to choose the latter approach and let the actor master the dialect with assistance from a dialogue coach.

Sentence Structure

One of the keys to creating characters with distinct dialogue is to focus on sentence structure. The first scene in Act Two of Anton Chekhov's *The Cherry Orchard* offers a series of characters whose various sentence structures provide insight into their personalities. Lopahin is a direct, open, and honest person who speaks in short, direct, and complete sentences. He tells Lyuboff, for example, "We must decide definitely, time doesn't wait. Why, the matter's quite simple. Are you willing to lease your land for summer cottages or are you not? Answer in one word, yes or no? Just one word!" (p. 203). A shy, socially inept, or insecure person may speak sparingly, apologize frequently, and talk in a very hesitant manner. The character of Epihodoff speaks in sentences that are full of qualifiers. For example, he says, "Strictly speaking, not touching on other subjects, I must state about myself, in passing, that fate treats me mercilessly, as a storm does a small ship" (p. 203). A pompous and arrogant character may pontificate, use big words, talk a lot but say little, and be condescending and irritating. When Dunyasha tells Yasha she loves him, he replies, "Yes, sir—To my mind it is like this: If a girl loves someone, it means she is immoral" (p. 203). After a pause, he continues, "It is pleasant to smoke a cigar in the clear air—" (p. 203). He then hears Lopahin and Lyuboff coming and tells Yasha, "Go to the house, as though you had been to bathe in the river, go by this path, otherwise, they might meet you and suspect me of making a rendezvous with you. That I cannot tolerate" (p. 203). Yasha treats her in a condescending manner, with no regard for her feelings.

Dialogue should capture a character's unique qualities. The use of sentence structure and the choice of words both help translate personality into dialogue.

Vocal Rhythm

The rhythm of the language must work for the character. As Edward Albee has stated, "It is sound and silence; it's a matter of durations" (Bryer, 1955, p. 12).

Punctuation is a key element in providing clues to the rhythm of a speech. A comma is a short pause. A semicolon is a longer pause. A period is a slightly longer pause. Three dots (an ellipsis) indicates a pause, in which a character is either thinking or trails off. A dash indicates that what follows is either an appositive—meaning the same thing—or an interruption. In either case, the words that come after are delivered faster.

An understanding of how to punctuate is essential to creating the rhythm desired for a speech. Look at the following example from Scene VI of Tennessee Williams's *The Glass Menagerie* (pp. 313–314):

JIM

(Grinning)
What was the matter?

TOM

Oh—with Laura? Laura is—terribly shy.

JIM

Shy, huh? It's unusual to meet a shy girl nowadays. I don't believe you ever mentioned you had a sister.

TOM

Well, now you know. I have one. Here is the *Post Dispatch*. You want a piece of it?

JIM

Uh-huh.

TOM

What piece? The comics?

JIM

Sports!
(Glances at it)
Ole Dizzy Dean is on his bad behavior.

TOM

(Disinterest)
Yeah?
(Lights cigarette and crosses back to fire-escape door)

JIM

Where are you going?

TOM

I'm going out on the terrace.

JIM

(Goes after him)
You know, Shakespeare—I'm going to sell you a bill of goods!

We can tell by the dashes in Tom's first line that he is thinking about Laura and choosing his words very carefully. Jim's answer to Tom's question about what part of the paper he wants to read is "Sports!" This one word, with an exclamation point, let's us know that the character is enthusiastic. We can tell sports are important to him. Jim's last line about "a bill of goods" also ends with an exclamation point and indicates a lively, enthusiastic delivery. Tom's use of short, declarative sentences about different subjects in every line shows his matter-of-fact, unemotional, and rather indifferent state of mind.

Details

What details does the character use in her speech? Generally, the more specific the details, the more vivid the speech. Giving a lot of specific details is a good way of telling a lie and convincing others that it's true. Giving a lot of details and getting them jumbled up or starting to tell one aspect of a story and then backtracking to fill in other details may be used to show a ditsy individual. Here are more examples:

> "When Mrs. Lucky arrived at the terminal, her luck had already left."

> "When Lady Luck arrived at the Miami Amtrak Terminal, she found the 4:15 for Baltimore disappearing on the western horizon."

> "When the old cow got to the Amtrak station, the train had just pulled out; all that was left was the stink of the diesel fuel and her perfume."

> "Well, I saw her get to the Amtrak station. She was dressed to the nines. You know what I'm saying? Black cocktail dress, jewelry—oh, wait! No, first I saw the train leave. Then she came running in. She had to stop and take her heels off. I watched her get to the platform, and she could see there was no train. She was steamed—I mean, I could tell she was mad 'cause she threw down her shoes. She kept pacing back and forth barefoot. Then she stepped on something and hurt her foot. I had to laugh. I did. I mean, it wasn't funny, you know, but it was."

Appeal to the Senses

What is your favorite color? How does color affect your mood? How does color affect your perception of space? Are there smells that you definitely do and do not like? What effect does the smell of a person have on the way you feel about him? How about the smell of a certain place? Do people from different cultures smell differently? Are you aware of textures in daily living? What kind of sound do you like? What kind of sound do you not like? How does the sound level affect you? What associations do certain foods have for you?

Ask these same questions about your characters. How may a character's speech appeal to the senses? Consider these examples:

> "I watched her pace back and forth on the platform, trying to figure out what to do."

"I watched her marching back and forth on the old gray planks of the platform, trying to think of what to do next. I don't know what she was doing there in the first place—dressed like that. She looked like a million, you know. People like that don't usually travel on trains."

"A man walked by."

"A man stumbled past me and I could smell the acrid stench of body odor and alcohol, even in the open air."

"Some dumb idiot staggered by. Jerk almost knocked me off the platform. Looked like he wet himself or worse. He said, 'Scuse me' when I looked at him with disgust. Wow, he stunk so bad I thought I was gonna puke. You know how a dog smells sometimes when it rolls in something rancid? That's what he smelled like."

Images, Slang, and Street Talk

What kinds of poetic images, slang, or street talk does the character use? Language characterizes people in terms of age, profession, education, social status, and religion. Look at the following lines from different characters as examples:

"Do you ever get cho acrylics done? Acrylics. You know, nails. Look at mine. I have them done every Thersday for my man. I bet yo' man would like that."

"Gargamel. The Smurfs didn't exist; they were a figment of the Gargamel's acid-induced hallucination. Little blue people? Come on. They all lived in colorful mushrooms. He used to always talk to his cat. Don't you know nothin'?"

"You're rude. I don't know why I let Joe talk me into this. You're rude, Wayne. Has no one ever told you that?"

"Boy, you are crossing the line. You are in my office, making an unwelcome disturbance, and I may need to call the police. Now, in the name of Jesus, get out of my office."

"I said *no* guacamole. I do not eat green things, nothing green."

Figures of Speech

Does the character use poetic speech? *Figures of speech* may be used especially to create comic characters. Richard Brinsley Sheridan created Mrs. Malaprop in *The Rivals*, a woman who misuses the English language in every way possible:

"Promise to forget this fellow—to illiterate him" (Act 1, Scene 1)
"Now don't attempt to extirpate yourself" (Act 1, Scene 1)
"There's a little intricate hussy for you!" (Act 1, Scene 1)
"My affluence over my niece is very small" (Act 4, Scene 1).

Using the wrong word that sounds similar but has a different meaning offers numerous comic possibilities: "She's in her middle flirties." "She's one of them illegibles snuck over the borders from Mexico." "Yeah, he's at the pineapple of success." Here we see substitutions for the words *thirties, illegal aliens,* and *pinnacle.*

Using *personification*—giving human qualities to inanimate objects—is a good way to make a comic remark or express sarcasm: "The coffee pot was unhappy like a spoiled child; it spit right in my face." *Hyperbole,* or exaggeration, is also a comic tool: "My wife has the disposition and bad breath of a shark." Metaphors and similes can also be used to convey vivid images. A *metaphor* states a comparison directly: "He struck his face in a car accident and turned it into mince meat." A simile uses the word *like* or *as* in making a comparison: "His smile was like the keys on a piano, the broken ones." "Her smile was like that of an old camel, yellow and brown."

The "Gems"

One of the things a playwright should consider is finding and honing the "gems" in dialogue. Metaphorically, most of the dialogue of any play will be "gravel," but every now and then, a line stands out as a polished and shining gem—a line that perfectly fits the character and the situation and offers us either insight into the character or the situation or theme. Playwright David Henry Hwang, in an interview in *The Playwright's Art* (Bryer, 1995), offered this quote, and while it is not from a play, it illustrates the idea. It's a gem:

> Jimmy Walker had a remark that I thought was great. He was saying that in the States we've got this thing between blacks and whites; then, when he went to Ireland, he saw the same thing between Protestants and Catholics and he said, "You know, if people don't have an enemy they'll improvise." (p. 139)

Richard Greenberg's *Eastern Standard,* written about the stress points of the generational meltdown, has several comic gems. When a character wants some service in a restaurant, he yells to Ellen, the chatty waitress, "Oh, actress." This line has stopped the show because many actresses in New York have day jobs as waitresses. Greenberg is a compelling writer who uses language and distinct character voices to draw out the humor and the pathos of the human condition.

Think of some of the famous movie lines that have become part of our everyday existence, such as Clark Gable's "Frankly, my dear, I don't give a damn!" Clint Eastwood's "Go ahead, make my day!" Arnold Schwarzenegger's "I'll be back!" and Dustin Hoffman's "Mrs. Robinson, you are trying to seduce me." There are stage lines that capture the same kind of moment and become part of theatre legends. Think of Williams's "I've always depended on the kindness of strangers" (*Streetcar,* p. 102). Think of Miller's "He's a man way out there in the blue, riding on a smile and a shoeshine. And when they start not smiling back—that's an earthquake" (*Death of a Salesman*, p. 225). Note Marlowe's "Was this the face that launched a thousand ships?" (*Doctor Faustus*, p. 330). What gems can you think of to crystallize a character's response?

The "F" Word

Should you use the "F" word and other curse words? I am well acquainted with words considered obscene—those relating to body parts and functions—and those that are considered profanity—words considered offensive because of religious beliefs. Many people use these words. However, in writing dialogue, it is important to consider not only the character but also the audience for whom you are writing.

If you're writing a one-act play and the intended market is high schools, it might be realistic to use curse words but it probably won't be appropriate or acceptable. If your play is intended for a general family audience, the same holds true. As a writer, explore your creative vocabulary and try to find other expressions that work for the character and the situation. On the 1970s sitcom *Alice*, Flo's expression "Kiss my grits" became a national sensation.

What expressions can you come up with instead of using curse words? Consider the use of references to food, animals, reptiles, birds, and inanimate objects: *tomato, onion head, mule-headed, dog breath, lizard-lips, hawk face, monkey nipples, computer brain.* "Hey, is your battery dead?" "Are your lights on?" "Zip it." "You like to toot your own horn? Well, toot this." "Your face is a stop sign, man." "You're like a vending machine. Sometimes you work, sometimes you don't."

Consider saving curse words for moments of extreme tension and conflict, when they will really have an impact. Consider the audience you hope will see your play. A strong drama with working-class characters, convicts, or soldiers may be more appropriate for expletives than a family-based comedy. Make the language work for the play, not against it.

First Impressions Count

Voice is very specifically useful when a character is first introduced in a play. Your parents may have told you before your first job interview that "First impressions count," and nowhere is that more true than in the theatre. Audiences make up their minds about whether characters are likeable in the first four minutes after they first enter. As a playwright, you need to give the audience a firm handle on the character right off the bat. They will make up their minds anyway—only they may decide the wrong things about the character if the writer is not very clear.

It is important to pay careful attention to how a character is introduced, and most particularly what they say in those opening moments, because voice can convey a lot of character information very quickly. See how Robert Harling introduces the character of Ouiser in *Steel Magnolias* (p. 37).

> OUISER
>
> This is it. I've found it. I am in hell.
>
> TRUVY
>
> Morning, Ouiser.
>
> OUISER
>
> Don't try to get on my good side. I no longer have one.

We know in these few sentences a great deal about who this woman is. And note that we find out through a combination of what she says, how she says it, and what she does as the scene continues:

> TRUVY
>
> You're a little early. You're not expected till elevenish.
>
> OUISER
>
> That's precisely why I'm here. I have to cancel.
>   (The phone rings. OUISER picks it up and hangs up on the
>   caller.)
> I have to take my poor dog to the vet before he has a nervous breakdown. My
> dog I mean. The vet is perfectly healthy.
>   (To ANNELLE)
> You must be the new girl.
>
> ANNELLE
>
> Hi.
>
> OUISER
>
> May I have a glass of water? I have been screaming this morning.

Harling gives us character quickly and concisely; we get a good sense of Ouiser's cutting irony and Truvy's deference right away. Ouiser's action of picking up the phone in this place of business that doesn't belong to her shows her custom of doing whatever she pleases wherever she pleases.

In his book *Shoptalk,* author Dennis Brown (1992) gives us profiles of twelve major American writers that he has interviewed. While I found the book offered fascinating insights into the personalities of the writers, I was also struck by Brown's observations:

> Ask Lanford Wilson a question and you'll get an answer, more often than not a long one. Ask Jason Miller a question and you'll get a pause, more often than not. . . .
> Lanford Wilson thinks while he talks. Jason Miller thinks and then talks. If Lanford Wilson spoke with the open delight of an Ozark mountain breeze, Jason Miller's

words were as wary, weighed, and measured as mercury. If Lanford Wilson conveyed an aura of accessibility, Miller's demeanor was intense, guarded. (p. 23)

This comparison gave me a clear idea of the two distinct voices and the different manners that these two men exhibit through their speech. Since Brown was able to record the interviews, he was able to quote the writers verbatim in the book. Tennessee Williams's voice is one of the most distinct, and the following two excerpts offer interesting samples.

And you know, St. Louis is a very materialistic city. It really is. It's very middle-American. Of course, when I was a kid the South still had an aura of romance about it. Not a *Gone With the Wind* sort of thing, but people still had *time* for each other. And they didn't judge you by the kind of car you drove or the street you lived on. . . . (p. 104)

Now, I am not . . . I never thought politically before. I don't even vote. I've never belonged to any party of any kind, and I don't subscribe to any "ism" at all. But I've just become recently, in the last few years, very conscious, very conscious, of this corruption, you know, of morals, and of the decay of democratic ideals which I think began as far back as Korea, which manifests itself through our political system, and which surfaced most dreadfully with the Kennedy assassination, you know. (p. 105)

Williams's rambling, broken-up speech, with repetition for emphasis, offers a strong contrast to the short, direct expressions used by Albee in this excerpt:

My brain gets tired. Or my concentration vanishes. Or I get a headache. Or I want to do something else. I find usually four hours is enough. Then I can go and correct for fifteen minutes. But I concentrate rather heavily when I'm working, so my brain gets tired. (p. 132)

Both men were major playwrights of the twentieth century. Yet they were very different, wrote in very different styles, and possessed very distinctive and unique voices.

The First Line

The first line of a scene should lead us directly into the essence of the scene, and that is especially true of the first line of a play. Give careful thought to setting the right tone and grabbing the audience's interest and attention immediately.

Henrik Ibsen's romantic drama *Peer Gynt* begins with his mother saying "Peer, you're lying" (Act 1, Scene 1, p. 5). This immediately gives us insight into Peer and connects with the whole action of the play, which involves Peer's inability to face things head on. The first line of August Wilson's *Fences* is similar. Bono says, "Troy, you ought to stop that lying!" (Act 1, Scene 1, p. 3). Later, we find that Troy has fathered a child by a young woman who is not his wife.

Thomas Ludwig's *7/11* begins with "Who left this pubic hair on my soap?" (Act 1, Line 1). This line lets us know we are in for a look at real life with a comic tone, and it jumps right into conflict. The opening of Clifford Odet's *Awake and Sing* begins with Ralph complaining "Where's advancement down the place? Work like crazy? Think they see it? You'd drop dead first" (p. 25). Sam Shepard's *Curse of the Starving Class* begins with the line "You shouldn't be doing that" (Act 1, p. 5). Whatever the makeup of your characters, whatever your premise, the first line spoken should start the conflict and the inevitable drive toward the proving of the premise. Dialogue is action. Dialogue reveals character.

The Lengths of Speeches

Keep speeches varied in length. Long speeches may grow boring and lose the point. Make certain that if you are writing a long speech, it is necessary for the play at that point. Ask yourself, Would other characters interrupt, ask questions, or respond during such a long speech? If so, include speeches by other characters to break up the monologue. Short to medium exchanges between characters keep all of them alive and make the play more crisp and vital. Variety provides different rhythms and keeps us interested and involved.

How long is *short?* Let the dialogue carry one idea per speech. Listen to the other characters while one person is talking and see who wants to interrupt. Keep the lengths of the moderate speeches generally under twenty words. Each speech should be driven by one specific objective or intention. The character is saying it for a reason. If you have a speech in which the character has several intentions, break it up and have the other characters in the scene respond after each intention has been completed. In some cases, another character will interrupt before the speaking character has completed his objective.

The mood and emotional content of a scene will affect the lengths of lines. A scene with a lot of activity or a very strong conflict usually has short speeches of a few words each. A deep discussion will have medium and short lines. A moment of revelation will often involve a long speech.

Ensuring a Smooth Delivery

Dialogue must be designed for actors to speak and audiences to hear. If after reading a part several times, an actor continues to stumble over certain lines, the playwright would be wise to examine those lines and try to make them more playable. It may be a matter of rhythm, a word that's difficult to articulate, or a sentence that is too long.

It may also be an actor problem—a word the actor doesn't understand, a peculiar reaction because of the actor's own personal life, or a poor association.

The playwright should talk to the director, not the actor—unless the director has established an open policy. The director may suggest that the actor do an action on the line, such as cross to the telephone or smell the flowers, without mentioning the line-reading problem at all. If an actor is made too self-conscious about a particular word or a line, she may get anxious, tense up when the line is coming, and never be comfortable with it again. If the actor continues to have problems with a line, the writer may want to simplify or rewrite it.

An actor knows what a word feels like in his mouth, what a speech feels like, how a relationship is played. Actors understand this practically, viscerally, in their guts. You may or may not be an actor, but by reading your material aloud, you will soon learn what the words feel like in your mouth, what is difficult to articulate, and what seems wordy or awkward.

Writing "On The Nose"

Avoid direct dialogue—that which expresses exactly what is on the character's mind, with no attempt on the part of the character to lie, be witty, or use a variety of subtle tactics. This is called "writing on the nose." It is a rare occasion that a person truly speaks exactly what's on her mind. Good dialogue expresses the will of the character indirectly. In reality, characters seldom say exactly what they mean.

Determine if your characters are witty, charming, and intelligent or stupid and inarticulate. Make them lie, tell fibs and half truths. Let them raise and lower their status. Let them stumble. Have a character avoid certain words in some way. For example, if a young man meets a woman with large breasts, he doesn't tell her he is attracted to her because of her breasts. He doesn't mention breasts, but an observer of the interaction should be able to tell his thoughts. Find behavior that reveals the character's mental processes. Make whatever the character is talking about on the surface different from the subtext, but include enough inferences, hints, and signs that we understand what the subtext is.

Poetic Language

Most contemporary American plays use standard English, and there is little effort to use elevated diction or language. Conversational realism is the norm. However, some plays experiment with poetic form or use a dialect or poetic language.

Tennessee Williams uses poetic language in his plays. While they are grounded in realistic acting, they also have a heightened use of language and metaphor and are particularly strong in imagery. Among his most poetic dramas are *The Glass Menagerie, A Streetcar Named Desire,* and *Summer and Smoke.* Maxwell Anderson explores the use of iambic pentameter or blank verse in writing both contemporary and historical plays, such as *Winterset, Anne of the 1000 Days,* and *Elizabeth the Queen.*

Today, we are most likely to find poetic language used in plays by Hispanic writers, such as Nilo Cruz; African American writers, such as August Wilson and Ntozake Shange; and in plays by non-American writers from Ireland and Africa.

I wrote *Shakespeare's Journey* using both blank verse and prose, as Shakespeare did in his plays. I wanted to capture the feeling, the language, and the style of the Elizabethan period, while making sure the meaning was very clear. Most playwrights use autobiographical elements in plays, so I reversed the process, reworking some scenes from Shakespeare's plays to fit his life. The play is structured like an Elizabethan play, as well, with comic scenes alternating with serious ones. Since the actors of that time also played more than one role, I designed the play for actors to play two or three roles.

Iambic Pentameter

Words are made up of one or more syllables, some of which are emphasized or stressed and some of which are relatively unstressed. When these words are joined into a line, their stressed and unstressed syllables work together to form an overall rhythmic pattern for that line. *Scansion* is the term for analyzing rhythm syllable by syllable.

The first step in scanning a line is to identify the stressed and unstressed syllables. Take this famous line from *Romeo and Juliet* (Act 2, Scene 2, line 1) as an example.

But soft! What light through yonder window breaks?

We put a *macron,* or line, over each stressed syllable and a semicircle, or *breve,* over the unstressed one:

˘ ‾ ˘ ‾ ˘ ‾ ˘ ‾ ˘ ‾
But soft! What light through yonder window breaks?

Even though we have marked the syllables as either stressed or unstressed, these are only very general categories. There is actually a great deal of variation within each. If we were to read all the stressed syllables one way and all the unstressed another way, the result would be a monotonous singsong. Only a few of the stresses in each line are major stresses.

Using the most common system of English scansion, *foot scansion,* you can identify the rhythmic pattern of a line. Scansion is not an exact science, however. Different people's choices will lead them to stress words or syllables that others might underplay. Stress is relative, and the amount of stress placed on a stressed syllable will vary. Readings would be monotonous if this were not the case.

To use foot scansion, we arrange the stressed and unstressed syllables into units called *feet.* There are a limited number of these arrangements of stressed and unstressed syllables, established by tradition. The "But soft" line is recognized as a foot called *iamb*. There are six traditional kinds of feet used in English verse, as represented by the acronym PITADS:

P   is for *pyrrhic*, which stands for the weakest and smallest foot.   *ta-tain*

I   stands for *iamb*, which has an unstressed syllable followed by a stressed syllable.   *ta-TUM*

T   stands for *trochee*, the opposite of iamb.   *TUM-ta*

A   is for *anapest*, which is different because it has three syllables, two unstressed and one stressed.   *ta-ta-TUM*

D   is for *dactyl*, the opposite of anapestic.   *TUM-ta-ta*

S   is for *spondee*, the strongest foot of all, with two stresses.   *TUM-TUM*

Of the six kinds of feet, we will only deal with the *iamb*, which has an unstressed syllable followed by a stressed syllable. If we look at the same line from *Romeo and Juliet* again, we see that it divides regularly into iambic feet. There are five feet in all. We call this meter *iambic pentameter*. Notice that the division of feet does not necessarily coincide with the division of words. Iambic pentameter is the most common English meter. When it does not rhyme, iambic pentameter is called *blank verse*. The iamb relates to basic rhythms of the human body. The iamb is the swift, strong, flowing beat of the human heart—*ta-TUM*. Shakespeare used basic iambic pentameter but deviated from it for his more sophisticated and subtle characters. These deviations give important clues to the nature of the character and his or her actions and reactions.

An *end-stopped line* is one in which the thought or idea ends at the end of the line. When lines run on into each other, they are called *enjambed lines*. These are expressions of thoughts and ideas that go beyond the ends of the lines. Enjambed lines are the opposite of end-stopped lines. Sometimes, they go to the middle or the end of the next line; sometimes they continue for as many as a dozen lines. Here are examples from Shakespeare's *Macbeth* (Act 2, Scene 1, lines 31–34):

Go bid thy mistress, when my drink is ready,   *This is an enjambed line.*

She strike upon the bell. Get thee to bed.   *This is an end-stopped line.*

Is this a dagger which I see before me,   *This is an enjambed line.*

The handle toward my hand? Come, let me   *This is an end-stopped line.*
    clutch thee!

Some students find it easy to write in iambic pentameter. Others do not understand it at all. Some write in language that is too Elizabethan and not modern. Try to open yourself up to this language. The idea is to write a modern scene with modern characters using contemporary dialogue in iambic pentameter, so that you begin to understand how to focus your attention on the language and heightened expression. The following is in prose:

If your father does live, I hope you'll try to make up with him. It's more difficult when a parent dies—if there's unfinished business—and there's no chance of saying "I'm sorry" or "I love you." When your last words are "Go to hell," it sucks big time. Believe me, son, I know.

The following is a rewritten version in verse:

> *My dad and I—we never got along.*
> *We had a fight a week before he died.*
> *I never had the chance to say "Goodbye"*
> *Or anything. The last few words he heard*
> *From me were, "I hope you do die quickly*
> *Because I sure as hell don't want to have*
> *To care for you or put up with your crap."*

Collaboration

Two imaginations are better than one. Think about collaborating with a partner. Two writers are more prolific in brainstorming. They can modify the each other's ideas, and combinations or modifications of previously suggested ideas often are superior to the initial ones. Working together reduces inhibition and defeatism, builds enthusiasm, and develops a competitive spirit in which each person wants to top the other. It can also help you through writer's block. Collaboration can help in developing better work habits. You have to show up and do the writing because the other person is. Writing with another person helps you stay motivated, focused, and productive.

For any collaboration, you need to begin by working out agreements to the process. Explore different spaces to see where you both work best—home, office, coffee shop, library. Work out your schedule for writing. Use your journals for noting ideas when you're not together. Consider the characters. Talk about people, character traits, habits, attitudes. Find photos to represent the characters. Make sure the characters are polarized. Decide what the story is about.

Set some ground rules for the process. Decide how you want to work together: co-writing every word together or dividing up the work into sections. In the latter approach, after one person has written a section, the other can rewrite it; then the two of you can act it out and agree on changes. Realize that some disagreement is bound to happen. It is an integral and valuable part of the process and often leads to important breakthroughs. Talk about how you plan to deal with disagreements and avoid hurt feelings. Perhaps the first writer of each section will make the final decision on that section. A good collaboration must have trust and respect, and it must focus on the work. The writers must have an agreement to talk things through and find ways to make decisions that both find acceptable. Many famous writers, such as George S. Kaufman and Moss Hart, collaborated for years and found great success.

In doing the following exercises, you will find that as you work on them, you become more conscious of the language, the choice of words, the imagery, and the sentence construction. These exercises force you to edit, to restructure sentences, and to choose other words to fit within the pattern.

EXERCISE 17

Beginning Level   Choose one of the following:

A. Form a partnership with another writer. Set the ground rules for the process and work together to write a ten-minute play, ten pages long, with two characters of very different voices, backgrounds, educations, and professions. Give them emotions caused by things they care about. Brainstorm to come up with a plot. Discuss each character's objectives, tactics, and subtext. Work together to make sure the dialogue is sharp.

B. Write a monologue of twelve to twenty lines, or about 125 words, and have Character A give advice based on his or her own experience. Rewrite the monologue in iambic pentameter. Do not use rhyme. Continue the thought beyond the end of the line (enjambed) as much as possible. Make the dialogue contemporary. Turn in both versions.

Intermediate Level   Choose one of the following:

C. Write a scene in which two characters never say exactly what they mean. Avoid direct dialogue. Good dialogue expresses the will of the character indirectly. Have each character attempt to lie, be witty, and use a variety of subtle tactics.

D. Select two characters with different professions. Make a list of fifty different words appropriate to each and write a scene using them. Perhaps the conflict is because the characters' professions have caused different outlooks. Perhaps one character is a workaholic or is learning a dangerous new job. Use differences in language to define each character.

Advanced Level   Choose one of the following:

E. Write a conflict scene between two modern characters of different social status over an object. Focus on the language, slang, images, details, and so on.

F. Rewrite a previous scene, making it comic by turning one of the characters into a talking animal. How does making the character a dog or a cat or a pig complicate the situation? Look at the comedy *Sylvia* by A. R. Gurney, Jr., about a man who has to choose between his wife and his dog.

Summary

Dialogue is action and reveals character. The audience wants to know how a character experiences the world and how that is reflected in both what the character says and how he says it. Just as the way a character behaves reveals who he is, so does the way the character speaks. Voice is one of the most potent character-building tools.

Every character, by the way she uses language, reveals something of her spirit, habits, capabilities, and prejudices. The choices of words, images, and sentence structures help create the character. The rhythm of the language must work for the character. Punctuation is a key element in providing clues to the rhythm of speech. A comma is a short pause. A semicolon is a longer pause. A period is a slightly longer pause. Three dots (an ellipsis) indicates a pause, in which the character is either thinking or trails off. A dash indicates that what follows is either an appositive—meaning the same thing—or an interruption. In either case, the words that come after are delivered faster. An understanding of how to punctuate is essential to creating the rhythm desired for a speech. The more specific the details, the more vivid the speech. The way in which details are included give clues to the character's perception. Figures of speech may be used especially to create comic characters. Language identifies character in terms of age, profession, education, social status, and religion.

Words that are considered obscene relate to body parts and functions. Words that are profane are considered offensive because of religious beliefs. Both obscenities and profanity are used by many people. However, in writing dialogue, it is important to consider not only the character but also the audience for whom the playwright is writing. Although it might be realistic to use curse words, it may not be appropriate or acceptable for some markets.

Now and then, a line stands out as a polished and shining "gem." Such a line perfectly fits the character and the situation and offers us insight into the character, situation, or theme.

The first line of a scene should lead directly into the essence of the conflict of the scene, and that is especially true of the first line of a play. Give careful thought to setting the right tone and grabbing interest and attention immediately.

When a character is first introduced in a play, the first impression counts. Audiences make up their minds about whether characters are likeable in the four minutes after the characters first enter the play. It is important to give the audience a firm handle on the character right off the bat.

Most contemporary American plays use standard English, and there is little effort to use elevated language. Conversational realism is the norm. However, some plays experiment with poetic form, and some use a dialect or poetic language. Words are made up of one or more syllables, some of which are emphasized, or stressed, and some of which are relatively unstressed. When these words are joined into a line, their stressed and unstressed syllables work together to form an overall rhythmic pattern for that line. *Scansion* is the term for analyzing rhythm syllable by syllable. The first step in scanning a line is to identify the stressed and unstressed syllables.

Collaborating with a partner provides two imaginations. Two writers are more prolific in brainstorming. They can modify the each other's ideas, and combinations or modifications of previously suggested ideas often are superior to the initial ones. Working together reduces inhibition and defeatism, builds enthusiasm, and develops a competitive spirit in which each person wants to top the other. For any collaboration, you need to begin by working out ground rules for the process.

CHAPTER

13 Monologues

In a play, a *monologue* is a long uninterrupted speech. Monologues can be quite flexible as to the forms they can take. A monologue may be given by one character to another. Usually, a monologue is not offered freely but given to answer a demand within a scene, such as Hickey finally telling the truth in Eugene O'Neil's *The Iceman Cometh* and Jerry telling about the dog in Edward Albee's *Zoo Story*. In William Saroyan's *The Time of Your Life,* Kit Carson tells Joe a colorful story that shows us a bit of his character (Act 2, pp. 425–436):

Told the Texas Ranger my name was Rothstein, mining engineer from Pennsylvania, looking for something worth while. Mentioned two places in Houston. Nearly lost an eye early one morning going down the stairs. Ran into a six-footer with an iron claw where his right hand was supposed to be. Said, You broke up my home. Told him I was a stranger in Houston. The girls gathered at the top of the stairs to see a fight. Seven of them. Six feet and an iron claw. That's bad on the nerves. Kicked him in the mouth when he swung for my head with the claw. Would have lost an eye except for quick thinking. He rolled into the gutter and pulled a gun. Fired seven times. I was back upstairs. Left the place an hour later, dressed in silk and feathers, with a hat swung around over my face. Saw him standing on the corner, waiting. Said, Care for a wiggle? Said he didn't. I went on down the street and left town. I don't suppose you ever had to put a dress on to save your skin, did you?

At the climax of Arthur Miller's *All My Sons,* Chris Keller demands answers from his father about why he sold defective airplane parts to the air force during World War II. Chris says, "I want to know what you did, now what did you do? You had a hundred and twenty cracked engine-heads, now what did you do?" Keller responds (Act 2, p. 58):

You're a boy, what could I do! I'm in business, a man is in business; a hundred and twenty cracked, you're out of business; you got a process, the process don't work, you're out of business; you don't know how to operate, your stuff is no good; they close you up, they tear up your contracts, what the hell's it to them?

You lay forty years into a business and they knock you out in five minutes, what could I do, let them take forty years, let them take my life away?
(His voice cracking.)
I never thought they'd install them. I swear to God. I thought they'd stop 'em before anybody took off.

Some monologues are delivered directly to the audience, such as the *soliloquies* in classical Greek, Roman, and Elizabethan plays. Today, such monologues delivered directly to the audience are frequently used in a drama with a narrator, such as Tom in Tennessee Williams's *The Glass Menagerie,* the Stage Manager in Thornton Wilder's *Our Town,* and Clifford in Warren Leight's *Side Man.* They are also used in contemporary comedies, such as Paul Rudnick's *Jeffrey* and Nicky Silver's *Fat Men in Skirts, Fit to Be Tied* and *The Food Chain.* The following speech is spoken by Phyllis at the opening of *Fat Men in Skirts* (Act 1, p. 7):

I loathe the beach. I am Phyllis Hogan and I do so loathe the beach. To me, it is the very definition of monotony. Just sand and water and sand and water. And more sand and more water. Ick. And look, a perfectly good pair of shoes, Susan Bennis/Warren Edwards, crocodile and completely ruined! I have never understood the appeal of the seashore: sand in your stockings and young girls with better bodies in skimpy swimsuits. When I was a girl I used to bury myself in the sand. Head first. I've no idea where I am. I was supposed to be in Italy by now, but I've been to Italy, and I always gain weight in Italy so here I am at the beach. My husband is in Italy, gaining weight no doubt, gorging himself on the local delicacies and the local girls—and perhaps, thinking, only fleetingly, "What could have become of Phyllis?" He's scouting locations for a new film. Something heartwarming about extraterrestrials I assume. My husband is a filmmaker. He was a director in the seventies, now he's a filmmaker. He makes heartwarming films about lovable extraterrestrials, mostly. My plane crashed. It's a miracle that I'm alive. I suppose. There were eight of us on the plane, including the pilot. Only Bishop and I survived. Of course one died of a heart attack during the in-flight movie. It featured Tatum O'Neal. I can't say I was frightened when the plane went down—the film was beastly. I just watched the ground getting closer and closer, spinning around outside my window like a top. I shut my eyes and waited for it to happen: the bang, the crash, the end. And knowing my life was over was kind of a relief in a funny way. The chore of my life was over and I could just relax and wait and see. . . . But then I opened my eyes and now a perfectly good pair of shoes is down the drain. Damn. You should meet Bishop. Bishop! He's my son. I sent him to go through the pockets of the others. I only have two packs of cigarettes with me and there's no telling how long it'll be before they find us. That was an hour ago. BISHOP! I'll go mad if I don't have some cigarettes.

Some writers try to create the impression that the character is alone, talking to himself or herself. This is a soliloquy, and it has a long history throughout classical drama. Perhaps the most famous is Hamlet's "To be or not to be" monologue. In plays by William Shakespeare, Bertolt Brecht, Lanford Wilson, and many other writers, the soliloquy is often addressed to the audience. In realistic plays, the character is usually not expected to look at the audience directly, since a soliloquy is generally considered to be thinking out loud. Edward Albee uses this kind of a monologue in *Who's Afraid of Virginia Woolf?* when Martha is alone and unable to find George. She's wandering around with a drink in her hand and does a rift after noticing the ice in her glass is going "clink." Other monologues happen when the character is talking to an imaginary person or persons, saying things that he always wanted to say but never had the chance, never had the courage, or perhaps is preparing to say.

The short monologue generally runs from two to six minutes. It needs to have a relatively uncomplicated story, with not too many characters. A successful short monologue is a highly condensed experience that can be thought of as the theatre's equivalent to poetry. Generally, such a monologue is written to be part of a larger play. Any monologue must be motivated by the situation and the character's emotional state. People just don't offer up their life stories to others for no reason. In a conflict situation, the monologue is usually the character's major explanation, plea, or excuse to clarify his or her behavior. Every monologue needs a clear reference point. We need to know who the speaker is addressing and what she wants. The character must have a passionate reason for saying this and needs to have different tactics that lead to achieving her objective.

Types of Monologues

Monologues and monodramas are often difficult to categorize because they are hybrids of style. The following distinctions are somewhat arbitrary but may be of some use in clarifying specific characteristics of both monologues and monologue plays.

Autobiographical Monologues

In this category, the writer recalls actual stories and events from his life. The actor/writer generally is the narrator in such a piece. There may be little or no attempt to perform different characters in the story. The emphasis here is on the telling of his tale.

One-Person Plays

A long monologue, or *monodrama,* is a one-person play. It may be autobiographical, fictional, or based on a real person. Monodrama can be a powerful form of theatre. Quite often, the writer uses elevated language and strong images to create a poetic enlargement of the characters and subject. A monodrama is like every play in that it has a beginning, middle, and end; contains concise dialogue; and expresses the writer's personal vision. Monodramas vary as to style, content, and time.

What makes monodramas so exciting and challenging to work on is that they are so flexible in terms of form. Although there is only one actor on stage, she can bring many characters into the piece by assuming their personalities and voices. Although it is difficult to incorporate conflict into a monodrama, some form of conflict is essential. The writer can rely on interesting characters, dialogue, a dramatic situation, and so on to make the piece theatrical, but there needs to be an expression of conflict, a struggle unfolded, a difficult goal finally reached, and adversity overcome.

Spalding Gray's autobiographical monologue, *Swimming to Cambodia*, is an example of this mainly narrative storytelling style. In it, Gray recalls his fascinating experiences working as an actor in the movie *The Killing Fields*. Charlayne Woodard's *Pretty Fire* is another example of the autobiographical narrative. She tells of her formative years and experiences as an African American girl who grew up with the same values, fears, and dreams as white girls. In this play, she remains the narrator throughout but also changes her voice and manner to portray the various role models in her life.

In monodramas such as *Freak* and *Sexaholics*, John Leguizamo uses only himself to tell an autobiographical story, but he sometimes transforms himself into others by assuming the voices, postures, and actions of family members and girlfriends. In his play *Mambo Mouth*, Leguizamo creates a series of character monologues. Each individual monologue features a family member or friend from his past. Each tells his or her own individual story, with a beginning, middle, and end. The form of these monologues has the character talking directly to the audience, conversationally. It is through the culmination of all of these individual monologues that the audience sees a larger story and understands what it was like being "a Latin from Manhattan."

Similarly, in *Spic-O-Rama*, John Leguizamo creates a series of wildly comic monologues portraying some of the people he encountered growing up in Jackson Heights, Queens. However, in this play, the monologues are all connected and the story as a whole has unity and momentum, moving toward one event: the wedding. Also an actor, Leguizamo has played all the characters in this satire of an urban Hispanic household, changing costumes and wigs as well as voices and movements to convey their distinct elements. In Leguizamo's play, Krazy Willie, a Desert Storm vet, is getting married. The looming event inspires the six members of the Gigante clan—nerdy nine-year-old Miggy, the bridegroom himself, Laurence Olivier wannabe Riffi, wheelchair-bound Javier, their sexy and sassy mother, Gladyz, and their foul-mouthed, philandering father—to reveal the love, pain, and frustration of unrealized dreams common to all families. As the actor changed costumes and prepared for each new scene, videos were shown to keep the forward motion accelerating. The videos bridged the plot and aided in camouflaging the costume changes, which ranged from the quickest of forty-five seconds to the longest of one-and-a-half minutes.

I Am My Own Wife is a new play by Doug Wright, who also wrote *Quills,* about the Marquis de Sade. The play is based on a true story and inspired by interviews conducted by Wright over several years. *I Am My Own Wife* tells the story of Charlotte von Mahlsdorf, a real-life German transvestite who managed to survive both the Nazi onslaught and the following repressive communist regime. The play is performed by a single actor, who portrays a host of characters, including Charlotte and an American writer who becomes intrigued by her. The play is a highly theatrical and subjective biography.

William Gibson's play *Golda's Balcony* is a one-woman bioplay about Golda Meir, who after a lifetime of public service, came out of retirement at age seventy to become Israel's fourth prime minister. Gibson (also author of *The Miracle Worker* and *Two for the Seesaw*) spent eight months with Meir in 1977, and the text of *Golda's Balcony* is largely derived from his conversations with her. There are parallels between the current situation in the Mideast and Meir's Israel of 1973.

Tea at Five, by Matthew Lombardo, is an intimate biodrama about Katharine Hepburn at home in her Fenwick estate in Old Saybrook, Connecticut. The first act takes place in September 1938. In spite of her Broadway appearances and Oscar, Hepburn has just been labeled "box office poison" after a series of film flops. With her professional future in doubt, she contemplates her childhood in Hartford, her education, and her start in show business. The second act takes place in February 1983, after Hepburn was injured in a car crash. The accident affords the now-legendary star an opportunity to reflect on the triumphs of her career and her heart-breaking romance with Spencer Tracy.

In the biocomedy *Say Goodnight, Gracie,* by Rupert Holmes, George Burns finds himself unable to join his wife, Gracie Allen, in heaven until he can give the final performance of his lifetime, completing his perfect track record of never having missed a curtain. The play—a last hurrah, as he might have presented on his one-hundredth birthday—is a guided tour through an American century, told through the eyes of a man who savored each day. From his impoverished youth on the Lower East Side of New York City to his career in vaudeville and his wooing of and unlikely marriage to Gracie Allen, the show illuminates Burns's life.

That Day in September, a solo play written and performed by Artie Van Why, chronicles his journey as he leaves behind an acting career and enters the corporate world. Being at work in New York City on the morning of September 11, 2001, across from the World Trade Center, and witnessing firsthand the horror of that day caused him to re-evaluate his life, quit his job, and begin chronicling his personal experience of being there. The greater part of *That Day in September* is given over to Van Why's graphic description of images from what he dubs the "war zone." He conveys the conflicting feelings of fear, awe, confusion, and helplessness as he recounts in graphic detail what he viewed. His recollections of his return to work, some two months after 9/11, are similarly vivid. *That Day in September* balances painful memories with a difficult healing process that encompassed a major life change for Van Why, who quit his job in November 2001 and returned to the career in theatre he had forsaken nearly two decades before.

Unlike a fictional monologue, an autobiographical one requires a somewhat different preparation. Since your life is the main source for the material, you'll need to review parts of it for material that will not only be informative to you but will also be a source of inspiration and illumination to your audience. Sometimes, the things that we consider to be the most private are in fact quite universal and can be understood by everyone in the audience.

Look through desks, drawers, and closets for photos, letters, old diaries, old toys, and any other sources of memorabilia that may trigger recollections. Try to recall your first romance. What was it about that person that excited you? How do you feel about the experience now? People face a number of turning points in their lives. Which ones have you faced? Think about what your life was like before each event. How did it change afterward? Think about an important job you once had. What was important about it? How did it change you? Recall the death of someone you really cared about. How did that affect you then? How does it affect you now? Think about a relative, friend, or teacher who influenced you and changed your life in some dramatic way. What was so special about this person? How did he or she influence your life? Thinking about past holidays usually brings up memories. Was there a particular holiday that will always bring back strong memories? What happened? Did you have a dream growing up, something that you really wanted to do? How has that affected your life? Did you make the dream come true, or did you change to another goal when you grew up? Have you or someone that you loved been ill with some life-threatening or incapacitating disease? What was the story surrounding that period? These suggestions are just memory triggers. If your monologue is about a specific period of your life, try to recall, in as much detail as you can, what was going on, both internally and externally, in the world around you. Recalling world events will create a context for your story.

Another thing to keep in mind is the list of characters that you're going to include from that period of your life. Recalling the exact things that they said is the ideal, but unfortunately we usually can't do that. But we can recall things like what they wore. If you think back, a particular day or moment may come to mind. Think specifically about what people were wearing. Try to remember every detail of each person's wardrobe—your mother, for instance. How did her hair look? Was she carrying a purse? Was she wearing earrings? What was her makeup like? Can you recall the smell of her cologne? Do you remember any specific mannerisms that she had? The way she held her head when listening to you? A look in her eyes when she ate something she liked? Her look of disapproval when she saw someone she didn't like? Try to remember any idiosyncratic things she did.

Try to remember how you felt about each character back then. Have your feelings toward any of these people changed? It's interesting how after people are gone, our feelings toward them change, sometimes dramatically. That change in feelings can be very helpful when writing about them. Interviewing relatives and family friends can be a useful source for gathering information that you may not recall. Return, if you can, to the old neighborhood that you grew up in. Walk around, look at familiar buildings and streets, and see what is conjured up. See if the people you knew then still live there. Perhaps pay a visit. Interview them, if it feels comfortable and is practical to do so.

Reality-Based Monologues

Some pieces are created from real-life events. This type of monologue uses the exact words of the people who were involved. In her play *Twilight: Los Angeles, 1992,* Anna Deavere Smith relates the experiences of forty-six characters in the wake of the Rodney King verdict on April 29, 1992, and the riots that followed. Smith portrayed all the characters when the play was performed. In writing it, she obtained information by tape-recording the actual people and taking notes on their speech tics and vocal inflections. In *Fires in the Mirror,* Smith explores the tensions between African Americans and Hasidic Jews after a Caribbean American boy was killed in Crown Heights, New York, on August 19, 1991, by a rabbi's motorcade, and a Jewish student was slain in retaliation. Smith again interviewed most of the principals involved and many others, presenting a series of characters with diverse points of view.

The *Exonerated,* a reality-based work by Jessica Blank and Erik Jensen, is about people who were sentenced to death, spent anywhere from two to twenty-two years on death row, and then subsequently were found innocent and freed by the state. Taken verbatim from court transcripts, depositions, and interviews, *The Exonerated* tells the true stories of six people who were wrongly accused, convicted of murder, and spent many years on death row before finally being proven innocent and released. Blank and Jensen edited their source materials to produce a series of monologues to tell their story (which is more about the loss of time than the morality of the death penalty) and fused everything into a seamless, compelling whole. The impact of *The Exonerated* is made more striking by the decision to stage the play as a reading. The actors sit on ten stools with music stands, facing forward. The direct contact helps the audience absorb the play's full weight.

Topical Monologues

Topical monologues rely heavily on the experience of the performer/writer. They are part autobiographical, part observation, and part opinion. There is a thin line between a topical monologue and stand-up comedy. Both generally incorporate anecdotes, jokes, and personal observations. The difference between the two lies in the writer's intention. The topical monologist's intention is to discuss a theme. His or her stories generally have a more cohesive quality. Stand-up comics primarily tell jokes, although on occasion, they will also include some anecdotal material. Comedian George Carlin generally focuses on a theme. He cites personal observations and specific incidents and then moves to the larger picture and his opinion of it. Kate Clinton's funny, feminist topical monologues express her particular view of the world. She has done both stand-up and topical monologues. Bill Maher also does topical monologues, often focusing on political issues.

Fictional Monologues

This is a fictional story performed by an actor. It is generally written in narrative form, in which the actor serves as storyteller. *Shirley Valentine,* by Willy Russell, is a very successful example. In it, Shirley ponders her unfulfilled life and eventually goes to Greece to find her "missing person" within. During the telling of the story, the actor will occasionally break the narrative form to momentarily become one of the characters, but then she immediately returns to the narrator/storyteller role.

St. Nicholas, by Conor McPhearson, is another example. In this monologue play, a fictitious character tells a chilling imaginary tale of a night of drinking and an encounter with a vampire. Although the story is told in a narrative form, occasionally, the man will re-enact a moment with present-tense dialogue. The story has a clearly defined beginning, middle, and end. It builds in tension, as we experience what the main character tells us about this scary night. Similar to a tale told around a campfire, we are in suspense as the storyteller takes us from one moment to the next.

Although Eugene O'Neill's *The Emperor Jones* has a scene with dialogue at both the beginning and end, it is essentially a monodrama, in which Jones is running through the jungle experiencing a nightmare of visions from his past and from the history of African Americans. He encounters the "little formless fears," the pullman porter he killed, the negro convicts, the prison guard, the planters, the slave market, the slave ship, the congo witch doctor, and the crocodile god. O'Neill uses monologues, masks, pantomime, suggestive scenery, lighting, costumes, and the increasingly faster throb of the tom-toms to outwardly express Jones's thoughts and emotions.

Talking Heads, written by British playwright Alan Bennett and produced in New York in the summer of 2003, showcased seven actors in a program of alternating monologues. Each monologue is a one-person, one-act play, complete with set and even costume changes. Even though they are united thematically and all explore the inner reaches of loneliness, they stretch the monodrama format in unexpected and new ways.

Audition Monologues

Sometimes, instead of using a monologue from an established play, a monologue is written especially for auditioning, usually by the actor performing it. Casting directors and agents pride themselves on their ability to make snap judgments, so if you write for auditions, it is best to remember that brevity is essential. An audition piece that unfolds slowly will still end whenever the director or agent says "thank-you." For this strange format, the material should not exceed two to three minutes. In some cases, an actor will be allowed only a one-minute monologue.

The purpose of an audition monologue is *marketing.* The actor is seeking to prove his talent. The actor/writer needs to choose a character that he is capable of playing and is realistically suitable for being cast. The monologue and the character need to show off the best assets of the actor. An actor/writer who is not good at physical comedy or gut-wrenching emotion should not try to create a character that requires such a portrayal. It is especially important for an audition monologue to have a clearly defined beginning, middle, and end. In a bare space, with no lights and costumes, the actor only has the words and his body and voice to indicate to the viewers the start of the performance, the high point, and when the piece is finished. Remember, directors and other casting agents, who often see dozens of actors, usually make these decisions quickly. A monologue must fit within the allotted time. If the call is for a two-minute monologue, it must work within that time limit. Less is more. Otherwise, the actor may be cut off before being able to really show his stuff.

While the monologue form is a flexible form with flexible rules, the audition monologue has more strictures, especially when it comes to time. A good, short audition monologue or character monologue should include several attributes:

1. It should generally be from one to two minutes in length. Because of its brevity, the story shouldn't be too complex.

2. It should not contain much exposition because that tends to drag the piece down and bore the audience.

3. It should avoid storytelling about a past event. An audition monologue needs to include strong, immediate dialogue; have an intense, passionate, and exciting reason for the character to be speaking; and employ clear tactics. Such a monologue is generally much more effective, especially for an audition where the goal is to wow the director or agent.

4. A limited number of characters should be mentioned in the piece. Too many characters will confuse the listener. Therefore, the number of characters involved in the story should be limited to no more than three.

5. Every monologue should have a clear *beginning, middle, and end,* and each of these three portions must be given its due. Without a strong adherence to this structure, problems will develop. A monologue with a faulty structure seems to hop all over the place, losing the audience along the way, and often seems just to stop rather than end. Such a monologue exemplifies the need for a strong beginning and end. A monologue that sets out to handle a large issue and then suddenly ends, without sufficiently dealing with that issue, generally needs a stronger middle. In most, though not all, monologues, the main character wants to achieve some goal. In the middle section, we see her struggle, which builds to a climax. Generally speaking, the middle of the monologue will dominate because it deals with action and plot development.

The monologue should include three elements. First is the character's *objective,* what she wants or must have. When we know what the character's *objective* is, the action of a piece can begin. Second, there must be an obstacle, which is any obstruction, hindrance, or opposition that stands in the way of a character's getting something that she wants. The third element, the *arc,* is the shape the monologue takes. It is the through line, from the beginning to the middle to the end. The arc is determined by the journey that the character takes to get what she wants or needs. The challenge and demand for the writer is to tell some sort of story and express some sort of meaning or message.

Unlike a play, a short monologue within a play does not always have to include a strong conflict. Striking characterization and dialogue are sometimes enough to keep the monologue interesting and theatrical. However, without conflict, nothing happens, and if nothing happens, it's not dramatic. This will not work for a longer monologue play.

The Questions

A monologue should make clear answers to the following questions: Who? What? Why? When? Where? To whom? How? I'm not suggesting that you write information out in some factual way. Avoid obvious exposition. You should be able to creatively reveal and show important information to your audience within the dialogue or narrative without stating all of it explicitly.

1. *Who is the character speaking?* You must know your character inside and out. You should be able to improvise in that character, if necessary. You should be able to imagine the character in situations other than the one you are presenting in your piece.

2. *What problems or complications arise for this character?* To make something dramatic, there should be some sort of conflict, something that stirs the character into action. What the character is trying to get and from whom will influence his choice of actions. As a writer, you must create a character with strong, specific wants. This is especially true in character-driven and narrative pieces.

3. *Why is the character telling this story?* Through the character's dialogue, let us know why the character is saying and doing the things he is. The audience must have some sense of what motivates the character; otherwise, they will become confused and eventually disinterested. Why does the character need to tell the story? The need cannot be general; it must be specific. The character may need to dispose of some guilt or pain from his past. Perhaps he has this hilarious story that simply must be told. Or maybe the character has discovered some profound insight that must be shared with the rest of the world—now! Whatever you select, remember, the need to tell and the urgency should be compelling.

4. *When is this happening?* Are we in the present, the past, or the future? What is the time of day? Is it 4:00 A.M. or 3:00 in the afternoon? Obviously, the time will affect how the character speaks, moves, and thinks.

5. *Where is it happening?* Where is the character physically when she is delivering this monologue? Letting the audience know the locale in the context of the story is helpful in their understanding and sharing of what you're trying to tell. In the case of an autobiographical monologue, the character may be back in the house that she grew up in. If you can clearly establish the location for your audience, or at least give them a sense of it, you will set a mood and bring them into your world. How does this location affect the character who is speaking? In some monologues, the actor may be the story's narrator and there may be no pretense that she is in a make-believe location. The character is just in the theatre, telling the story of your monologue to the audience. In an audition monologue, there are no pieces of scenery, no costumes, and no props. Therefore, it is the job of the storyteller to fill the stage with images that will evoke the world needed.

6. *To whom is the character speaking?* If the character is talking to someone, who is this person? What is their relationship? The secret to dealing with this aspect is not to clutter the monologue with a lot of facts about the person being addressed. How the character relates to this person, what she says, and how she says it will give the audience most of the important information. Certainly, some relevant facts about the relationship may be necessary. But by calling someone "Mom" or "Honey," you immediately give obvious clues about the relationship.

7. *How does the character resolve the complication?* The way the character goes about solving his dilemma or conflict is one of the main components of story-telling. Specifically, how a character resolves his problem is often an indication of whether we are watching a comedy or drama.

Dramatic Style

It's important to understand the difference between *narrative* and *dramatic* writing, since both styles are interwoven throughout most monologues. In the narrative style, a narrator tells a story. Background material, with detailed descriptions, is presented. Character, set, and plot are developed in these detailed descriptions. Generally speaking, autobiographical monologues use more of the narrative style than other types of monologues.

In the dramatic style, we are shown the story through strong dramatic actions, rather than told the story. The writer frequently begins with the character in the middle of an action—a conflict situation. For instance, the character may start the monologue ranting about some issue or appealing to the audience for something. The story is happening right there, right now, in the moment. In this case, there is no need to go through the beginning, middle, and end of the *narrative;* regardless, the piece still needs to have an *arc* to it.

Your Personal Style

Your voice is your *style,* your way of expressing yourself. Your voice stems directly from your sense of truth. It is your unique choice of words and phrases, your rhythm, the way you speak, your vision, how you tell your story. It is your trademark style. It is a major factor in determining the tone of your work. All good writers have their own distinct voice. Finding and developing your personal voice is an integral part of your work as a monologist.

The trap for most beginning monologists it that they try to emulate their favorite writer's style, consciously or unconsciously. To avoid this, always stay focused on specifically what it is you want to say, on your need to tell your story, and create your characters exactly the way you see and feel them.

Finding the Character's Voice

A writer needs to develop a distinct voice for each character in a play. One way of doing this is to get the characters talking. Let your imagination take you inside each character's head. Stay there a while; breathe it in; live in her shoes. Imagine what it's really like to be this person. Notice the differences and similarities between who you are and who she is. Notice how the character thinks and feels about things.

When you feel that you really know the character, viscerally, let the character speak. Write exploratory monologues, in which each character is in the present and talks about the ten most important milestones in her life and what effect each one had. Explore how the characters feel about the moments of crisis and change. Let the characters get emotional. Envision how each character looks and acts upon making her first entrance. Concentrate on her thought patterns, word choices, and command of language.

Many playwrights have said that they really don't write their plays but that the characters tell them what to say. Let your characters lead you where they want to go. Let your characters tell the story that they want to tell. Get out of the way; just "play." Always try to simplify things; bring them down to their basic truths. Nothing is more boring on stage than a long-winded, unnecessary narrative that could easily have been stated in a line or two.

Keep in mind that you are writing for the stage, not for a book. You don't want to become too literary, too cerebral; your audience will fall asleep on you. People in real life sometimes struggle to find the right word. They repeat themselves. They interrupt themselves and change directions. They don't use complete sentences. They use contractions and slang, and their grammar isn't always correct. Write as the character thinks, feels, and speaks. Visualize the character going to school, eating dinner, listening to music. What does the character's face look like? His teeth? Lips? Find the voice.

Characteristics of Good Monologues

A good monologue play should have a well-defined structure, just as a good play does. There is no one rule as to how a monologue must be structured, however. The story should always dictate the form.

A monologue play, like a short monologue, should have a clear beginning, middle, and end. No matter what form it takes, the monologue play is a way of telling a story, and all good stories have a clear through line.

The story that you're telling should be able to sustain interest for however long it takes to tell. This means that since there is an audience, there must be entertainment value. Make sure that the monologue is theatrical, not something that the audience could have stayed home and read. When you're writing for the theatre, you must take into account your audience.

Images are one of the main things that capture an audience. The more specific and descriptive you can be, the better. How the character feels about the event of the story that he is telling is another important thing to keep in mind. Storytelling is about saying something out loud to people who are listening. Words, images, and ideas are what we communicate to make stories alive, vibrant, and interesting.

The short monologue or monologue play should include an objective, an obstacle, and an arc. It should have conflict, for it to work theatrically. You may create as many characters as you want. Just be sure that each one is necessary to your story; you don't want to overpopulate the piece. Each character should be fully developed and different from the others. If you have a play with a series of character monologues, such as Leguizamo's *Mambo Mouth,* each may have a different setting, as long as the locales are simple and set changes can be made in less than a minute. Sometimes, with a no-set show, locale changes are indicated within the dialogue, but the writer must be sure that the audience always knows where they are.

At some point, your audience should become aware of your point of view, of what you're trying to say. For any play to succeed, the audience should have some sense of why the writer took the time to create it in the first place. One of the main reasons to create your own monologue should come out of the need to express something that deeply concerns you. It may be a burning issue or some event in your past that you need to resolve. The important thing is that during the monologue, you attempt to come to grips with the issue or the meaning of the event. The most important thing to keep in mind is that every monologue and monologue play must have an interesting story to tell, a good yarn, a reason for the audience to want to be there.

EXERCISE 18 (Optional)

Beginning Level   Choose one of the following:

  A. Write an autobiographical monologue in which Character A talks about a significant object given to him by Character B, a person no longer in his life because the person is dead, estranged, or moved away. Use an object that an actor can have in his hand when performing the monologue. The significance of the object is not its monetary value but its importance as a symbol of something the character values because it represents the relationship—the love, sadness, joy. Possible objects include a ring, key, shirt, candy box, watch, photo, or a letter.

  B. Write a fictional monologue in which the character spins a whopping, fantastic story that has just enough elements of truth so that the audience might be sucked into believing that it is not a total lie, but it is. This might be a fantasy trip, an experience with an alien, an urban legend, a wild west story, or a brief love affair with a romantic stranger.

Intermediate Level   Choose one of the following:

C.   Write an audition monologue. Imagine a conflict situation in which the character has reached the end of his or her rope. The character is confronting a best friend or lover about a serious addiction problem with food, drugs, alcohol, or sex. Who is the character speaking? What is the problem for this character? Why is the character telling the story? What time of day or night is it? Where is it happening? To whom is the character speaking? How does the character resolve the complication? The monologue should have a beginning, middle, and end. It needs an arc that builds to a climax.

D.   Write a monologue specifically designed to focus on the character's voice. Pay careful attention to the choice of words and phrases, slang, and regionalisms. Craft the sentence structure to reflect the personality. Is the character tough, shy, uneducated, urban, rural, overconfident, brash, sassy?

Advanced Level   Choose one of the following:

E.   Pick a serious monologue from a play. Rewrite the monologue to fit a comic character with attitude and a distinctly different voice and vocabulary.

F.   Write a fifteen-minute monodrama about a well-known contemporary or historical figure. Explore one major event in that person's life in one space at one time. Although there will be only one actor on stage, he can bring other characters into the piece by assuming their personalities and voices. There needs to be expressions of conflict, a struggle unfolded, a difficult goal finally reached, or adversity overcome.

Summary

A *monologue* is a long, uninterrupted speech delivered by one character to another or directly to the audience. Some writers try to create the impression that the character is alone, talking to himself. This is a *soliloquy*. A successful short monologue is a highly condensed experience that can be thought of as the theatre's equivalent to poetry. Any monologue must be motivated by the situation and the character's emotional state. In a conflict situation, the monologue is usually the character's major explanation, plea, or excuse to clarify his behavior. A long monologue, or *monodrama,* is a one-person play.

Monologues and monodramas are often difficult to categorize because they are hybrids of style. The following distinctions are somewhat arbitrary but may be of some use in clarifying specific characteristics of both monologues and monologue plays.

In an autobiographical monologue, the writer recalls actual stories and events from his life. The actor/writer generally is the narrator in such a piece. Examples include John Leguizamo's *Freak* and *Sexaholics*. A variant of this form is a series of monologues portraying different people, all played by one actor, and centered around one event in his life, such as Leguizamo's *Spic-a-holic*.

A long monologue, or monodrama is a one-person play. *Golda's Balcony* (Gibson) and *I Am My Own Wife* (Wright) are two examples. This type of play may be autobiographical, fictional, or based on a real person. Monodrama can be a powerful form of theatre.

A reality-based monologue is created from a real-life event. The monologist uses the exact words of the people who were involved, as in *Fires in the Mirror* (Smith).

A topical monologue is part autobiographical, part observation, and part opinion. There is a thin line between a topical monologue and stand-up comedy. Both generally incorporate anecdotes, jokes, and personal observations. The difference between the two lies in the writer's intention. The topical monologist's intention isn't only to get laughs but to center the material with a cohesive theme.

Fictional storytelling monologues are fictional stories performed by actors. They are generally written in narrative form, in which the actor serves as storyteller.

Sometimes, instead of using a monologue from an established play, a monologue is written especially for auditioning, usually by the actor performing it. The characteristics of a good, short audition monologue or character monologue are as follows: (1) It should generally be from one to two minutes in length. In some cases, an actor is only allowed a one-minute monologue. (2) It should not contain much exposition because that tends to drag the piece down and bore the audience. (3) It should avoid storytelling about a past event. An audition monologue needs to include strong, immediate dialogue; have an intense, passionate, and exciting reason for the character to be speaking; and employ clear tactics. (4) A limited number of characters should be mentioned in the piece—no more than three. (5) It should have a clear beginning, middle, and end.

Every monologues should make clear answers to the following questions: (1) Who is the character speaking? (2) What problems or complications arise for this character? (3) Why is the character telling this story? (4) When is it happening? (5) Where is it happening? (6) To whom is the character speaking? (7) How does the character resolve the complication?

A good monologue has a well-defined structure. The story should always dictate the form. A monologue play, like a short monologue, should have a clear beginning, middle, and end and a clear through line. The story should be entertaining. The monologue should be theatrical, not something that the audience could have stayed home and read. The words, images, and ideas used to communicate must make the story alive, interesting, and capture an audience. The short monologue or monodrama includes a clear objective, obstacles, and an arc. It has conflict. It works theatrically.

14 Settings, Costumes, and Other Technical Matters

What is the period in which you plan to set the play? What about the people, manners, country, time, culture, sounds, and clothing? What kind of world does the play create? What is the visual environment? How can the playwright deal with this visual world in a manner that is practical for the theatre?

One of the problems I encounter with student playwrights is their lack of knowledge about the practical issues of theatre from a design and technical standpoint. Recently, a beginning playwright turned in three scenes with three very realistic and different locales. The first scene took place on the edge of a cliff, the second scene was set in an office, and the third was in a bedroom. Among the stage directions was the note "Half an hour goes by." This playwright was used to film but had no understanding of the stage. As such, the writing he had created on paper wasn't possible or practical for the theatre.

Theatrical Forms

The physical setting of a play is often determined by its type of theatrical form. A professional musical production—with its presentational style, spectacular scale, numerous sets, and large cast—generally requires a large theatre with a seating capacity of at least 1000 to 1500 in order to make a profit at the box office. A straight (nonmusical) play, which is more intimate in nature, needs a smaller-sized stage and house, with seating from 99 to 850.

Both types of theatrical productions have clung to the traditional *proscenium* theatre, with the audience facing the stage. However, there are small theatres with flexible seating arrangements off-Broadway, off-off-Broadway, and in many universities and communities throughout the United States. These theatres are able to change the audience/actor relationship by having the audience on two sides of the stage (*alley staging*), on three sides (*thrust stage*), surrounding the stage (*arena staging*), or in an L-shape around the stage.

In the past hundred years, new theatres of all forms have sprung up all over the country. The black box theatre, which allows for flexible staging and changing the audience stage relationship for each play, has become popular. These smaller theatres have reduced the ornate splendor of the old proscenium theatres for a simpler "form follows function" approach. These theatres minimize the scale of production.

Most student playwrights start out with a ten-minute play or a one-act. Often, such a work is presented with no scenery and a minimum of furniture and props. An evening of two long one-acts may have sets, if produced in a professional theatre or occasionally in an educational or community theatre. This is more apt to occur if the playwright is well known or if the theatre is focusing on new work. Colleges and universities are more apt to produce an evening of four or five short plays directed by students, with just furniture and props.

Settings

Because of the enormous costs of producing a straight, nonmusical play—comedy or drama—most plays today are restricted to a single or unit set. Most straight plays take place in living rooms. Many use a kitchen setting. Some are set in cafes or bars. Some are set outside houses. Only a few plays call for a really unique or different kind of locale. For instance, *Out of Gas on Lover's Leap,* by Mark St. Germain, and *The Unseen Hand,* by Sam Shepard, are each set outdoors with a car on stage. Arthur Miller's *The Price* is set in an attic filled with junk. Tennessee Williams's *Cat on a Hot Tin Roof* and Alan Ball's *Five Women Wearing the Same Dress* are each set in a bedroom. Tennessee Williams's *Orpheus Descending* and Ed Graczyk's *Come Back to the Five and Dime, Jimmy Dean, Jimmy Dean* are each set in a general store. Doug Wright's *Quills* and Peter Weiss's *Marat/Sade* are each set in a mental asylum. *Steaming,* by Neil Dunn, is set in a Turkish bath. Herb Gardner's *I'm Not Rappaport* is set in Central Park. Miguel Pinero's *Short Eyes* is set in a prison. David Rabe's *Streamers* is set in a paratroopers' barracks. Patrick Meyers's *K2* is set on the side of a mountain covered with ice. Leroi Jones's *Dutchman* takes place in a subway car. Other locales include locker rooms, offices, brothels, gas stations, and even beaches. Most contemporary plays are tied to realism. The exceptions are those plays with a number of locales, which are then produced with a unit set, an imaginative and creative approach that is suggestive rather than realistic. My advice to the playwright is to try and find a setting that is more unique than the typical living room or kitchen.

A *unit set* provides a basic structure and allows minor changes in the set, props, and lighting to suggest different locales. There are many different solutions to the problem of multiple locales. A revolving stage with three sets in a pie shape may work for some plays. Another approach is to have a major set on stage with inserts, which may be on a wagon that rolls through an opening. Another way is to anchor sets on the right and the left. Once the main set is rolled upstage, the set on the right or the left swings on stage, like the opening of a knife. Another approach is to have one major set piece with some areas on the stage that are neutral. By adding a chair or a bar or a bed, the neutral space can be used for short scenes in other locales. Some contemporary plays with intriguing unit sets are Peter Shaffer's *Royal Hunt of the Sun* and *Equus,* Arthur Miller's *After the Fall,* and Tony Kushner's *Angels in America.*

Royal Hunt of the Sun uses a large raked circle. (*Raked* means that the back of the area is raised higher than the front so it is tipped up, allowing the audience to see better.) The circle opens up to suggest a blazing sun. *After the Fall,* by Arthur Miller, uses an abstract platform stage to represent many different locales. *Equus* uses a platform in the center with benches to represent the psychiatrist's office, the Strang home, a stable, a movie theatre, a field and so on. The area around the center platform is used for other locales. The center platform also revolves. In the background around the stage, there are benches for the actors to sit on when they aren't involved in the action. There are six towers that each hold a horse mask. When the actors are to play horses, they move to the towers and put the masks on in a ritualistic fashion.

Angels in America: Millennium Approaches is a three-hour play in three acts that has about ten different locales and thirty set changes. In some scenes, there are simultaneous actions in two different locales. This design, by J. David Blatt, is a unit set with most of the furniture on stage throughout. Two turntables downstage—small revolving circular platforms—and a wagon upstage are used.

After the Fall, *performed at Berry College, Rome, GA. Directed and designed by Leroy Clark.*

Angels in America: Millennium Approaches, *performed at Wichita State University. Directed by Leroy Clark, Set and Lighting designed by J. David Blatt, Costume Design by Betty Monroe.*

Changes are made on the turntables during intermission. A few items are brought on and off by actors. Lighting focuses the audience's attention on the area of the stage associated with each specific locale. White drapes provide an opportunity to show off dramatic color in the lighting as well as to visually provide a theatrical metaphor for the angels in heaven, the white of a hospital room, and the snow-covered landscape of Antarctica.

Working with student playwrights, I've encountered the same major problem over and over again—that the writer has no understanding of the stage or the limitations of live theatre, the small budgets, and what is practical. Most important, however, is how this lack of understanding translates into poor approaches to structuring plays and poor choices concerning settings and technical production. In every playwriting class I've taught over the last twenty years, a number of the students turn in first drafts of plays with multiple locales and time changes. Most beginning writers are very influenced by film, and they write in a cinematic way, with a series of scenes in different locales and the expectation of a realistic set and an immediate change for each locale. They also do not take into account the needs for costume and prop changes. Thought must be given to the time, labor, and cost such changes would require. In most cases, I am able to show the students how their plays can be rethought to work in one location or a unit set with fewer time changes.

Such plays, when produced—even if a unit set is devised—often seem choppy. If there is a blackout between scenes, it drops the audience out of the play, and when this happens over and over, it alienates the audience. If the stage doesn't go completely to black between scenes but stage hands appear and change props, that also takes the audience out of the play. When I am directing, I try to incorporate prop changes within the activities of the characters in the scene. If props are used and left on stage at the end of a scene and should not be there in the next scene, I try to find a way of dealing with them in the stage business of the actors during the scene, so that stage hands are not seen on stage until intermission or after the play.

It is nearly impossible in most theatres today to produce a play with multiple full stage sets. There isn't the space to store sets, and the cost is prohibitive. The time it would take to change the scenery would destroy the flow of the play. In many university, community, and professional theatres, the personnel who are available to build, paint, decorate, find or make props, and run the set and prop changes are too small in number to manage such a large-scale production adequately or effectively.

Therefore, the wise writer should think small. A play by an unknown writer that requires a spectacular, complex, and expensive setting (or several of them) isn't likely to ever be produced. The beginning writer should focus on the characters, the plot, the structure, the dialogue, the rhythm, and most important, the conflict. Depend on the characters to tell the story. The setting and technical requirements need to be kept simple. This doesn't necessarily mean boring, but it means the writer needs to be practical and creative. She needs to learn what is possible and practical, to be resourceful, and to find a setting that is unique and not overcomplicated. The same cautions apply to the playwright who wants numerous lighting and sound effects or music playing during the play. Any production that focuses on these elements, rather than the story, the acting, and the characters, is likely to have major problems.

Visual design in the modern theatre is concerned with the total visual effect of a dramatic production. It involves not only the scenic background—the colors and shapes of framed pieces of scenery—but also the selection and style of the furniture and set dressings, the quality and intensity of the lighting, and the easy movement of the actors. The careful consideration of the actor's costumes to contrast with the background; to represent the personality, age, period, sex, and status of the character; and to fit with the overall style of the production is also part of the visual design. Visual design is the creating of a form to fulfill a purpose. Scenic, lighting, costuming, and sound design all provide a visual/aural support of the dramatic form. The form of the play should guide the designers in understanding the relationship of the scenery to the action, to the style, to the moods, to the theme, and to the story in general.

Jo Mielziner, one of the most notable stage designers of the twentieth century, avoided realism. He did not believe literalism had any place in the theatre. He omitted the nonessentials and accented the details he believed were the most revealing. His designs for the original productions of *Death of a Salesman* and *A Streetcar Named Desire* became world famous and reproduced in countless theatre books internationally. His design for Tennessee Williams' *Cat on a Hot Tin Roof*, a realistic play set in the bedroom of a Southern mansion, was originally represented on the stage with just platforms and furniture in front of a cyclorama. There were no walls, no attempt to present a realistic bedroom in a Southern mansion. Women's costumes were poetic and stylized, not realistic. Playwrights can learn how less is more by looking at his designs in his book, *Designing for the Theatre,* published by Bramhill House (1965) or *Mielziner: Master of Modern Stage Design* by Mary C. Henderson, published by Watson-Guptill Publications (2001).

As you think of the locale or setting for your play, seek to find unique places. In *The Knack,* by Ann Jellicoe, the setting is basically an empty room, in which one character is painting the walls during the play. Edward Albee's *Seascape* is set on a beach, and his *Sandbox* is set in a sandbox. William Saroyan's short play *Hello Out There* is set in a jail. The possibilities extend as far as your imagination.

It is also helpful to understand what is practical in the theatre. As noted earlier, the practical problems of staging will affect play selection by a producer or a theatre, even when the play under consideration is clearly a good play. Practical factors include the number of sets and the style and detail of the sets. Whether there is a large stock of ready-made flats and platforms to use or whether all must be built from scratch may also determine the acceptance or rejection of a play. The playwright's script may be extremely set-specific, such as *A Streetcar Named Desire* or *Equus.* The original sets for these plays were so successful in creating the environments for the plays that the designs for most other productions continue to be strongly influenced. The directions for staging within the scripts also make it difficult for any director of designer to ignore them or produce the plays in a different way. However, many plays lend themselves to a variety of approaches. A revival of *An Inspector Calls,* by J. B. Priestley, on Broadway in 2001 showed how a typical kind of mystery play, set in a 1912 drawing room, could be creatively reimagined with an expressionistic exterior setting. When the play opened, it was raining. The floor of the stage was paved with stone, so that the water could be channeled. In the background was a miniature English manor house. This moved downstage toward the audience, and the family members emerged from the house. The approach to any play depends not only on what the playwright is saying and how he is saying it but also on the vision of the director and designers. The director's concept, the theatre space, and all that is in the script—the demands of the action, the literary style, the characters—affect the vision of the designers. The more you as the playwright know about staging, about scenery, and about costumes, the more stageworthy your work will be.

I always ask the students in my playwriting classes how many have never seen a play. I remember that in a recent class, two people had never seen a play. They were familiar with television and film, but here they were, taking a playwriting class without ever having seen a live theatre production. Both of them also presented scenes in class that were cinematic and not really developed or practical for the stage. One wrote a scene that called for darkness, then a nuclear explosion, lighting that kept getting brighter and brighter, and two soldiers in silhouette fighting with swords. There were only a few lines of dialogue. The soldiers dropped their swords, but the swords moved in slow motion and disintegrated before they touched the floor. There was dialogue about the heat, the numbness in the body, and the end of the world. The soldiers hugged each other and disintegrated. It would be very difficult to show these things on stage, of course, and the lighting, projections, and special effects would be very time consuming and expensive. The assignment was an exercise calling for students to write a scene focusing on the use of a creative and unique kind of setting, with a character making a major decision. The writer of the scene just noted focused on the setting but wasn't able to describe it in stage-worthy terms. His description was more suitable to a movie, and the only decision made was the soldiers throwing down their weapons. The soldiers were not developed as characters. They were cardboard types. There was no clear protagonist. There was no distinction between the two characters. Understanding what is possible and practical in the theatre will help you tell a story in a way that will work.

If you don't understand what is practical, you may find your play will be considered unproducible and tossed aside. This nearly happened to a play called *Under Fire,* by Catherine Keyser. I want to tell this story for two reasons: First, I want to make it clear that you don't always have to have one simple set and only a few actors. If you have a clear vision, follow your dream. Second, if you have a vision but are not sure if it will work, find someone to help you—someone you trust and who has faith in you. Otherwise, you may be wasting your time. *Under Fire* was produced at Central Florida University. Without the support and help of director Lani Harris, the play would have been discarded.

The play had been selected from a student competition. Professor Lani Harris was part of the selection team. Some of her colleagues felt the play was unproducible. It focused on Hillary Clinton and her election to the U.S. Senate, it had a strong role of the very well-known Bill Clinton, it had many locales, and it had a huge cast of about 150 characters. Casting, staging, costumes—all presented many problems to be solved. Nevertheless, there was much about the play and what it had to say that intrigued Harris, and there was no doubt that the twenty-one-year-old student writer from Harvard was talented.

Harris worked with the author to cut down the number of characters and make the play more focused. She cast the play with individual actors playing the major roles and a chorus of other actors playing five or six characters each. Each chorus member had one basic costume, and by adding a hat or a sweater and changing his or her physicality, each actor was able to convey different characters—real contemporary people, historical figures, and the imagined group of reporters, aides, secretaries, and other people Senator Clinton dealt with. Harris found solid, experienced actors to play Hillary and Bill, who were made up to capture the likenesses of the real people. Her set designer created a multilevel, abstract set with terrific acting areas and used five screens—television and large projection screens—for slides and video. The student lighting designer lit the actors and the set brilliantly. It was a good story, but without the daring and skill of the director and designers, whose collaboration helped shape this enormous project, the play would not have been produced.

This situation of a first play being produced with a huge cast, a very complicated setting, and the extensive use of slides, film, and live mics was an exception. Similarly, there may have been one-hundred other successful plays that have broken the rules, but there have been tens of thousands of plays produced that have followed the rules. The beginning playwright with no track record and no recognizable name should work to create a dynamic play that focuses on the characters, story, structure, and dialogue, using a small cast and a simple set. A play that focuses primarily on spectacle is like one of those overhyped movies with amazing special effects that leaves you disappointed. We must care about the characters and the story first—the rest is just window dressing.

A playwright may write a play that is extremely realistic, but the director and designers may come up with a production concept in which the setting and lighting is not realistic. The acting style of Arthur Miller's *The Crucible*, for example, as well as the costumes and props, may be realistic while the setting is abstract. Since the locale changes from Betty's bedroom to Proctor's house to the courtroom, to outside in the woods, then back to the courtroom, and finally to a jail cell, the play is frequently staged using a unit set—platforms, a raked stage, or suggestive fragmentary scenery. Theatres seldom try to create completely realistic settings for all five locales.

The director and designers normally seek to find a concept that works with the playwright's style, provides unity, and supports the message of the play. For a drama, they will seek to create the proper atmosphere and meet the needs of the action. For a comedy, they will seek to use color, line, and form to accentuate the genre. However, the budget, the stage space, or the timing may demand a more creative and simpler approach to the visual style. A Shakespearean play might be done in modern dress, with projections of modern locales, without changing a word of the dialogue. A seventeenth-century Molière play might be produced in a lavish, period style, with historically authentic costumes and opulent painted drops, or very simply using nonspecific costumes and stock flats.

When I directed Sam Shepard's realistic play *Curse of the Starving Class*, I kept the acting realistic but wanted an expressionistic setting to suggest the old farmhouse kitchen, and so we used a wooden framework with slats for walls. The slats were placed about an inch apart, like a lathe. Keeping the natural wood color contributed to the rustic atmosphere.

The Magic "If"

If you were this character in this situation, what would you do? What is within the capacity of this character? What would he really do? These questions address the magic "if" that Constantin Stanislavsky told actors about in his famous acting school. It is a question invoked to stir the actor's creative imagination. It also works for the writer. What would happen if you put these characters in a creepy basement, in a subway tunnel, or on a cruise ship? You need to consider all the possibilities your character would consider. Suppose Rachel is hopelessly in love with John, a married man who she has worked with for nine years at an office. She has been pining away for him without ever saying a word. Nothing has happened. Nothing is happening. Think of all the things Rachel could do if she takes action:

> She might have a friend intervene for her.
> She might telephone John and disguise her voice.
> She might join his church choir.
> She might befriend his wife or decide to kill her.
> She might get tipsy at a party and make a pass at him.
> She might decide to end her life.
> She might decide to stalk him.
> She might . . .

What setting would be appropriate for each decision? If the character is to be believable, you must ask, Would she really . . . ? Think of clever and resourceful alternatives for your character. Ask yourself: What would I do if I were this character in this situation? Would she really do that? Is it within the capacity of that character? What else could she do that would be more ingenious, dramatic, surprising, or funny?

What would happen if you used an actual place for the setting? Eugene O'Neill's *Long Day's Journey into Night* takes place in the Monte Cristo Summer Home, where O'Neill lived in Connecticut during the summers of his youth. Paul Rudnik's *I Hate Hamlet* is set in the apartment of the actor John Barrymore in a brownstone off Washington Square in New York. Herb Gardner's *I'm Not Rappaport* is set in Central Park. Doug Wright's *Quills* is set in the Charenton Asylum in France, where the Marquis de Sade spent his last days. It is possible even to visit specific places and take pictures. If you can't photograph a locale, you can draw sketches and describe the place for future reference. If you have a clear vision of the locale, it will be easier to write the play. However, realize that a designer may want to provide an interpretation, rather than a literal reconstruction.

Take a camera and explore your neighborhood. Find unique and interesting locales that might serve as inspirations for stage settings: a park bench, a place where homeless people sleep, an abandoned house, inside an old garage, a hospital room, the backyard of a home, a front porch, a cave, a junkyard, a rock quarry, a clearing in the woods, an abandoned store, a garden supply store, the front stoop of a building.

In preparation for choosing a setting, explore books that have pictures and discussions of stage designers such as Jo Mielziner, Boris Aronson, Lee Simonson, Ben Edwards, John Lee Beatty, and Heidi Landesman. In most stage settings, there are three to five acting areas—that is, different sections of the set where the furniture is grouped to provide realistic reasons for characters to gather together. With exterior settings and sets designed as abstract formalism, platforms, steps, and ramps are often used to provide different levels to areas of the stage. The floorplan

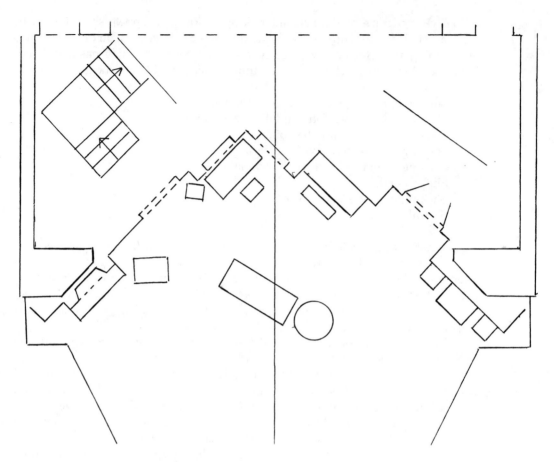

FIGURE 14.1   Floorplan for *Blithe Spirit,* performed at Berry College, Rome, Ga. Directed and designed by Leroy Clark.

of the set for Noel Coward's *Blithe Spirit* in Figure 14.1 shows several different acting areas.

For a production on a proscenium stage, the relationship of each area of the stage to the audience creates an order of importance (see Figure 14.2). The *downstage center* area is the strongest because it is closest to the audience and provides the best visibility to all. *Stage right* is usually considered stronger than *stage left* because of the conditioning of our eyes, since we are programmed to read from left to right. (Remember, these designations are from the actors' right or left as they face the audience. Therefore, stage right is actually on the audience's left as they look at the stage.) *Up left* is the weakest area on the stage. It's most often used by directors for scenes that are judged hard for the audience to take. For example, the scene with Stanley's rape of Blanche in Tennessee Williams's *Streetcar Named Desire*

5 Upstage Right	4 Upstage Center	6 Upstage Left
2 Downstage Right	1 Downstage Center	3 Downstage Left

Audience

FIGURE 14.2   Areas of the Stage and Their Order of Importance

is usually staged up left. Scenes of violence and taboo situations that might shock the audience are staged up left in order to distance them from the audience, soften the unpleasantness, and avoid nervous laughter.

What other pictures, research materials, films, or other sources might be helpful to you as a playwright or to your actors or designers? If you plan to use a nonrealistic setting, your description of a nonrealistic or abstract setting needs to give us a combination of the shapes you imagine on the stage and the feeling you hope the whole arrangement will evoke.

Costumes

When a script is considered for production, all aspects of costumes will be carefully weighed—the number of costumes, whether they are contemporary or period, whether they are simple or elaborate, whether there is a large stock to draw from, whether they can be borrowed or rented. Nudity in a play may make it unacceptable for many theatres. You must take into account what is theatrically effective, stage worthy, and realistic as you are writing. *The Diary of Anne Frank,* by Frances Goodrich and Albert Hackett, has a single setting but takes place over a long period of time. It presents a number of quick-change problems for actors, which require careful planning to make sure the costume changes can be made efficiently. With each production the costume designer, director, and actor must work out a plan for what clothing can be underdressed or overdressed. *Underdressed* means the actor wears one costume over the top of another so that they can remove the top layer quickly. *Overdressed* means the actor adds a second costume over the first. Set designers must be aware of the needs for costume changes, as well, so that they provide access to offstage areas where the actors can be accessible to the wardrobe crew.

The playwright must take into account costume changes during writing. If a character ends one scene in a wedding dress and returns four lines into the next scene, set the following day, in a completely different costume, it will not work. To get into or out of any costume takes time. An elaborate costume such as a wedding dress takes even more time and probably at least two people on the wardrobe crew to assist the actor. The more the playwright knows about the realities of the theatre, the better she can prepare for the technical necessities.

In *The Miracle Worker,* author William Gibson has Annie Sullivan lock Helen Keller in the dining room for twenty minutes, where she tries to teach Helen to eat with a spoon. There is no dialogue. Just action. The costumes must allow free movement and be constructed so that seams will not easily split. In Lerner and Loewe's *My Fair Lady,* Eliza is transformed from a filthy guttersnipe to an elegant lady. Not only is this change manifested in the character's dialogue and behavior, it is also seen in the costumes.

Fran Lautenberger (2002), a costume designer that I worked with for many years at the University of Alaska Anchorage offers the following costume advice for the playwright:

1. *Keep it simple.* Unless your script revolves around a piece of costume, do not try to describe every little thing you would like an actor to wear. It is more helpful if you give an indication of character if that is what you are looking for. EXAMPLE: *Mary enters wearing a black lace, low-cut blouse with sleeves and a short, black leather skirt.* This might be more specific than you need. If these specific items of clothing are not crucial to the plot, you could say *Mary enters wearing a really low-cut blouse and a short skirt* or even *Mary enters in a sexy outfit,* if that is what you want, or *a really tacky outfit,* or *She looks like a hooker.*

2. *Give the designers room for imagination and collaboration.* Don't do their work for them. Think about quick changes before they happen. Realize that humans can only move so fast, so if you need to have a character change into something or someone else, give them time to do it. EXAMPLE: In the play *Corpse,* by Gerald Moon, one actor plays two different characters. At one point in the play, there was a problem for the actor to change from one to the other quickly enough. Thus, we made clever use of another actor as a body double to give the actor time to change. This technique has been used in many different plays and is fun to use. Otherwise, giving the actor even a few seconds between changes really helps in the long run.

3. *As always, don't use a cast of thousands.* More people mean more costumes. However, doublecasting an actor also means more costumes. Remember, every time you have another character, whether or not that character is played by an actor in another part or a separate actor, he or she will need a costume. Think about the cost of each new character. It makes a big difference as to whether anyone will want to do the show.

The costume designer is extremely important in helping to create the characters. The designer can change the shape and size of an actor by using line and color as well as padding, special shoes, and wigs. The costume will also affect the movement of the character. The designer's choices also will reflect the character's socioeconomic status. For example, in *Shakespeare's Journey* I wanted Will to appear rustic and poor in his first act costume. Figure 14.3 shows the conceptions by two different designers for two different productions.

FIGURE 14.3   *Left:* Will, Act I, Shakespeare's Journey, performed at Wichita State University. Costume designed by Betty Monroe. *Right:* Will, Act I, Shakespeare's Journey, performed at Florida International University. Costume designed by Marilyn Skow.

In this same show, ten actors play eighteen roles. The costumes in both productions helped the actors by giving them completely different looks for each character. In the Florida International University production there were two designers. Christina Perdomo played Shakespeare's daughter, Susanna, in a plain blue dress with a white collar, designed by Marilyn Skow (see Figure 14.4). It was in the style of the Puritans. As the whore Donna Holland, designed by Marina Pariji, Christina was dressed in a rust-colored skirt with a low-cut, off-white blouse, a vest that laced up the front, and a long, reddish-brown wig. As Mrs. Cross, she wore a very

FIGURE 14.4   *Left:* Costume sketch for Susanna. *Right:* Costume sketch for Donna. From *Shakespeare's Journey,* performed at Florida International University. Costumes designed by Marilyn Skow and Marina Parigi.

dark Puritan-style dress with a fitted white cap that tied under her chin, designed by Skow, and her hair was pulled back into a bun. Danny Suarez played Gilbert Shakespeare in a fat suit, designed by Parigi, and a shoulder-length brown wig. His brown doublet with a white collar was padded in the front to give him a pot-bellied look. When he switched to playing Cuthbert Burbage, he wore regular unpadded doublets of blue or burnt umber and used his own hair.

The contemporary play *Angels in America: Millennium Approaches* was written by Tony Kushner to have some of the actors play two or three characters. Two of the women also play men's roles. In the production at Wichita State University, with costumes designed by Betty Monroe, the actress Amity Hoffman played Hannah Porter Pitt, Ethel Rosenberg, and Rabbi Isidor Chemelwitz. Karen Hinkle played Joe's wife, Harper, and the Reagan man, Martin Heller. They had to be convincing as men in their looks, movements, and voices. The rabbi wore a beard and moustache, a wig, glasses, and a man's suit and tie and shoes. Martin wore a wig and moustache and a man's suit, tie, and shoes.

Such double-casting may also work for your play, particularly if you need a large number of characters who only appear for one scene. Double-casting is also appealing to producers because it cuts costs. It is appealing to actors because they get to show their versatility in playing more than one role. It is also a fun challenge for the costumer to create totally different looks for the same actor.

Props

There are three kinds of props: set props, props for set decoration, and hand props used by the actors. *Set props* are the larger items and furniture needed for the action; they are usually selected by the designer as part of the overall set. *Set decorations* are the additional props used on the set to help make the visual environment seem authentic. They must be approved by the set designer and are often selected by him. *Hand props* may be called for in the script or added by the director. For example, pumping real water is essential in the final scene in William Gibson's *The Miracle Worker*. Cooking is called for in Gerald Moon's *Corpse*. Ears of corn for shucking are needed in Sam Shepard's *Buried Child*. Working on the characters' hair is an important activity in Robert Harling's *Steel Magnolias*. Actually having an actor do an activity with hand props is often used to bring reality to a scene. A director sometimes adds such activity to help the actor perform with a sense of truth or to spice up a rather talky or static scene. Folding laundry, ironing, washing dishes, sewing, and making a bed are typical examples of such activities with props.

As a playwright, consider what each character would always have with him. Building a scene around an activity may help bring the characters to life. Consider a group of women all working together in sewing a quilt. What about a group of men playing basketball or playing poker? What about a group of women at a gathering to learn about sex toys? What about a family decorating a Christmas tree? A particular prop and the way in which a character uses it can give clear insights into the character's habits, outlook, and emotions. What creative ideas do the following props inspire?

Towel	Feather boa	Whip
Clipboard	Rollerblades	Bicycle
Mannequin	Briefcase	Grocery cart
Horse's skull	Rubber gloves	Mask
M-16 rifle	Bag of apples	Prosthetic leg
Thermos	Chocolates	Severed hand
Boom box	Large painting	Bottle of pills
Sunglasses	Paper shredder	Bowl of ice
Paperback	Newspaper	Pail of water
Cat skeleton	Pillow	Playing cards
Saxophone	Coffee cup	Dead rat
Bottle of wine	Machete	Purse
Urn	Garbage bag	Pair of shoes
Pitchfork	Skin lotion	Shopping bag
Laptop computer	Kite	Walking cane
Ten watches	Airline ticket	Bird cage
Kimono	Camera	

Transformations

Characters in conflict often transform an object in some way by modifying it, destroying it or using it in a manner for which it was not intended. Objects are not always used for the purposes for which they were intended. In Billy Wilder and I. A. L. Diamond's screenplay for *The Apartment*, C. C. Baxter (Jack Lemmon), clowning to amuse a depressed guest, uses his tennis racket to make pasta, demonstrating its applicability both to straining spaghetti and serving meatballs. At the end of the film version of *The Graduate,* directed by Mike Nichols, Benjamin rescues Elaine from an inappropriate marriage, grabs a big cross from a stand in the church, and swings it at the wedding guests to keep them from charging. The cross becomes a sword. When the guests emerge from the building, he uses the cross again to bar the church doors to prevent their pursuit. In both of these movies, the filmmakers not only made the characters' relationships to other characters vivid through the use of an object, but they also jolted the audience by transforming that object so it could perform a new and unanticipated function. In Jason Miller's *That Championship Season,* four former teammates meet for a reunion with their high school basketball coach. As the evening progresses, what these men were and have become is revealed. They are frauds—morally bankrupt men living poisoned lives. The object transformed is their championship trophy into which one of them vomits. Transformation often involves using a high-status object for a low-status purpose or vice versa, further violating the audience's expectation. The cross in *The Graduate* is a high-status object, and part of the scene's power lies in the use of a sacred artifact first as a crude weapon and then a barricade. The same is true of the trophy in *That Championship Season*.

Comics often subvert the usual functions of props. Part of comedian Jonathan Winters's act featured him approaching a table full of objects and using a mixing bowl, for example, as a football helmet or a banana as a telephone. This is hardly a new idea, of course. In *The Second Shepherds' Play* from the Middle Ages, a thief, hoping to elude discovery, wraps the lamb he has stolen in swaddling clothes, puts it into a cradle, and tries to pass it off as a baby. In Rodgers and Hammerstein's *South Pacific*, the character Luther Billis, in drag for the number "Honey Bun," wears two coconut shells on his chest to simulate femininity. When a fellow serviceman lifts up one of the coconuts, it turns out that it serves another purpose—as a hiding place for his cigarettes. So the coconuts are transformed into a bra, and the bra is further transformed into a stash for cigarettes.

In murder mysteries, we often see objects transformed into murder weapons—the letter opener, a plant pot, the heavy candle holder, the paperweight, the poker from the fireplace. Someone picks a lock with a paper clip or a hair pin. In prison dramas we see a razor blade added to a toothbrush to create a weapon or other common objects changed into shanks. A candle or a cigarette can become a torture device.

Transformation is particularly striking in the theater. But then, the theater is about transformation. This points to one of the key differences between stage and film: No matter how realistic the setting and staging of a play, this element of transformation applies. When you go to the theatre, you have to agree to translate in your imagination the elements on the stage into what they are intended to represent. In film, although technical gimmickry is employed, the idea is to persuade you that you are seeing something that is real, even if what is represented is palpably preposterous.

Another interesting transformation is to have one character transform on stage into another. The son in Sam Shepard's *Curse of the Starving Class* transforms himself into his father by putting on his father's clothes. In *The Mystery of Irma Vep*, by Charles Ludlum, a character turns into a werewolf on stage. In the mystery *Corpse,* by Gerald Moon, the play begins with an old woman talking to the landlady. Then the old woman enters the apartment, takes off her wig and dress, and turns back into a man.

There is no more radical way you can transform something than to destroy it. Imagine that you have only one copy of your play and you lose it on the street. A homeless person finds it and uses it to make a fire to keep warm. In Henrik Ibsen's *Hedda Gabler,* the character of Hedda burns the manuscript of the man who idolized her. In Beth Henley's *Crimes of the Heart,* Meg opens her sister's box of candy and sticks her finger in each one. The unicorn in Williams's *The Glass Menagerie* is changed into an ordinary glass horse when its horn is broken off. Transformations such as these provide major dramatic moments.

Sound Effects

Music and sound effects are often important elements in plays. For a play such as Peter Shaffer's *Amadeus*, which explores the lives and music of composers Wolfgang Amadeus Mozart and Antonio Salieri, music is a central element. However, even in the average straight play, music is used to provide transitions from scene to scene, set the mood, intensify emotion, transmit the impact of offstage events, heighten the reality of a scene, and suggest the outside world and environment. To establish the nervous tempo and the spirit of life in the French Quarter for *Streetcar*, many offstage sounds are used, such as train whistles, street cries, and cat screeches. Tennessee Williams wrote into the script that every time Blanche thinks of her husband's suicide, there is the polka tune "Varsouviana," which is only heard by Blanche.

When Elia Kazan began directing the Broadway production of *J. B.*, by Archibald MacLeish, there were thirteen sound cues written by the playwright into the script. These included the sound of a distant voice, the crash of a drum, and a rushing sound in the air. Kazan added music where the human drama was at its most intense. He wanted the music to intensify the human feelings. In addition, he added many more sound effects, bringing the number to thirty-nine. He added circus calliope music, laughter, doorbells, jazz music, a siren, car door slams, and a trumpet sound.

Although much of the sound is added to a show in production, the playwright should be aware of how such effects can enrich a play. If a particular piece of music is desired to serve as a recurring motif, such as the "Varsouviana" in Williams's *Streetcar* or Rachmaninoff in Axelrod's *The Seven-Year Itch*, it should be noted in the stage directions. Sound effects that suggest the outside world should also be included. Offstage laughter, a dog barking, breaking glass, cars arriving or leaving, explosions, and cricket sounds all can help establish mood and time of day. They can also bring a reality to what is happening on stage. Imagine a scene that begins with the sound of a drunken young man, banging a garbage can lid on wrought-iron fence. A dog barks. The man knocks on a door and then pounds on it. The barking becomes louder, more intense. The protagonist is awakened, goes to the door, opens it, sees the man, and tries to close it. The man forces his way in. They shout at each other; the dog continues to bark. The tension mounts.

Design and Production Meetings

Once a script has been finished and scheduled for production, a design meeting is held with the director and designers. By this point, the production team has analyzed the play and done the necessary research on the period, style, set, and costumes. They discuss all the elements of the production and how to approach them. The purpose of the meeting is for all the team members to bring their ideas to the table for discussion and eventual agreement on the concept. Usually, the director leads the way, but sometimes the set designer is the one who finds the right approach. Frequently at this meeting, the focus is on images, and participants may bring pictures or a collage to the table for discussion.

When Elia Kazan directed *After the Fall*, by Arthur Miller, he told designer Jo Mielziner that he saw the play as the story of a man who discovers he has survived by the deaths of other people, especially those he loved. Kazan noted his thoughts on the setting: "It should seem primordial, as old as murder itself. . . . It should be stained with old hatreds, old bloodsheds. . . . It should be cavernous, deep and dark. It should be made up of the corners of his memory into which his mind has never penetrated before, because it never dared to." As the discussion continued, there was a steady progression toward the elimination of physical detail. While Kazan and the team considered a sort of collage, this was eventually discarded in favor of abstract platforms and simple boxes.

When Kazan was hired to direct Arthur Miller's *Death of a Salesman*, the script contained over forty scenes with numerous locales. There were instantaneous time changes, from the present to the past and back again. Actors playing a contemporary scene suddenly went back fifteen years in the same setting. Miller had described the house as once surrounded by open country and trees but now hemmed in by apartments. Mielziner's solution was to have a backdrop showing the house encircled by ugly brick tenement buildings for contemporary scenes and to project leaves on the backdrop and parts of the house for scenes in the past. Kazan agreed with Mielziner that the most important visual symbol in the play was the house. All the other scenes—the hotel room in Boston, the business office, the lawyer's consultation room, the bar, the cemetery—were, therefore, played on the forestage. Kazan's vision for *J. B.*, by Archibald MacLeish, was as follows: "The set is not a circus. It looks like a circus. It is not an illustration of anything. It is the plastic rendition of essences."

Once the concept for the show has been agreed on, the designers go off and work, putting their ideas on paper. Sketches and models are made and brought to later production meetings, until all problems have been solved and all aspects have been agreed upon. Everything needed for the play—sets, costumes, props, lighting, and sound—is decided at these meetings. Sometimes, this also involves rewrites by the author. As Kazan and Mielziner developed the plans for the set for *Death of a Salesman*, Arthur Miller continued rewriting to make the script work with each new change.

EXERCISE 19 (Optional) _____

Beginning Level   Choose one of the following:

A. Select a real locale that you can use for the setting of a scene, and observe its distinct qualities. Describe it. What is the atmosphere? What are the textures? The sources of light? The furniture? The colors? Where are the entrances and exits? What levels are there? Use this setting and write a scene in which a character faces a major life decision.

B. Describe a real environment, using as many details as possible to evoke the atmosphere. Write a conflict scene between two or three characters, in which their problem centers on the environment and their present condition, fate, fears, and so on. Make one of the characters pregnant or injured to increase the stakes.

Intermediate Level   Choose one of the following:

C. Create a dreamscape—a locale that exists in a dream. What objects are visible? Perhaps it is in an open field, a field of old appliances, or a field with lots of easels, paintings, and models. Describe the locale, which doesn't need to be realistic, and then write a dream scene. In dreams, characters, objects, and actions are free from the restrictions of reality. Dreams do not obey linear thought or structure. Do not worry about interpreting the dream. Give us the actions, sounds, and images.

D. Look at books with color photos or reproductions of great paintings. Find a picture with a striking environment, and write a conflict scene between two or three characters in which this setting is important. Include at least one transformation. Use the painting as your central image or metaphor for the scene. What effects do you want the scene to have on the audience? What emphasis is the scene to have? What is special about this setting? Turn in a copy of the picture with the scene.

Advanced Level   Choose one of the following:

E. Write a scene in which there is a physical obstacle within the locale. This obstacle must affect the characters in the scene, such as a disabled woman in a wheelchair in her home seeking to escape a drug addict trying to rob her, a character that has been kidnapped and tied up by another, or two people struggling to move a large object. Maybe the characters are trying to open a box, defuse a bomb, unblock a cave-in. The setting must be vitally important to the characters.

F. Write two contrasting mood scenes about two pages each. Both scenes should be in the same locale, but they may use the same or different characters. The time of day should be different, as should the tone, the atmosphere, and the lighting. For example, perhaps the scene is on a street in the daylight and the other is on that same street deserted and dark at 2 o'clock in the morning. What sound effects could be helpful? Props? Costumes? Music?

Summary

The playwright must have a clear understanding of the period in which the play is set. He needs to know about the people, manners, country, time, clothing, and whatever else is important in understanding the time, place, and events. The playwright needs a clear vision of the world in which the play takes place.

The physical form or setting of a play is generally determined by its genre and theatrical form—whether the play is a musical or a straight play, a comedy or a drama. The size of the piece may dictate the venue in which it is produced. The space may dictate what is practical to produce.

Playwrights need to be aware of what is practical and have a realistic grasp of what is stage worthy. Those with only a literary background or a knowledge of films will have no understanding of theatre and how it works. As such, they may find their expectations impractical. The size of a show—the number of characters, the number of sets and set changes, the kinds of costumes and the number of costume changes—may cause a play to be tossed aside as unproducible.

Visual design is concerned with the total visual effect of a dramatic production. It involves the scenic background—the colors and shapes of framed pieces of scenery, the selection and style of the furniture and set dressings, the planning of the quality and intensity of the lighting, and the easy movement of the actors. It also involves the careful consideration of the actor's costumes to contrast with the background; to represent the personality, age, period, sex, and status of the character; and to fit with the overall style of the production.

Characters in conflict often transform an object by modifying it, destroying it or using it in a manner for which it was not intended. *Transformation* often involves using a high-status object for a low-status purpose or vice versa, further violating the audience's expectation. The usual function of a prop is often subverted or changed for some comic purpose. Another interesting transformation is to have one character transform on stage into another or change gender through a change in costume, makeup, and wigs. This use of disguise is a major device in numerous plays, especially comedies.

CHAPTER
15 Genre and Style

This chapter explores how plays are classified as dramas or comedies or tragedies. These are *genres*. We will also explore *style*, which refers to the treatment or approach to the play by the author, including her individual style and the theatrical conventions she selects to use. Most styles fall within three areas: presentational or classical, representational or realistic, and one of the revolts against realism. We will also look at the value and risks of writing nude scenes as well as the latest in-your-face style of theatre.

Genre

Genre refers to a play's classification: comedy, tragedy, or drama. Each of these can be further divided into many subcategories. A *comedy* may be a comedy of manners, satire, farce, situation comedy, burlesque or parody, or fantasy or romance. A *tragedy* is a serious work of some significance, in which the protagonist seeks to overcome formidable obstacles and is overcome, in the end, despite having taken the morally right path. A tragedy may be historical, mythological, romantic, horrific, or melodramatic. A *drama* is a serious play, which may have a sad or happy ending.

Tragedy and comedy began with the Greeks. Drama began in the eighteenth century and takes its name from the *drame* in France. These were serious plays dealing with everyday people, written in prose, and focusing on domestic and romantic matters. This was the coming together of domestic tragedy and sentimental comedy. In the late 1880s, Emile Zola, Henrik Ibsen, August Strindberg, Leo Tolstoy, and others created modern realistic drama, centered on the philosophy of *determinism*—that all things were determined by heredity and environment. These plays were *naturalistic*, taking realism to the extreme. Settings were highly detailed and included everything that would be in that locale, whether it was needed or used in the play.

For the one hundred years since then, drama has been primarily grounded in *realism*, with sets that are realistic, less extreme than naturalism, and more selective, usually including only those things actually needed in the play. In the 1940s, Tennessee Williams and Arthur Miller combined realism with *expressionism* in plays such as *The Glass Menagerie* and *Death of a Salesman*. In Europe after World War II, realism was combined with the philosophy of *existentialism* in some of the plays by Jean-Paul Sartre, Albert Camus, and Jean Giradoux. From the 1950s on, realistic drama continued in the works of nearly all the major writers. In the 1990s, Tony Kushner mixed realism with fantasy in *Angels in America*. Dramas may be problem plays, "whodunits" or mysteries, soap operas, tragicomedies, or melodramas. They may even include elements of fantasy.

Melodrama came into vogue in the midnineteenth century. These plays centered on an innocent victim whose life was endangered by a villain. They were plot driven and characterization was limited. The plays included many realistic elements, however, such as real animals and special effects to create fires, buildings collapsing, and waterfalls. The complexity of the productions required a director who could coordinate all the various elements into a unified whole. When these plays are produced today, the approach is generally to stage them as campy, comic plays, but in their day, they were presented very seriously.

Today, melodrama is often associated with crime dramas, such as Sidney Kingsley's *Detective Story*, mysteries such as Mary Roberts Rinehart's *The Bat*, and thrillers such as Fredrick Knott's *Wait Until Dark*. These are serious plays with happy endings, in which the focus is on overt conflict, suspense, and physical action. Plays with extreme behaviors, such as savage murders, suicides, and lunacy, are often called melodramatic. *Melodrama* is now often defined as characters overreacting to what's going on. When writers look at something they've written and realize it is melodrama, they often cut back on the big scene and try to lessen the over-the-top quality. However, melodrama isn't really about a character overreacting; it's caused by the writer not providing appropriate motivation for the character's behavior. The problem isn't the reaction but the lack of motivation.

If a man (Character A) comes home to his apartment and finds his wife, girlfriend, partner, or friend (Character B) screaming, throwing things, and slashing the furniture with a knife, what are we to think? We might think, Hey, this is way over the top. This is too much. However, what if we had seen Character B in an earlier scene that foreshadowed this reaction? What if we had seen Character B in an earlier scene upset because of her father's bad driving? What if this person had had a sibling killed in a highway accident and was trying to connect with her father to make him stop driving? What if Character A had condescendingly undermined Character B's concern? Now in this final scene, the father is dead and Character B is distraught.

A *comedy of manners* draws its main characters from the upper strata of society and looks at how they behave in their social world and the consequences that befall them when they lack common sense. Whenever a character is at odds with the expected norm—overblown, affected, pretentious, hypocritical, pedantic, self-deceived, or vain—he or she is set up for ridicule. Such plays usually focus on love plots and witty dialogue. Language and style are very important.

Satire is comedy of the mind, for it makes us laugh through the mind. Satire makes us look at our current civilization and its public policies, figures, and events. It awakens thoughtful laughter. When people—because of their greed or lust or stupidity—act in ways that violate the unwritten laws of society and become the objects of public inquiry or scandal, they are candidates for satire. Satire often focuses on a specific situation, such as the Monica Lewinsky affair, the Enron scandal, or Watergate. A play by Mindy Kaling and Brenda Withers in the fall of 2003 in New York called *Ben and Matt* satirized Affleck and Damon. Plays by Aristophanes, such as *The Birds* and *The Clouds*, satirized current events and figures in ancient Greece. In the 1960s, Barbara Garson's *Macbird* poked fun at President Lyndon B. Johnson and Lady Bird. In the 1970s, there was Larry Gelbart's *Mastergate*, which satirized the Watergate scandal.

At the Coconut Grove in Miami each year, there is a parade called the King Mango Strut. Although it doesn't present plays, it shows groups of people in costumes and each group satirizes a local, state, national, or international event from the past year. In a recent parade, the local mayor, who supposedly threw a teapot at his wife, was one of the targets. Another was the terrorist Osama Bin Laden. A large group of people dressed in Middle Eastern garb and wore signs satirizing Bin Laden and members of the Taliban. The Capital Steps is another group, which stages scripted political satires in Washington, D.C.

The laughter of comedy is impersonal. We understand and are able to relate to a character or situation intellectually, but if our emotions are truly aroused, the humor is lost. We see a man run into a pole. It is funny as long as the man reacts to it and responds in a way that shows the event as harmless. If we believe he is truly injured and have concerns for his well-being, the fun will be gone.

Low comedy, or *farce*, depends on physical action, ludicrous situations, unexpected happenings, and especially physical humor. Two characters sneaking on stage and backing into one another is a physical joke. Two characters backing up and missing each other is another. Three characters who are sneaking around and all run into each other at the same moment and scream is another. Laughter is open to perversion. Imagine the exterior of a house on stage. A character sneaks into the yard and steps in dog poop. He opens a window in the house and climbs in. We hear the growls and barks of a large dog. Neil Simon's *Rumors* and Michael Frayn's *Noises Off* are popular recent farces.

Gene Perret (1990), in *Comedy Writing Step by Step*, defines a sense of humor as having the ability to see life as it is, to recognize life as it is, and to accept it as it is. If you are losing your hair, baldness may not be a funny topic to you. Some people think that if they part their hair on the side and comb it over the bald spot, no one will notice. There's a new spray you can use to paint the bald spot. Some people do not see reality, or recognize the truth, or accept the fact that they are growing bald. Once you can look at it from the perspective of Perret's three abilities, it can be funny.

Human attitudes, gestures, and movements are laughable when the body reminds us of a mere machine. Rigidity of character—obstinacy, absentmindedness, an obsession, or a particular vice—is funny. A character with a rigid virtue, as in Molière's *The Misanthrope*, shows us this kind of humor. Comic characters are comic in proportion to their ignorance of themselves. Organ, in Molière's *Tartuffe*, is blind to the real nature of the religious hypocrite, Tartuffe. He wants to do something good for Tartuffe, and he is completely out of touch with reality. Organ responds like a jack-in-the-box in one scene. Dorine tells Organ of his wife's illness, and he interrupts her time after time with questions about Tartuffe. No matter what she says about his wife, he asks "And Tartuffe?"

Vices have the same relation to character that rigidity has to intellect. The character is pulled by the vice as though he were a puppet, an automaton. In George Axelrod's *The Seven-Year Itch,* the leading character is trying to quit smoking. After he throws his cigarettes on top of a tall bookcase, he tries to find something to stand on so he can retrieve them. The idea of lying is set up with the turning on of a blender in Jonathan Tollin's *The Last Sunday in June.* Every time someone tells a lie, someone else turns the blender on.

A ceremony or ritual has potential for comedy when things goes wrong. When the bride falls backward into the pool, the seat of the groom's pants is torn out by a dog, or the mother-in-law falls on top of the cake, a wedding becomes funny. Although a drama, William Gibson's *The Miracle Worker* offers a lesson in ritual that is both fierce and funny. The ritual of the family dinner is interrupted by Anne when she stops Helen from grabbing food from her plate, an unacceptable custom that has been tolerated by the family. Helen pitches a fit. The father is angry. Anne makes the family leave the dining room, locks the doors, and for the next twenty minutes, engages in a physical action scene, in which she teaches Helen how to eat with a spoon and fold her napkin.

Humans are comic. We find it funny when an animal exhibits a human attitude or expression. A. R. Gurney's play *Silvia,* about a dog, is funny in the ways in which Silvia takes on human characteristics. Since Silvia is played by a woman, it is also funny when she takes on dog characteristics.

Characters are funny when they exhibit mechanical qualities. When a character continues to perform in the same way when something else is called for, it is funny. When a character goes to a door expecting it to open but then finds it locked, her body continues the momentum and she runs into the door. An absent-minded person is always thinking of what she has just done, never what she is doing. Runners after the ideal who stumble over the reality are funny.

The *dancing Jack*—a character who believes himself to be acting freely but is actually a puppet—also makes us laugh. When this character thinks he is speaking and acting on his own, he retains all the essentials of life, but from another perspective, he appears as a toy in the hands of another who is playing him. Knowing how he will react, he is set up in such a way as to act just as expected. In Molière's *Scapin,* the fathers of Leander and Octavio are tricked by the servant, Scapin, to assure the happiness of the sons. In *Fit to Be Tied,* by Nicky Silver, Boyd acts as a puppet controlled by Arloc. Arloc offers a bribe of five hundred dollars if Boyd will let Arloc tie him up for five minutes. Boyd agrees and Arloc ties him to a bondage chair and then won't let him go. Two or more people who move in unison, dance or gesture together, or strike the same attitude are comic because they are like marionettes.

The periodic repetition of a word or a bit, the systematic inversion of the parts, and the geometrical development of farcical misunderstanding can create great fun. However, each must be suitably motivated to preserve an outward aspect of probability.

The *snowball effect* is a technique—like a snowball rolling downhill, growing bigger and bigger—that puts something into effect which then grows by arithmetic progression. It might be a letter that is written and sent and then must be recovered. Recovering it creates a series of other problems, results in numerous lies, and eventually causes the very thing that recovering the letter was supposed to prevent. *The Italian Straw Hat,* by Eugene Labiche and Marc-Michael, and *The Servant of Two Masters,* by Carlo Goldoni, are two entire plays based on this snowball concept. Another approach is for the letter to be found and misinterpreted, as happens in Shakespeare's *Twelfth Night,* when Maria plants a letter for the servant Malvolio, who mistakes it for a love letter from the lady of the house. This then sets off a chain of events. Such comic techniques appeal to the intellect, not the emotions. Larry Shue sets up *The Foreigner* with the lie that Charlie Baker is a foreigner who doesn't speak English. This results in a series of delightfully funny incidents.

As noted earlier, comic characters are generally comic in proportion to their ignorance of themselves. The comic person is not aware of what makes him or her funny. Once a character realizes she has a defect that is ridiculous, she attempts to modify it or appear to have changed. What life and society demand is that we constantly pay attention and adapt. We must have elasticity of mind and body to enable us to adapt. If these are lacking in a character, we have rigidity of character, and that creates laughter.

When the body, facial expressions, or character as a whole is imprinted, contracted, or made mechanical, the effect is comic. The attitudes, gestures, and movements of the human body are laughable in proportion to the extent that the body reminds us of a machine. When one person is imitating the gestures of another, he or she is imitating the mechanical uniformity of those gestures—the automaton. Fashion that exceeds the norm is comic. The fop in Restoration-era comedies is always dressed too elaborately. A man or woman in disguise is comic. The worse the disguise, the funnier it is. A man with a mustache and hairy legs in a dress is funnier than a man without a moustache and without hairy legs because of the contrast. A woman dressed as a man is more outrageous when the shoes are too big, the pants are held up by suspenders that are too big, and the eyebrows and the moustache are painted on.

A good comic scene needs an idea, a few complications, and an ending. Try to think of a *premise:* a statement of what the scene is about. For example, a person who refuses to adjust to change will suffer the consequences, and a person who responds on a mechanical or habitual level will get what she deserves. Once your premise is set, put it into motion. If you have promoted a goal to be accomplished, introduce some complications. John is in a hotel and covered with mud; his clothes are not wearable. He must get dressed for a meeting with his boss. He opens what he thinks is his suitcase, but it contains only women's clothes. He tries to find what will fit. A family is at the airport saying good-bye to their daughter, who's going off to college. The situation progresses from sadness at her leaving, to impatience that the flight is delayed, to an argument over what is the best college, to an argument over money, to name-calling, to a fist fight, and finally back to the loving good-bye.

Base your jokes on characters and situations. The ending should progress naturally out of the scene and the characters, tie the scene into a neat package, and end with a big laugh.

Style

Style refers to the treatment or approach to the play by the author, including his individual style and the conventions he selects to use. There are three types of style: representational or illusionistic; presentational or classical; and one of the revolts against illusionistic plays, such as expressionism, surrealism, theatricalism, stylization, epic theatre, or absurdism. Representational styles include naturalism and realism.

Naturalism, the extreme form of realism, developed in the late 1880s, uses the philosophy of *determinism,* or the idea that man is determined by heredity and environment. The structure follows a slice-of-life approach. Settings are extremely detailed. Examples of naturalistic plays are Leo Tolstoy's *The Power of Darkness,* Henrik Ibsen's *Ghosts,* August Strindberg's *Miss Julie,* and Gerhart Hauptmann's *The Weavers.*

Realism is an approach that incorporates selective realism within the well-made play. Artistic choices are employed to give the play a well-developed struc-

This general store set is in the naturalistic style, with dozens of props selected for the overall visual effect. Orpheus Descending, *performed at Wichita State University. Directed by Leroy Clark, Set and Lighting Design by J. David Blatt, Costume Design by Betty Monroe.*

Beth Henley's realistic comedy Crimes of the Heart, *performed at University of Alaska Anchorage. Directed by Leroy Clark, Set and Lighting Design by Frank Bebey, Costume Design by Fran Lautenberger.*

ture and the appearance of reality, but only those elements needed for the play are actually used. In both of these approaches, the actors and audience pretend that what is happening on the stage is real. The audience is viewing the play through an imaginary fourth wall, so to speak. Most plays today fall into the category of realism. Examples of realistic plays include Kenneth Lonergan's *This Is Our Youth*, Beth Henley's *Crimes of the Heart*, Brian Friel's *Dancing at Lughnasa*, William Mastrosimone's *Extremities*, and Lanford Wilson's *Burn This*.

Presentational styles acknowledge that this is the world of the theatre. The characters speak directly to the audience in asides or soliloquies. There may be a chorus or other theatrical conventions employed. These styles include all classical plays up to the end of the nineteenth century: Greek tragedy and comedy, Roman tragedy and comedy; plays of the Middle Ages, Elizabethan and Jacobean and Caroline plays, French neoclassic, Restoration and eighteenth century, and Romantic plays. Each period had its own theatre conventions, style of theatre, and kinds of

Shakespeare's Twelfth Night, *performed at Wichita State University, was set on the planet Illyria in a place where the sea had receded, leaving a pink coral landscape. This science fiction approach allowed for many strange costumes, as well. Directed by Leroy Clark, Set and Lighting Design by J. David Blatt, Costume Design by Betty Monroe.*

scenery and costumes. Today, we may try to recreate those conventions and approaches to staging, or we may produce the play in a very modern way.

Realism emerged in the late nineteenth century. Once it had become the established style, there were revolts against it, continuing into the second half of the twentieth century. The new forms included expressionism, surrealism, theatricalism, stylization, epic theatre, absurdism, and abstract formalism.

Expressionism as a style presents a subjective view of the world, as seen through the eyes of the central character. These plays are episodic in structure and include themes dealing with man's place in the world and the evil effects of industrial technology on humanity. Only the central characters are developed; the others are types, frequently one dimensional, and often identified by just their roles in the story, such as bank teller, wife, judge, or bicycle rider. Masks are often used. Sets and costumes are distorted and exaggerated, showing the world as seen through the subjective eyes of the main character. Expressionist settings and costumes are sometimes used even for realistic plays. Examples of expressionistic plays include Eugene O'Neill's *The Hairy Ape*, August Strindberg's *Ghost Sonata*, Georg Kaiser's *From Morn to Midnight*, and Elmer Rice's *The Adding Machine*.

Surrealism was both a literary and art movement influenced by Sigmund Freud and dedicated to the direct expression of the unconscious as revealed in dreams, free of the conscious control of reason and convention. The movement, founded in 1924 in Paris by André Breton, was primarily confined to France. Surrealist writers were interested in the associations and implications of words, rather than their literal meanings; dreamlike perceptions of space and dream-inspired symbols dominate their work. Among the leading surrealist writers was Jean Cocteau. Surrealistic plays include Cocteau's *Orphée*, Guillaume Appollinaire's *The Breasts of Tiresias*, and Fernando Arrabal's *Picnic on the Battlefield*.

Theatricalism is a style that calls attention to the theatre itself using a play within a play, a direct address of the audience, the appearance of a stage manager

Curse of the Starving Class, performed at University of Alaska Anchorage. Although this play by Sam Shepard is realistic, the setting was approached in an expressionistic way and the farmhouse interior was created with a skeletal framework and slats on the walls. Directed by Leroy Clark, Set and Lighting Design by Frank Bebey, Costume Design by Lois Aden.

For the outer-space musical Starmites, *performed at Wichita State University, the setting used an abstract metal structure and cartoon-like costumes. Directed by Leroy Clark, Set and Lighting Design by J. David Blatt, Costume Design by Betty Monroe.*

or other crew member, or direct references to theatrical devices. Examples of plays in this style include *Our Town* and *The Skin of Our Teeth* by Thornton Wilder, Christopher Durang's *An Actor's Nightmare,* and Maxwell Anderson's *Joan of Lorraine.*

Formalism is a return to the architectural stage, similar to the classic forms of the Greek, Roman, and Elizabethan theatres. This style creates a new abstract unit setting, using platforms, steps, ramps, columns, and other devices to mold the space. Like the fixed stage of the classical theatre, this formal abstract setting doesn't change during a production. It might even be used for all the plays presented in a given season. The designs of Adolphe Appia, Gordon Craig, and Jacques Copeau, as well as those of some American designers such as Robert Edmond Jones and Lee Simonson, brought this new style to the theatre.

Stylization involves imposing a style on a work that calls attention to itself. For example, the musical *City of Angels,* by Larry Gelbart, Cy Coleman, and David Zippel, on Broadway had scenes in which everything was in shades of black and white and gray, as though it were a black-and-white movie: the set, the props, the costumes, even the actors' skin. Similarly, designer Cecil Beaton used all black-and-white costumes for the horserace scene in Lerner and Loewe's *My Fair Lady.*

Erwin Piscator was the first director to explore a militant approach to the theatre and create a proletarian drama called *epic theatre;* however, the term is now primarily associated with Bertolt Brecht. Brecht arrived at his characteristic style with the play *Man Is Man* in 1926. Brecht called his approach "epic" because of its broad sweep and mixture of narrative and dramatic techniques. He wanted the audience to watch critically, not passively. Consequently, he developed the concept of *alienation*, making the audience constantly aware that they are in a theatre and participating in a work relevant to them. Epic theatre was developed so that spectators did not watch the show as if it were a real event; rather, they were distanced and made aware intellectually of relating what they saw on stage to the outside world.

Brecht's plays and the techniques of epic theatre became synonymous. This type of play was episodic, and each scene was distinct in itself. Frequently, a scene could be cut and it wouldn't affect the rest of the play. The scenes were connected not just by the continuing events surrounding the protagonist but also by the theme. These plays incorporated characters speaking in the third person along with theatrical settings and costumes. No attempt was made to hide lighting instruments or devices of the stage, and various nonrealistic devices were used, such as slides, placards, film clips, masks, and songs.

Theatre of the absurd became popular particularly in Paris in the 1950s, after the existential angst caused by World War II. *Absurd* means "out of harmony with

The Good Person of Setzuan, *performed at Viterbo University. Directed by David Gardiner, Set Design by J. David Blatt, Lighting Design by Greta Haug, Costume Design by Jeff Stolz.*

reason or propriety, incongruous, unreasonable, illogical." Martin Esslin (1986) in his book *The Theatre of the Absurd,* provides the major comprehensive examination of this kind of theatre. Eugene Ionesco, one of the most notable absurdists, showed that life was devoid of all meaning. In his plays characters are cut off from religious, metaphysical, or transcendental roots. As a result, man's actions become senseless. This absurdity of the human condition is the theme of the plays by Samuel Beckett, Arthur Adamov, and Jean Genet, as well. Absurdist theatre also destroyed the conventions of the well-made play, action, and development of character. In an absurdist play, characterization is left on a surface level. There is no deep character because no meaningful decisions or choices are made. Characters don't change and are sometimes interchangeable. Dialogue is meaningless. The world presented in this type of play is meaningless and absurd. There is no meaningful plot, structure, action, or dialogue.

The audience makes decisions based on their expectations of the author's intentions as to the type of play. It is the author's intent, as perceived by the audience, that determines the genre and style. Today, the theatre is eclectic. It may use any of the conventions of the past, mix elements in new ways, and combine the traditional with the new. Some genres succeed in the marketplace more than others. Today's public seems to prefer musicals to other forms of drama. Comedies are also more popular than dramas, although a really strong and highly acclaimed drama can be a strong draw. Plays tied to realism are more prevalent than any other form. Surrealistic fantasies and experimental forms draw the least appreciation, but nonlinear structure combined with realistic characters and dialogue is growing in popularity.

Style and genre define both the writer's and the actor's approaches to the play. In general, the beginning writer is most knowledgeable and comfortable with realism. Some writers, such as Eugene O'Neill, experimented and tried many different genres and styles. *Beyond the Horizon* was naturalistic. *The Hairy Ape, The Great God Brown,* and *The Emperor Jones* were expressionistic. *Ah, Wilderness!* and *A Long Day's Journey into Night* were realistic. *Mourning Becomes Electra* and *Desire under the Elms* were adaptations of classical works. *Strange Interlude* borrowed from the novel and included long internal monologues. O'Neill experimented with a different approach for nearly every play.

Nudity

> I think on-stage nudity is disgusting, shameful and damaging to all things American. But if I were 22 with a great body, it would be artistic, tasteful, patriotic and a progressive religious experience.

I found this quote by actress Shelley Winters on the Internet. It points up the dual perspectives common to audiences in the United States.

What is the value of onstage nudity? Is it shock or art? Nudity can be a natural part of a play and essential to the story and the character, or it can be gratuitous, added primarily to sell tickets. Nudity is more powerful on stage than in film. In the presence of a live person, you are sharing the same environment and breathing the same air; all things are unpredictable, and more is unknown. Nudity in general doesn't always have a sexual context. It's normal life. People get naked to bathe, to have medical examinations, and to change clothes, as well as to make love.

In the theatre, as in many arts, there is a premium on "pushing the envelope," and using nudity is one of the ways of doing that. For Tracy Letts, author of *Killer Joe* and *Bug*, nudity is a way to strip away the skin of respectability as a way of getting to what is really important. Letts uses three nudes scenes in *Killer Joe* and two in *Bug*. They help him tell his stories in an efficient way, without having to use a lot of words to substitute. Sharla is wearing only a T-shirt when she opens the door to admit Chris in the beginning of *Killer Joe*. We know immediately something about her character without having a lot of exposition. This also sets the tone for the play, letting the audience know that they're in for a graphic ride that is loud, raucous, and in your face. There is a tender, vulnerable, and powerful scene with Dottie appearing nude. Killer Joe Cooper also appears nude later on in the play. That immediately establishes his relationship with Dottie. Letts began his career as an actor. He appeared nude himself in the 1992 Buffalo Theatre Ensemble production of D. H. Lawrence's *Lady Chatterley's Lover*, adapted by Nick Lane.

Nudity can be a device for character revelation, but it is often added to a production primarily for the box office. A recent New York presentation of Shakespeare's *Macbeth* had Banquo baring everything but his throat, which was encircled by a bloody Elizabethan ruff, while the ambitious Lady Macbeth dropped to the floor during her sleepwalking scene and let everything hang out of her nightgown. Nicole Kidman's fleeting nude scene in *The Blue Room*, by David Hare and Kathleen Turner's nude scene in *The Graduate*, adapted for the stage by Terry Johnson, were too brief and overhyped to be more than a distraction. A major selling point in the musical *The Full Monty*, by Terrence McNally, was the promise of on-stage nudity, but there is only a fleeting glimpse, and that view is quickly obscured by a strong backlight. Other contemporary plays using nudity include: David Henry Hwang's *M. Butterfly*, Tony Kushner's *Angels in America*, Joshua Sobol's *Ghetto*, Terry Johnson's *Hysteria*, Rick Cleveland's *Danny Bouncing*, Eric Bogosian's *Griller*, Michael Sutton and Cynthia Mandelberg's *Looking Glass*, Mary Zimmerman's *Metamorphoses*, Anthony Burgess's *A Clockwork Orange*, Tracy Letts's *Bug*, Margaret Edson's *Wit*, Sam Shepard's *Curse of the Starving Class*, Doug Wright's *Quills*, and David Grimm's *Kit Marlowe*. In some cases, it's essential to the story, and in others, it is used to titillate. "If you want to put bums on seats, then put bums on the stage," wrote David Benedict in the *London Observer* (2002).

Benedict went on to note that the peculiar business of stage nudity is different for women and men. The playing field is not level for both genders. Stage censorship was abolished in England in 1968 and about the same time in the United States. "Suddenly the gloves, and everything else, were off," noted Benedict, in productions of *Hair*, by James Rado and Gerome Ragni, and Kenneth Tynan's *Oh, Calcutta!* Since then, actresses have been harassed, hoodwinked, and blackmailed into baring it all for wily directors. Women have been asked to strip for action far more often than men have. Nicole Kidman's nudity in *The Blue Room* was a *cause célèbre*, but Iain Glen's cartwheeling in the nude every night in the same play went unnoticed.

However, gay theatre is changing that. Recently, numerous American plays have presented buff and toned men. This "boys-keep-swinging" kind of play reached its highest or lowest form to date (depending upon your perspective) with shows such as *Naked Boys Singing* with book, music, and lyrics by Stephen Bates, Marie Cain, Percy Hart, Shelly Markham, Jim Morgan, David Pevsner, Rayme Sciaroni, Mark Savage, Ben Schaechter, Robert Schrock, Trance Thompson, Mark Winkler, and Bruce Vilanch. *Naked Boys Singing* is a musical review done with the entire cast nude. However, highly respected dramas including Terrence McNally's *Love, Valour and Compassion*, Richard Greenberg's *Take Me Out*, and Edward Albee's *The Play about the Baby* contained significant scenes with nudity.

In addition to the exploitation of actors, the dramatic dividends of nudity may not be worth it, in some cases. Nude scenes make some actors and audience members uncomfortable. Nudity for some actors is no big deal, but there are many actors who will not appear naked on stage, no matter what the play or what the role. For the audience, even if the nude scene is essential to the plot, being faced with a naked actor makes it difficult to concentrate on the scene. Because we are rarely allowed to stare dispassionately at a real naked person in the United States, it is difficult for audience members to stop their extracurricular thoughts of lust or loathing. Rather than seeing the *character*, audience members are looking at the *actor*, noting the size of his penis or her breasts. The result is that the suspension of disbelief—and the focus on the characters and story—disappears. Instead of being involved in the world of the play, people are self-conscious, embarrassed, and distracted.

John Istel writes in "The Naked Truth," in *American Theatre Magazine*, that fire and nudity in the theatre make the audience uncomfortable and take them out of the play. He urges a moratorium on nudity, believing that it is not only distracting, it is antitheatrical. He explains that it is difficult to get swept up into the illusionary world of a play in the first place. We have to accept all kinds of crazy theatre conventions such as families who crowd around only three-fourths of a dinner table and people who, no matter what they're doing, always seem to face in the direction of the audience. For naysayers such as Istel, nudity raises unnecessary questions that are just further distractions. Audience members may be wondering, for example, Is she cold? Did he take a shower before the show? What do her parents think about this? or Do they get splinters?

The test of obscenity that usually wins for artists relates to the question of whether the play is utterly without redeeming social, artistic, and literary value. A work of art has artistic value by definition. However, playwrights need to remember that there are still many communities and theatres that do not allow nudity. Any show that is more tart than art may have difficulty getting produced. Some believe the magic of the theatre is more intriguing, more romantic, and more imaginative if the actors keep their costumes on.

In-Yer-Face Theatre

A current style is in-yer-face theatre, which is defined as something blatantly aggressive or provocative, impossible to ignore or avoid, and confrontational. It implies being forced to see something close up, having your personal space invaded. It suggests crossing normal boundaries. In short, it describes the kind of theatre that puts the audience in just such a situation.

In-yer-face theatre has been notably prevalent in Great Britain and has really taken off in the last decade. Just as the theories of Antonin Artaud inspired provocative and confrontational theatre in the 1960s, in-yer-face theatre became the dominant style of much new writing in the 1990s. Among the writers of in-yer-face theatre are Sarah Kane, Mark Ravenhill, Nick Grosso, Tracy Letts, Martin McDonagh, Patrick Marber, Philip Ridley, Naomi Wallace, and Richard Zajdlic. Mark Ravenhill is the author of *Shopping and Fucking, Handbag, Some Explicit Polaroids, Faust Is Dead,* and *Mother Clap's Molly House.* Critic Michael Billington wrote in *The Guardian* (2001) about the last play, "Mark Ravenhill clearly likes to have it both ways. In this wonderfully exuberant new musical play, he celebrates Sodom like there is no Gomorrah. But the satirist in him also attacks the commodification of sex and the resultant loss of love. The result is an evening rich in rudery and ambivalence" (p. 14).

In the United States, in-yer-face theatre is exemplified by plays such as *Killer Joe* and *Bug* by Tracy Letts, *Bash* and *The Shape of Things* by Neil LaBute, and some of Sam Shepard's work, but the majority of audiences in the United States seem to prefer comedies and musicals; they want to be entertained, not shocked. Nevertheless, in-yer-face theatre has found an audience, and the plays of Letts and LaBute have met with critical acclaim and sold-out houses.

How can you tell if a play is in your face? The language is filthy, there's probably nudity, people have sex in front of you, violence breaks out, one character humiliates another, taboos are broken, unmentionable subjects are broached, and conventional dramatic structures are subverted. At its best, this kind of theatre is so powerful, so visceral that it forces you to react. Its themes include society's standards, hypocrisy, and values as well as attitudes toward extramarital sex, drugs, fraud, violence, and marriage.

Summary

The term *genre* refers to a play's classification: comedy, tragedy, or drama. These classes can be further divided into many subcategories. A comedy may be comedy of manners, satire, farce, situation comedy, burlesque or parody, fantasy or romance. A tragedy is a tragedy, but it may also be historical, mythological, romantic, horrific, or melodramatic. A drama is a serious play, which may have a sad or happy ending. A drama may be a problem play, a "whodunit" or mystery, soap opera, tragicomedy, or a melodrama. It might even include elements of fantasy.

Style refers to the author's treatment or approach, including his individual style and the conventions he or she selects to use. Theatre styles include approaches that are representational or illusionistic, presentational or classical, or revolts against realistic plays, such as expressionism, surrealism, theatricalism, stylization, epic theatre, absurdism, and abstract formalism. Representational styles include naturalism and realism. Presentational styles acknowledge that this is the world of the theatre. Characters speak directly to the audience in asides and soliloquies. There may be a chorus or another theatrical convention employed. These styles include all classical plays up to the beginning of modern drama in the late nineteenth century. Once modern realism became the established style, there were revolts against it, but it remains dominant.

Nudity can be a natural part of a play and needed for the story and the character, or it can be gratuitous, added primarily to sell tickets. Nudity that is integral to the believability of the action helps tell the story efficiently, shows the audience about a character without having to use a lot of words, shows the relationship of the characters, and conveys the tone of the play.

In-yer-face theatre is defined as something blatantly aggressive or provocative, impossible to ignore or avoid, and confrontational. It implies being forced to see something close up, having your personal space invaded. It suggests crossing normal boundaries. In short, it describes the kind of theatre that puts the audience in just such a situation. In a play of this kind, the language is filthy, there is nudity, people have sex in front of you, violence breaks out, one character humiliates another, taboos are broken, unmentionable subjects are broached, and conventional dramatic structures are subverted. At its best, this kind of theatre is powerful and visceral, pushing the audience to react.

CHAPTER

16 The Spine and Premise

The playwright should ask, If I were the audience, watching this play, what conclusions would I come to about the story, about the characters, and about life? Each play says something through what it shows. In this chapter, we will explore the spine and premise of a play. The *spine* is defined as the basic action of the play. The *premise* is the major idea behind the play—what it shows. If we define a *dramatic story* as the transformation of a character through a crisis, the premise is a succinct statement of that transformation. One of the essentials to good playwriting is to show, not tell. The premise, or theme, comes through not by having the characters talk about it but by having the play illustrate it, so that the audience can discover it.

The Spine

Plays that succeed do so because they nail the basics and build from there. One basic is that central thread around which all the other threads are woven—the spine. The *spine* of a play refers to a coherent and focused storyline—the basic action of the play, the critical path along which the story moves, what the play is about from the standpoint of the characters' principal conflict. Like a train following its rails to its destination, the spine keeps the play on track as the script unfolds. This can be a useful tool when troubleshooting a play that has lost its focus at some point.

Harold Clurman (1972) in *On Directing* writes, "The director chooses the spine of the play, the key or springboard of his interpretation, according to his own lights, not to mention the actors he has at his disposal, the audience he wishes to reach and the hoped for affect on that audience" (p. 30). He learned this concept from Richard Boleslavsky, who had been trained by Stanislavsky at the Moscow Art Theatre. The body's spine holds the vertebra in place just as the main action in a play must hold all the smaller events and actions. For example, he explains that Eugene O'Neill's *A Touch of the Poet* focuses on characters who are immigrants to this country, and the spine was for these characters "to make a place for themselves" (p. 221). For his production of O'Neill's *Long Day's Journey into Night,* he determined that each character was alone with his own secret or guilt but that each had his or her eye on everyone else. For him the play was a self-examination, a search into oneself and into others. The spine was "to probe within oneself for the

227

lost 'something'" (p. 255). For Carson McCullers's *The Member of the Wedding*, he said the spine was to get connected.

For a playwright, the spine must be the dramatic core of the script, extended from beginning to end. It is created as one scene builds on the next, as one event follows another, as characters act and interact. It is a dynamic mix of story and dramatic elements that provides the source of energy that drives the story forward. It is also the path along which the energy flows, a central and critical element in the anatomy of a play.

After finding the spine of a play, Clurman (1972) then determined the spine of each character and how it related to the main action. For example, if the spine in McCullers's drama was to get connected, he then asked, "What does the protagonist Frankie do about it?" To Frankie, getting out of herself means growing up. As she is growing, she faces twists and turns, joy and torture—in short, growing pains—but at the end, she has achieved her aim. She's ready to get out of herself and get connected (pp. 189–190).

The spine provides a path for the inner moral/spiritual journey of the central character. The protagonist will reach various destinations along his or her path, each of which advances the story. The spine triggers the major question in the play: Will the protagonist get what he or she wants? We learn the answer when protagonist and antagonist meet face to face at the climax.

So, in the final analysis what is the spine? It is organic, generated during the writing process itself, not built or assembled according to some handy blueprint. It doesn't pre-exist. It comes into being as the play unfolds. Its creation is an evolving process. Character is the heart and soul of the spine, dramatic structure provides its skeleton, and dynamic storytelling adds the flesh and blood. The presence or absence of a clear spine can be felt on a very basic level: "It's working" or "It's not working."

The Premise

A good spine needs a strong dramatic premise to set it in motion. The *premise* is the controlling idea of the play, expressed in a single sentence. Think of the dramatic premise as the prime mover—the source of momentum that causes the story to unfold and the dramatic elements to function at maximum efficiency. The dramatic premise is active like a fully charged battery waiting to transform its energy into action.

The potency of a dramatic premise derives from an inherent imbalance or conflict that demands to be addressed and set right. This imbalance—a form of dramatic instability—forces the protagonist into action, relentless and unstoppable, until equilibrium is restored. A good dramatic premise springs from something being out of balance, and the protagonist takes it upon herself to set it right. In Shakespeare's *Macbeth*, the title character's world goes out of balance as soon as the witches' first prophecy comes true. It is then that his ruthless ambition starts to take hold.

The dramatic premise is postulated in the setup and always involves the main characters facing a very specific set of circumstances, which ideally spring from both internal and external sources. A viable dramatic premise is a statement of what the whole play is about.

The dramatic premise is the starting point, providing the motive to drive the story forward. In Sophocles' *Oedipus the King,* Oedipus wants to save his people from the plague, even if it is to his own peril. For Annie Sullivan in William Gibson's *The Miracle Worker,* the goal is to make Helen Keller understand how to communicate, and the successful completion of the task is one on which her own self-worth depends. For Macbeth, it is to become king, no matter what the cost. For Shakespeare's Hamlet, it is his duty to avenge the murder of his father, above all else. In the play *Extremities,* by Mastrosimone, a woman named Marjorie is attacked and nearly raped but eventually overpowers the rapist, Raul. She ties him up and barricades him in her fireplace. Raul tells her that he will be out of jail quickly because he didn't really rape her, and then he will come back and finish the job. She tortures him and then decides to dig a hole and bury him. Eventually, her two roommates return and try to convince her that the most reasonable action is to call the police. She then sees the situation rationally and demands that Raul confess in front of her roommates. He must do so before she will call the police to ensure her future safety from him.

In these plays, the classic elements for dramatic action are in place: The main characters are in extreme jeopardy, the obstacles are seemingly insurmountable, the goals are clearcut, the need to take action is overwhelming, and the clock is ticking. This familiar mix of ingredients can be found in the setups to a great many plays. It creates a solid dramatic footing that is then spun into a play.

The premise also clarifies what the author has to say. It shapes the ending. It answers the central question of the play and tells us what happens afterward. For example, Macbeth does become king, but his ruthless ambition leads to his destruction. Oedipus does save his people, but to do so, he must realize his own faults. He learns that he killed Laius and is the cause of the plague, and to fulfill his promise to punish the evildoer, he blinds himself and goes into exile. We might offer several premises for *Extremities:* "He who digs a pit for others, falls into it himself," "He who commits violence on others will suffer in equal measure," or "Reason leads us away from destruction." The central character is on her way to destruction, but reason prevents it.

But whatever the conflict, it is meaningless until it has been *personalized.* It needs to have a significant impact emotionally on the audience, and for that to happen, they must care about the characters. The story must grab hold of its audience early and not let go.

The relationship of the characters must compel our attention and concern. We need to identify with or sympathize with the protagonist. We must see how he struggles and what the quest costs him. Taking on the quest should cause the protagonist trouble, pain, and suffering.

The antagonist must make the protagonist's life miserable and be so strong that we're never sure of the outcome until the end. We must also learn how terrible the consequences will be if the protagonist fails. In classic fashion, the protagonist will probably lash out at those she loves to protect herself and shelter the core of inner pain that has become the defining aspect of her character.

A good dramatic premise has three C's; character, conflict, and consequences:

1. A *character* (protagonist) who takes action and is a prime mover.
2. An impulse to action that results from the direct *conflict* between the protagonist and the forces of opposition, whether internal or external.
3. Clearly defined *consequences*.

The antagonist must be as determined to win as the protagonist. The antagonist must also be determined to confront, expose, and stop the protagonist from getting what he wants. They need to dance around each other like a pair of boxers probing for weaknesses and openings, landing an odd jab here, a solid punch there, until through the progression of their scenes, each becomes more exposed and more vulnerable to the other. They must battle with their hearts and minds. This kind of unwavering focus on the central issue of the story will generate tremendous strength and sustain the spine.

There is a strong link between the spine and the overall structure of the play. The structure may be as simple as beginning, middle, and end. It may involve multiple story lines, multiple timeframes, or a deliberately fractured or scrambled narrative line. It may utilize unusual narrative devices, like the three-part "repeated with variations" rape in *Rashomon,* by Fay Kanin and Michael Kanin, or the multiple story lines of a Shakespearean play. But good dramatic structure goes beyond architecture to something more akin to musical composition.

The playwright, as well as the director, needs to approach structure in terms of what happens when, for how long, and at what intensity. Creating this sense of pacing, duration, and dramatic impact is an intuitive process. It has to do with *rhythm,* and it also has to do with *expectations.* We expect to see the conflict set in motion and the first complication—the protagonist's first step into quicksand—within the first twenty pages. By the end of Act One, we need to see the protagonist fall into the next quagmire, so that we go out at the intermission wondering what is going to happen next. The second act needs to take us to a third and even worse situation that will lead to the climax. If there are some surprises, some new discoveries by the protagonist or antagonist that take us to unexpected places, that is even better.

The structure is designed to compel and focus questions in the audience's mind. The inciting incident propels the first question: How will this turn out? What is going to be the outcome? The audience wants its expectations reversed. They didn't come to see what they already know. They want a surprise—a reversal. If a play turns out to be exactly what the audience expected and unfolds exactly how the audience expected it, then they will be disappointed. If you, as the playwright, can answer the main question in a way the audience doesn't expect and can surprise them such that they can truly understand and accept the outcome, then you will have brought about a successful resolution. This sense of pacing, momentum, and overall shape is a vital part of dramatic structure and the one that links most directly to the effective functioning of the spine.

Think of the *premise* as the controlling idea of the play expressed in one sentence. It is the root idea or central idea of the play, suggesting how the idea controls and guides the writer's choices. The controlling idea is the one we take away from the play.

It is unlikely that the writer will begin with a clear idea of the premise, unless the inspiration for the play is a message she wants to tell. Usually, a writer begins with an experience, an image, a vague idea of a story, or a character. She writes a few scenes. The characters may take the writer places she didn't expect to go. The writer discovers the controlling idea as the focus of the play develops. As the writer continues, the characters make choices and the writer's vision becomes clearer. Eventually, the writer must decide what the controlling idea is and what the play will show when all is said and done. Through the controlling idea, the writer reorganizes and reshapes the story and gives it meaning, creating a metaphor for life.

A. R. Gurney, Jr., states in an interview with Jackson Bryer (1995) in *The Playwright's Art* that he really has to have some idea of where he wants to end up but that he often doesn't end up there. In writing *The Dining Room,* he didn't know how it would end. He says,

> All I knew was that I wanted to have a play that took place in one room during the course of a day. It had to get more exciting, and something important had to happen toward the end of the day. What could you have take place in a dining room as the light is beginning to wane? I suppose it had to be something about death, which has become a kind of penultimate scene in *The Dining Room,* as the table is being set for the final dinner party, the ultimate scene. (p. 95)

Gurney goes on to note that with *Later Life,* he had a specific climax clearly in mind and what he thought was a wonderful ending. The second draft, however, took him in an entirely different direction and resulted in a different ending. Similarly, Edward Albee (1995) states in *The Playwright's Art,* "When you write something, you're working from both your conscious and your unconscious mind, and you don't necessarily always know what you have until someone points it out to you" (p. 15).

The responsibility of the writer is not to uplift society or to be politically correct. The responsibility is to tell the truth as you passionately believe it. Do you believe what you have written? Do you believe what the end shows?

The audience wants a reason to go to the theatre. Why should they go through the ritual of driving to the theatre, buying a ticket, sitting in the dark in a public room with a bunch of strangers, and putting in a great amount of concentration and energy to experience the story? They want to experience a meaningful metaphor for life.

The premise, message, or theme may be stated briefly, but it doesn't mean that the idea behind the play or the theme is simplistic. A ten-minute play or a one-act is capable of mind-stretching thought. It can carry a significant subject and theme just as a full-length play can. What's important is that the play shows *thought*. What does the play in its entirety say?

Every story, novel, or play must have a premise. A play without a premise is like a car without a steering wheel. It should be avoided. Think of the premise as the love in a marriage. It is the reason you are writing what you are writing. It is the major point that your play shows when the final curtain has come down. Thomas Price (1992), in *Dramatic Structure and Meaning in Theatrical Productions*, claims the play's argument is "fundamentally the projection of a spiritual struggle within the soul of its creator" (p. 7). In his view, the playwright develops a *proposition* that is a brief statement or syllogism and then develops the action of the play to demonstrate it. Lajos Egri (1960) calls it *premise* or *purpose* and defines it as the "theme, root idea, central idea, goal, aim, driving force, subject, plan, plot, or basic emotion" (p. 2). The premise of Shakespeare's *Romeo and Juliet* is "Great love defies even death" (p. 12). Henrik Ibsen's *Ghosts* shows us that "The sins of the father are visited on the children" (p. 13).

In Neil Simon's *Barefoot in the Park*, newlyweds Corie and Paul Bratter move into a fifth-floor walk-up. Corie is a free spirit. Paul is a conservative, stable lawyer. When Corie tries to get Paul to lighten up, have fun, and walk barefoot in the park, he resists. They fight. Finally Paul gets drunk, walks barefoot in the park, and then climbs on the roof above the skylight. Corie is terrified he will fall. In the end, she is enlightened. The premise of the play is "Compromise on both sides is necessary for a successful marriage."

Don't Tell, Show

One of the essentials to good playwriting is to show it, not tell it. Your premise or theme will come through not by having your characters speak about it but by making the play illustrate it. The audience must be able to observe the interactions of the characters, discover the story, and come to their own conclusions. It is crucial that your story actually illustrate the themes you want it to through the dramatic action. If the play does not illustrate the themes you planned, you have a choice: change the themes or change the story. Look at your scenario closely and ask yourself, If I were the audience, watching this play, what conclusions would I come to about the story, about the characters, and about life?

For example, Shakespeare's *Macbeth* clearly illustrates the terrible conflict and tragedy caused by obsessive ambition and greed. It is not just about how things go awry when you listen to your spouse. If it were about that, the first scene would not show Macbeth meeting the witches and reacting strongly when they tell him he will be thane and king. Instead, it would give us a scene between the married Macbeths right off. This doesn't mean that all plays are thesis plays (some are just good yarns, with theatricality) or propaganda, although your play may come across that way if your story and characters don't have plausibility and dramatic probability. They must be consistent within the dramatic conventions of the world you set up. Examine each scene that you've written in terms of its premise. Make a list of the titles of the scenes and state the premise of each one. What does each scene show?

Note that the premise is not stated directly in the scene but implied in a subtle way. Once you have a clear understanding of what each scene shows, then try to determine the overall premise of your play.

EXERCISE 20 (Optional)

Beginning Level   Choose one of the following:

A.   Write a comic scene with a strong premise. The premise might be "A person who cannot make up his or her mind will suffer the consequences" or "A person who responds in a way to baffle, confuse, and astonish others will get what he or she deserves." Once your premise is set, put it into action. What complications can you use to put obstacles in the protagonist's way? What is the worst that could happen? Make it happen. Again, base your jokes on characters and situations. The ending should have a big laugh and tie the scene into a neat package.

B.   Rewrite a previous scene. Make it comic by turning one of the characters into an imposter who gets confused, lies through his teeth, and goes off on tangents. Imagine a comic such as Robin Williams, Kathy Griffith, or Dave Chapelle playing the character.

Intermediate Level   Choose one of the following:

C.   Select a familiar classic comedy by Shakespeare, Molière, Etherage, Sheridan, or another dramatist. Select a scene and rewrite it, changing the characters and setting to today. Molière did this by adapting *The Pot of Gold*, by Plautus, into *The Miser*. Plautus's *The Twin Menachmi* was adapted by Shakespeare into *The Comedy of Errors,* which was adapted into the musical *The Boys from Syracuse* by George Abbott with music and lyrics by Rodgers and Hart. *Sly Fox*, by Larry Gelbart, is an adaptation of Ben Jonson's *Volpone.* The contemporary film *10 Things I Hate about You* was based on Shakespeare's *The Taming of the Shrew.*

D.   Select a playwright and write a scene in the style of that playwright. For examples, look at the following plays: *Lend Me a Tenor* or *Noises Off* by

Michael Frayn (farce), *Cat on a Hot Tin Roof* by Tennessee Williams (realism), *The Hairy Ape* by Eugene O'Neill (expressionism), *Bug* by Tracy Letts (in-yer-face drama).

Advanced Level   Choose one of the following:

E.   Write a scene in which it would be realistic and believable for a character to be nude. Look at Tracy Letts's *Killer Joe.* Make sure the nudity is essential for the story and the character. Include an important physical action, whether serious or comic.

F.   Write an in-yer-face scene that focuses on social standards, hypocrisy, greed, or old-fashioned attitudes that you believe should by changed. Maybe you want to draw attention to the problems of date rape, extramarital sex, drugs, fraud, violence, or marriage. This is experimental theatre, where you make the rules regarding language, nudity, violence, taboos, theme, character, and structure. Your goal is to write a powerful and visceral scene that pushes the audience to react.

Summary

The *spine* of a play refers to a coherent and focused storyline—the basic action of the play, the critical path along which the story moves, what the play is about from the standpoint of the characters' principal conflict. Like a train following its rails to its destination, the spine keeps the play on track as the script unfolds. This can be a useful tool when troubleshooting a play that has lost focus at some point.

Harold Clurman (1972) writes "To give active direction a formulation in the simplest terms must be found to state what general action motivates the play" (p. 27). He used the word *spine* to indicate the major struggle that is at the core of a play, and he used a single sentence to describe the spine of each play. For example, Shakespeare's *Hamlet* is a story of a man's search for the truth. William Saroyan's *My Heart's in the Highlands* is the story of people eager to give things to one another. Clifford Odets's *Night Music* is the story of the search for a home.

Every story, novel, or play must have a *premise.* It is the reason you are writing what you are writing. It is the major point that your play shows when the final curtain has come down. The play needs to have form. It needs to be organized in such a way, scene by scene, to make clear the action and theme. The premise suggests three things: the central character, the conflict, and the ending of the play. If we define a *dramatic story* as the transformation of a character through a crisis, the premise is a succinct statement of that transformation. In William Mastrosimone's *Extremities,* the premise is "Reason leads us away from destruction." In Shakespeare's *Macbeth,* it is "Ruthless ambition leads to destruction." In Martin McDonagh's *The Beauty Queen of Leenane,* it is "The inability to face reality brings about isolation and destruction."

One of the essentials to good playwriting is to show, not tell. The premise will come through not by having the characters talk about theme but by making the play illustrate it so that the audience can discover it. Examine the story closely and ask, If I were the audience, watching this play, what conclusions would I come to about the story, about the characters, and about life? If the play does not illustrate a writer's desired themes, he or she has a choice: change the themes or change the story.

CHAPTER

17 Writing and Rewriting

In this chapter, we will explore many of the areas you need to address in writing and rewriting. Once the first draft is done, it is then important to determine what changes are needed to improve and clarify the plot, characters, and dialogue as well as to correct punctuation and spelling. We will focus on comma problems and also look at information on copyright.

The First Draft

If you are putting together a series of scenes written in response to the exercises for your first draft, you will need to pay careful attention to transitions, entrances and exits of characters, and costume changes. If you have used different locales, you will need to decide how to rewrite the scenes to make them work in a single or unit set. If you have more than six characters, you should rethink the roles and try to combine and/or eliminate characters. Make certain that each scene is essential to the story and that something is different at the end of a scene from the beginning.

Using the average of one and one-half minutes per page, remember that a thirty-minute short play is about twenty pages, a forty-five-minute play is about thirty pages, a sixty-minute play is about forty-five pages, a ninety-minute play is about sixty pages, and a two-hour play is about seventy-five pages. Carefully work through your play, line by line, and edit. Eliminate unnecessary repetition and verbosity, and rewrite for clarity. Make sure that you follow the professional format (see Chapter 4), and proofread for typos, spelling, and punctuation. Make sure that the pages are numbered correctly.

Also, don't forget to have fun with your play. If you aren't having fun with it, then neither will anyone else. And if you aren't having fun with it, you probably won't be writing much of it. So as Buff says in *Suburbia*, "Go with the flow." Listen to and obey the unexpected whims of your characters.

EXERCISE 21

All Levels

Complete your first draft:
  A. Beginning Level: 30 pages minimum

B. Intermediate Level: 45 pages minimum
C. Advanced Level: A full-length play, 60 to 75 pages

Follow these guidelines for writing your first draft:

1. Your title page should have the title and the name of the author centered:

STUDENT BODY

By Lola Montes

2. Your second page should have the same title and name of author plus copyright and contact information in the lower-left corner.

© Lola Montez
11684 Lincoln Rd.
Miami, FL 33199
(305) 555-4321
lola1982@hotmail.com

3. Your third page should include the character descriptions, setting, and time.

4. Your scenario may be on the fourth page.

5. The first page of dialogue should be page 1. Make sure you include the page number at the top-right of each page, beginning with the first page of dialogue. If your one-act has only one scene, you should number the pages consecutively: 1, 2, 3, and so on. If you have more than one scene, provide the number of the scene using a numeral, a hyphen, and then the page number. Always number the pages consecutively. Do not start over with 1 at the beginning of each scene or act. If you have more than one act, use numerals for both the acts and the scenes and continue the numbers consecutively for the pages. Examples: 1-1-1, 1-1-2, 1-1-3; 1-2-4, 1-2-5, 1-2-6; and so on.

6. Each scene starts on a new page. The word SCENE and the number are centered at the top of the scene. Example: SCENE 1.

7. At the end of the scene, the words END OF SCENE 1 should be centered.

8. Make sure you follow the correct format. Stage directions in parentheses are indented 1.5 inches and character names are all in caps and indented 3.0 inches.

9. Make sure that you proofread your script and correct all misspellings, punctuation errors, grammatical mistakes, and the like.

10. What editing needs to be done?
   A. Cut repetitive words.
   B. Cut elaborate, long-winded stage directions.
   C. Edit every speech, removing any unnecessary words.

When you see a performance of a play, nothing should be distracting. You should notice the set, and then it should go away. You shouldn't be aware of the acting, the directing, the sets, or even the playwriting. If, instead of being caught up in the experience, something distracts you, then somebody has not done his job properly. Similarly, when a teacher, or hopefully a literary manager, agent, director, or producer reads your play, nothing in the manuscript should distract from the story. The format, spelling, and punctuation should be as clean and professional as possible.

The best way for a playwright to determine the strengths and weaknesses of her play is to hear it. The playwright who's working independently can make this happen by enlisting friends and relatives to read the play aloud in her living room. The student in a workshop or university playwriting class will most likely have a teacher who makes this happen in the classroom by enlisting the participation of the other students. Following these kinds of readings, whether they are for a scene or the whole play, the participants and observers generally provide feedback to the writer. The playwright should listen, take notes, and ask questions, but under no circumstances should she get defensive when others offer criticisms and suggestions for change.

Rewriting is part of the process. Even the most astute playwrights rewrite their work many times. Lanford Wilson's play *Burn This* was four hours long when it went into production. It needed to be cut considerably to shorten the playing time, as did Sam Shepard's *A Lie of the Mind* and Tennessee Williams's *Night of the Iguana*. If you look at *The Season*, by William Goldman, and *Playwrights in Rehearsal*, by Susan Letzler Cole, you will see numerous case studies of rewriting situations.

The Second Draft

Once the writer has heard the first draft read, he must decide what changes are needed to improve the plot, characters, and dialogue as well as to correct the punctuation and spelling. During the writing process, the writer must be emotionally connected to the material and follow his instincts. He should also realize that finishing the first draft of the play is just the beginning. Then comes rewriting.

After becoming subjectively and personally involved with the play during the writing process, the writer must be able to distance himself and be able to look at each draft with a more objective eye. In the beginning, this may require listening to other theatre professionals who have more experience and can guide you. The more knowledge you have of the theatre and the more experience you have as a playwright, the more independent your decisions will become. However, we all have blind spots. Thus, having someone else read the play or having a public reading can bring you feedback and insights from others.

William Whitehurst, a former student, wrote a ten-minute play called *Chinese Takeout* in which a consultant, Jeff, calls in a phone order of Chinese food while finishing an all-night "megaproject." The Chinese man answers yes to Jeff's order but no food ever comes. Jeff finally gets so angry that he finds the address he had called from looking in the Yellow Pages, drives there, and attacks the Chinese man. What he thought was a restaurant turns out to be a laundry, and the Chinese man says yes to everything. It is the only English word he knows. Jeff is thrown in jail and then, much to his consternation, the Chinese man shows up and he must share the cell with him.

When Whitehurst's play was read aloud, it became apparent that it didn't work to actually have the phone calls, different locales, and a passage of several hours. Whitehurst described the experience as follows:

> It sounds like I have described a lot of action: phone calls, growing conflict, an attack. Yet, the response I got was: "Nothing interesting happens until we get to the jail cell." On reflection, I realized the characters did not really interact until the jail cell. I revised the piece beginning in the cell. All of the previous action was easily captured as "backstory" in a few references by Jeff. And these passages weren't empty exposition: since the characters were in dramatic conflict, Jeff's comments on their immediate past were "motivated speech." The principle was clear: begin at the point closest to the dramatic climax—a lesson particularly valuable in a ten-minute short. (Personal communication, November 12, 2002)

There are many reasons a play may not work. Each play has its own specific rules and structure and language. Since a writer often doesn't know where it's going on starting a play, she may not figure that out until near the end of the first draft. It may be that she can't solve the major problems until several drafts later. Most writers do not start writing with the beginning, middle, and end already decided. The idea may come from an image, an event, a character, or a situation. It may metamorphose into something quite different. A scene may be too long or underdeveloped. A character may not be interesting or dynamic enough. The exposition may be clumsy. There may be two many stories or characters or locales mixed up in the play. All of this must be sorted out.

In addition to improving the play itself, the writer must take care of the mechanics. It is difficult to read a script that has errors on every page. Few literary managers and dramaturgs will read such a manuscript. It will be left on the shelf or tossed. Before a writer sends the script off to a theatre, an agent, or a contest, he must edit the work. This important aspect of rewriting is like cleaning house before guests arrive. It's not much fun in itself, but you feel really good when everything has been completed.

If you read your script from a computer screen, you will miss problems with formatting and spacing. You need to print a paper copy to read so you can better see the mistakes. A well-written and edited manuscript flows smoothly. There should be nothing in terms of format, grammar, spelling, or punctuation that distracts from the story. Also consider the following:

1. Make sure you are showing, not telling. Exposition is telling. Action is showing. We don't want to be told what happened offstage. If it is important and possi-

ble, make it happen on stage. Show a character's emotions by his or her actions. Don't tell us how the character feels. Don't have John say, "You really make me angry." Show it. Have John throw the book at the door and yell, "Take the book and get out!"

2. Establish each character gradually. A character doesn't need to enter the stage and deliver a monologue about her past life. Although a character may make a reference to another character's behavior or personality or attitude before entering, once that person arrives, we need to see her in action and others responding to her. Bring in background information only when it is vital to the current scene—on a "need to know" basis. Make sure that your characters do not offer information that would already be known by the other characters. Make sure they don't offer information to another person they normally wouldn't confide in: "Hi, husband. Aren't you going to work today? I'm sure they're going to need you to look at the dials at the nuclear power plant."

3. Are your stage directions clear and brief? Remember that many actors and directors do not read stage directions. Some directors even blacken out all the stage directions when they direct a show. Limit the stage directions to the characters' specific actions. Avoid telling actors how to play lines (e.g., "sarcastically").

4. Read your dialogue out loud to make sure your characters have specific voices. Cut any words and phrases that are repetitious. Are you saying the same thing several different ways? Remember that ellipses (three dots) are for gaps and dashes for interruptions. Are some lines too long and difficult to articulate? Do you have one idea per speech? If you have more than one, add a response by another character to the first idea before expressing the second.

5. Are you trying to tell too much with dialogue? Have you made the dialogue count? Can you eliminate expository dialogue? How much of your story can you tell visually?

6. Point of attack is important for the play itself and for each scene within the play. Are your scenes starting too early? Do the scenes run too long past their completion? Each scene should have a beginning, middle, and end. You can usually hone a scene effectively by eliminating all the setup at the beginning and starting at the first point of conflict. Don't try to bring each scene to a neat, comfortable completion. Leave some scenes open, ending with unresolved conflict. In the structure, pay close attention to the discoveries your central character makes. Where you place the discoveries or turning points in the progression of the story is very important. Have you looked at the transitions? What is the hook that takes us from scene to scene? Have you looked at the contrasting rhythms and tones of your scenes? No two scenes should be the same length or have the same emotional feeling.

7. Have you checked for unintentional repetition? Do you have two scenes that accomplish the same end? Does a character give the same information more than once? Is the same word repeated too closely in the dialogue? Do you have too many italics, exclamation points, dashes, metaphors, or uses of profanity? These items are most effective when used sparingly. Use them too often, and they will lose their impact.

8. Check your general mechanics. Check your spelling with a spellcheck. If you don't have one, get one. Make sure you are using the right forms of words. The following are often confused:

> their/there/they're
>
> its/it's
>
> who's/whose

On a final read through, check for errors such as two periods per sentence, two spaces between words, and words your spellcheck missed. For instance, perhaps you've typed *the* instead of *them*. Your spellcheck won't get this because *the* is a correctly spelled word, even though it's not the right word.

Editing involves an ability to look at your work with an impersonal eye. For some, this is difficult. Find another person who's willing to proofread your script, as well. It is often helpful to let your manuscript sit for a while; then go back and do a final edit. Time and distance can give you a clearer view of your dream. Always remember that a play is not just written; it's rewritten.

Rewriting is like finding the meaning of life. We go on a quest with the first draft, and in the subsequent drafts, we get to relive that life over and over until we get it right.

Using Commas

The comma is the most widely used of all punctuation marks, since it serves so many different purposes. Because of its varied and distinct uses, however, it is also the most troublesome of all punctuation marks. Its overuse and misuse obscure meaning more than the misapplication of other punctuation marks. In fact, comma usage varies so greatly that only a few rules can be considered unchanging. Regardless, this mark of punctuation, more than any others, can help to clarify the meaning of writing.

The writer needs to keep in mind several important facts about the comma. It is a weak mark compared to the period, semicolon, and colon. It is always used *within* a sentence. It has three primary purposes:

1. To *separate* sentence elements that might be misread
2. To *enclose* or *set off* interrupters within a sentence
3. To set off certain *introductory* sentence elements

Using Commas to Separate

Use commas to separate words and other sentence elements that may be misread. The single most important use of the comma is to prevent misunderstanding. Look at this statement: "Mr. Robinson our neighbor is an acting teacher." Is this a comment *to* or *about* Mr. Robinson? You can make the meaning clear by writing "Mr. Robinson, our neighbor is an acting teacher," which translates as a direct address, or "Mr. Robinson, our neighbor, is an acting teacher," meaning that Mr. Robinson is both our neighbor and an acting teacher. In each of the following sentences, if you omit the commas, the meaning becomes confused:

> In 2002, 102 directors produced this same play.
>
> Outside, the theatre needs a coat of paint; inside, the walls need plastering.
>
> The day after, our director was absent herself.
>
> Soon after, Lesley Ann got up on her crutches and stormed out of the room.
>
> The cost increased five dollars, to twenty-one. (The comma makes it clear that the range of advance was sixteen upward, not between five and twenty-one.)

   1. *A comma is used to separate two main clauses joined by a coordinating conjunction.* A comma between two such clauses prevents misreading, as in the following sentences:

> We ate fruit and our leading man ordered eggs and bacon.
>
> Last week I was sick with a cold and my understudy took over.
>
> I am not interested in staying for the role is dull.

Adding a comma each after *fruit, cold,* and *staying* will prevent readers from thinking that the subject of the second clause is part of the first clause. If the clauses are short, the comma before the conjunction may be left out. But how short is *short?* If each clause consists of only a subject and a predicate or of only three or four words each, then the comma may be omitted:

> Roberto did not win the Irene Ryan Scholarship nor did Lina.
>
> The audience came and the actors performed.

Long clauses may be written without a comma between them if both have the same subject and if the thought connection is close:

> Philip looked at the stage set quickly and then he began a close inspection of it.

   2. *Do not use a comma to separate a subject from its predicate or a verb from its object or complement.* No comma is needed in any of these sentences:

> Jack gave out copies of the script and asked me to read the stage directions.
>
> We asked to hear the scene read by the actors and then improvised.
>
> Hal found that writing for an hour was not so hard after all.

3. *Use commas to separate the elements in a series.* One kind of series is represented by A, B, and C—three or more words, phrases, or clauses, with a conjunction (usually *and*) joining the last two members. Book publishers use the comma before the conjunction. Some writers omit the comma before the conjunction and use A, B and C. Present practice in the playwrighting field favors this pattern:

> Melissa, Megan, Ramon and Christina are terrific actors.
>
> That director is noted for his wild concepts, cinematic music and long rehearsals.

Another kind of series is represented by three or more words, phrases, or clauses without any conjunctions.

> The room is bright, clean, quiet.

4. *Do not use commas when conjunctions join the items in a series.*

> I have read no plays by O'Neill or Inge or Odets or Lilliam Hellman.
>
> All makeup must meet the same standards for safety and strength and purity.

Use commas to separate two or more adjectives when they equally modify the same noun:

> This beautiful, rich, athletic woman could actually act.
>
> For the performance, Katie wore an old, ragged dress and an ugly, cheap hat.

When the adjectives do not modify equally—that is, when they are not coordinate—use no commas:

> A large green centipede crawled on the dry waxed floor.

If you cannot tell whether modifying adjectives are really coordinate, test it by mentally inserting the coordinate conjunction *and* between adjectives; using a comma is correct only if *and* fits naturally. In the preceeding sample sentence, you can fit *and* between *large* and *green* and between *dry* and *waxed,* but the fit does not seem natural. *Large,* for example, seems to modify *green centipede.* Also, truly coordinate adjectives can be reversed: *dry waxed floor* makes sense whereas *waxed dry floor* does not.

5. *Use a comma to separate contrasted elements in a sentence.* Such contrasted elements may be words, phrases, numbers, letters, or clauses:

> Jorge begins his name with a J, not with an H.
>
> Your punctuation problems are due to carelessness, not to ignorance.
>
> Food should be kept in the green room, not in the theatre.
>
> The harder it rained, the faster they ran.

6. *Use a comma or commas to separate an absolute phrase from the remainder of the sentence.* An *absolute phrase,* or group of words that has no grammatical relationship to any word in the sentence, consists of a noun and a participial modifier. (The latter is sometimes omitted but understood.) For example:

> The performance having been finished, we started on the trip home.
>
> I went to the main office, my resume in hand, and asked for the stage manager.
>
> We need another actor for the show, Rachel having moved to another town.

7. *Use commas to separate elements in place names, dates, and titles of people:*

> Troy left on May 27, 1999, to go to Norman, Oklahoma, for the interview.
>
> He lives in Rome, Georgia, having been transferred there from Miami, Ohio.
>
> Schriner, B. F., Allen, P. G., and Marreo, T. B., head the list of producers.
>
> The son of Tim James, Sr., is listed as Tim James, Jr., in our records.

The second comma must be used when the state follows the town or city and when the year follows both the month and day. When only the month and year are used, the use of commas around the year is optional. Use two or do not use any: *Betty was born in June, 1981,* or *Betty was born in June 1981.* In the dateline of a letter, punctuation is optional. It was formerly common practice to write *July 7, 1977;* increasingly popular is the form *7 July 1977.* Both are acceptable. For clarity, always separate two numerals; where a word intervenes, the comma may be omitted, if you prefer.

Using Commas to Enclose or Set Off

Use commas to set off or enclose interrupting constructions. **A word or phrase that** comes between a subject and its verb is an interrupter of sentence sense. So is any element that comes between a verb and its complement or object. Some interrupters are necessary and, when used, should be set off in order not to confuse the basic pattern of the sentence.

Use commas to set off nonrestrictive phrases and clauses. A *nonrestrictive* (nonessential) phrase or clause is *not necessary* to the meaning of the sentence. It merely adds information about a word that is already identified:

> Rafe Silva, who lives across the street, is the most exciting designer.

In this sentence, the nonessential clause *who lives across the street* is not needed to identify Rafe Silva. Since it could be omitted from the sentence, it is nonrestrictive and thus set off by commas.

A *restrictive* (essential) phrase or clause, on the other hand, contains information that is *necessary* to the meaning of the sentence. An essential element limits or restricts the meaning of the word it modifies by identifying the particular one that is meant:

> The person who lives across the street is the local eccentric.

In this sentence, the descriptive clause is needed to identify the person. It is essential and therefore not set off by commas.

Consider these pairs of examples:

> The Laramie Project, telling about the death of Mathew Shepard, is well written.
> The play that tells about Shepard is well written.

> The actress my brother met in Los Angeles has traveled extensively.
> Angela Summerfield, whom my brother met in Los Angeles, has traveled widely.

> Tourists, who can usually be recognized by their cameras, seem to outnumber the native population on Miami Beach.
> Tourists who visit Miami for vacations are treated like special guests.

Remember that commas are used to enclose nonrestrictive (nonessential) phrases and that no commas are needed if the phrases are restrictive (essential).

1. *Use commas to set off parenthetical words, phrases, and clauses.* A test of a *parenthetical* expression is this: It can be omitted without changing the basic meaning of the sentence. Here is another test: Frequently, though not always, its position in the sentence can be shifted without any change in meaning:

> However, we do not disagree very much about quality writing.
> We do not, however, disagree very much about quality writing.
> We must, on the other hand, consider every aspect of the production.
> I believe, if anyone should ask my opinion, that opening night should be postponed.

Parenthetic elements vary in intensity, and you show their relative strength by means of punctuation (commas, parentheses). Some expressions are so weak that they require no punctuation.

2. *Use commas to set off words in a direct address (vocatives).* A *vocative* is a noun, pronoun, or noun phrase used in a direct address. That is, a vocative indicates the person to whom something is said. A vocative may appear at various positions within a sentence:

Hey, you, come over here.

John, will you perform for us next?

Will you please, sir, speak more distinctly?

We are here, pig face, to discuss an important problem.

3. *Use commas to set off words in apposition.* A word in *apposition*—that is, an *appositive*—is a noun or pronoun (word or phrase) that identifies a preceding noun or pronoun using different words. Usually, the appositive is explanatory and therefore nonrestrictive. But occasionally, it is restrictive in meaning; then, the commas are omitted:

His father, a television director, retired from Channel 6 last spring.

This is Dean Cantrell, our newly elected Equity representative.

Nell Gwyn was the famous mistress of the English king.

Haidee Gunderson, our supervisor, was a considerate woman.

My task, to write a ten-minute play, seemed hopeless.

Using Commas to Set Off Introductory Elements

Several introductory sentence elements need to be set off from the rest of the sentence with a comma. In effect, these elements act as interrupters, delaying the main thought of the sentence. The comma serves both to separate these elements and to introduce the main idea that follows.

1. *Use a comma following an introductory adverbial clause.* Remember that a clause expresses a complete thought, but in this case, it becomes a modifier. Among the many words used to begin the adverbial clause are *because, when, while, if, before* and *after:*

Before Martin started memorizing his lines, he highlighted just his dialogue.

If I arrive first, I'll wait for you in the lobby.

Many introductory adverbial clauses are simply transposed elements. Inserted in their customary order, they may or may not have commas, depending on their meaning. Inserted elsewhere, they are enclosed by commas:

After you arrive at the theatre, the stage manager will guide you.

The stage manager, after you arrive at the theatre, will guide you.

When the adverbial clause follows the independent clause, omit the comma if the adverbial clause is necessary to complete the meaning of the sentence:

> The stage manager will guide you after you arrive at the theatre.
>
> Marilyn wrote her own one-woman show because she was sick of waiting tables.
>
> Many actors have jumpstarted their careers because they have learned how to write.

Note that an introductory noun clause is not set off by a comma. Also, an adjective clause *follows* the noun or pronoun that it modifies:

> That your final script was turned in late is unfortunate. [Noun clause]
>
> The playwright whom you were talking to is my aunt Simone. [Adjective clause]

   2. *Use a comma following a series of introductory prepositional phrases and following a long prepositional phrase:*

> On the stage, in the aisles, in the lobby, litter was everywhere.
>
> After a long walk across the city to the theatre, we were glad to rest before the curtain went up.
>
> In a funky little shop in Greenwich Village, we bought a long piece of red silk.

Use a comma following an introductory participial phrase:

> Acting on the advice of the producer, we bought some stock in the company.
>
> Standing in the line at the front of the stage, Lacey knew where she belonged.

   3. *Use a comma to introduce a short quotation, especially in writing dialogue:*

> Frankie said, "Get outta my face or I'll hurt you."

If the *he said* or its equivalent follows the quotation, it is separated by a comma, provided that a question mark or exclamation point is not demanded:

> "I ain't leaving without my money," said Paula.
>
> "If I give it to yah, will you leave me alone?" asked Frankie.

If the *he said* or its equivalent is inserted between the parts of a quotation, it is enclosed by commas:

> "I'll leave you alone forever," he said, "until I run outta money."

When the quotation being introduced is long or formal, a colon replaces the comma.

Sam Shepard is quoted in *Playwrights in Rehearsal* about ending a play:

> I never know when to end a play. I'd just as soon not end anything. But you have to stop at some point, just to let people out of the theatre. I don't like endings and I have a hard time with them. . . . A resolution isn't an ending, it's a strangulation. (Cole, 2001, p. 25)

Make a careful distinction between quotations that are really quotations of speaking or writing and quoted material that is the subject or object of a verb or is material identified by quotation marks, such as titles, slang, and special word uses. See the following examples:

> His usual remark is, "Up your puppy with a meat hook."
>
> "Make friends quickly, but make love slowly" is the motto that came to my mind.

If the "he said" comes between parts of a quotation, it is enclosed by commas.

> "Stink pot" is not the exact phrase to use for a warm greeting.

4. *Don't use unnecessary commas.* Be able to account for each comma in your writing. A comma must be *needed* for sentence construction, clarity, or effectiveness. Do not use commas needlessly to separate closely related sentence elements. Some of the most common misuses or overuses of the comma are discussed in the following:

- *Do not use a comma before an indirect quotation.* No comma is needed in this sentence: *The stage manager asserted that she stood squarely by the rules.*
- *Do not use a comma indiscriminately to replace a word that has been omitted.* The word *that* in an indirect quotation, the word *that* in introducing another noun clause as an object, and the relative pronouns *who, whom, which,* and *that* are frequently omitted in informal writing. They should not be replaced by commas. In *Like a star Lina replied, she would return next week,* the comma is incorrectly used for *that.* (The comma also comes between a subject and its verb.) In *The person, I met was a friend of a friend of mine,"* whom should replace the comma or the comma may be omitted. *She thought, that the man was dead* should be written *She thought that the man was dead.*
- *Do not use a comma between two independent clauses; a stronger mark of punctuation (semicolon, period) is needed.* Confusion is always caused by this misuse, sometimes called the *comma fault* or *comma splice.* Use a period or semicolon in place of the comma in a statement like this one:

My director told me to come to rehearsal early, I told her I couldn't.

■ *Do not use a comma or pair of commas with words in apposition that are actually restrictive.* The following bold words really limit, identify, or define; they should not be enclosed with commas:

Eugene O'Neill's play **A Long Days Journey into Night** is one of his greatest.

My cousin **Cameron Diaz** is a lovely actress.

Richard Maxwell **of the Juggerknot Theatre** was a follower of Kozinsky.

■ *Do not use a comma in any situation unless it adds clarity and understanding.* Comma usage is slowly growing more open. In the following sentences, every comma can be justified, but each could be omitted, since clarity would not be affected in the slightest degree:

After the play, Maria and I went home, by taxicab, because we wanted, at all costs, to avoid subway crowds.

Naturally, the last thing you should do, before leaving the theatre, is make sure the coffee pot is off.

Of all marks of punctuation, commas are the most frequently used and the most important for clarity. Use them when necessary to make your meaning clear. Avoid using them when they slow down thought, interrupt, or make your writing look as if you have used a comma shaker.

Editing

A play that is tight has nothing superfluous. Editing is important. After completing your first rough draft and getting feedback, decide what changes are needed for the second draft:

1. What must be done to revise the script for the final draft?

2. What characters can be eliminated or combined?

3. Do you need to change the gender of a character?

4. What editing needs to be done?
   a. Shorten or eliminate scenes that are too long or static.
   b. Cut lines that are wooden, unbelievable, or repetitive.
   c. Make cuts to shorten the playing time.
   d. Clarify your intent or meaning.
   e. Cut elaborate, long-winded stage directions.
   f. Edit every speech in the play to remove unnecessary words.
   g. Reduce the number of scene changes and time changes.

5. What specific problems must be addressed?
   a. Create a more distinct voice for each character.
   b. Raise the stakes.
   c. Develop a scene more.
   d. Develop a character more to add depth.
   e. Provide a different ending.
   f. Add more physical activity.
   g. Correct all typos, misspellings, and grammatical errors.

EXERCISE 22

All Levels

Write the second draft, making all the needed changes and corrections.

Copyright

Once you have completed editing your script, you may want to send a copy to the Library of Congress and register it formally for copyright protection. Copyright information is easily available on the Internet and in books and other resources. (You can find the United States Copyright Office at http://lcweb.loc.gov/copyright and the Copyright Website at www.benedict.com:80.) I am not a lawyer and cannot give you legal advice. But as a teacher, I strongly recommend that you check out the sites just mentioned for more detailed information.

Granting a *copyright* is how the law protects people who create original works of authorship. It gives the copyright owner the right to determine who can use his or her work and how. This right can be sold or licensed to someone else. It can be bought in advance for work someone has hired you to do, as in *work for hire.* The copyright exists as soon as the original work is created in a tangible form. Ideas and thoughts cannot be copyrighted, but as soon as you put them in tangible form on paper, on a disk, in an e-mail, or in computer code, they can be copyrighted.

In general, a copyright established after 1978 lasts until seventy years after the author's death. The work also has to be creative, not just factual. But any original play you write is considered creative. And even though factual data can't be copyrighted, a play based on those facts can be. (That doesn't mean, however, that you can use the actual wording from other documents without permission.)

No printed copyright notice is required on copyrighted material. If you wonder why there are copyright notices on plays and other works, it is because doing so serves as a warning to people not to violate the copyright.

Things like titles, names, characters, slogans, blank forms, and information that is common property (i.e., taken from public documents and other common sources) cannot be copyrighted. However, titles, slogans, and the like can be trademarked, but that involves a different process.

Copyright has to do with protecting your right to profit from your creative labors. Obviously, if you write a play, you want to be the one to benefit from the public performance or sale of published copies of your work. Copyright infringement suits usually don't happen unless some serious money is involved. So really, to be enforced, a copyright should have some commercial value to it. A regular e-mail, for instance, usually has no commercial value, but when a play is posted anywhere on the Internet, it definitely means it is being published. Anyone with access to the Internet can read it, and by giving it away free, you can damage that value.

When you formally register a play with the Library of Congress, a public record is created of the basic facts of that particular copyright and additional protection is provided. You may have evidence that a work is yours, but registering it gives you statutory and more easily enforceable rights. Should you desire to file an infringement suit, formal registration of the copyright is necessary. If you register a work within three months of publication or before infringement, you can receive statutory damages and attorney's fees in court actions. Otherwise, you get only actual damages and profits. To register your play costs thirty dollars and involves filling out a form and sending a copy of your work to the Library of Congress. The forms are available online.

Do not confuse *publication rights* and *copyright*. The right to publish something is what you offer when you submit a play to Dramatists Play Service, Inc.; Samuel French, Inc.; Broadway Publishing; or one of the other publishers of plays. Your copyright already exists; you are offering a publisher the permission to publish it. You are selling the exclusive right to publish your work one time and for the first time. Geographic limits may also be stated: *First North American, World,* and so on. You retain all other rights. If you sell "All Rights" to your work, it means you are selling your right ever to use the material again in any form.

It is important to consult with the Dramatists Guild before signing any contract for a professional production of your play and to consult a theatre lawyer before signing away future rights related to recordings, film, television, video, or the Internet.

Summary

Writing and then rewriting your first draft mean more than just correcting typographical errors. Editing involves many decisions about revising the script for the next draft. Can you reduce the number of characters by eliminating or combining some roles? Do you need to change the gender of a character? Other editing questions to ask yourself include the following. Do you need to:

1. Shorten or eliminate scenes that are too long or static?
2. Cut lines that are wooden, unbelievable, or repetitive?
3. Make cuts to shorten the playing time?
4. Clarify your intent or meaning?

5. Cut long-winded stage directions?
6. Reduce the number of scene changes and change the time?
7. Provide a different ending?
8. Add more physical activity?
9. Bring the outside world into the play more through the use of sound effects, props, and lighting?
10. Raise the stakes?
11. Find a more distinct voice for each character?
12. Write more believable dialogue?
13. Develop a scene more?
14. Provide more depth for a character?
15. Edit each speech of the play, removing all unnecessary words?
16. Correct all typos, misspellings, and grammatical errors?

The comma is the most widely used of all punctuation marks and serves many different purposes. Because of its varied and distinct uses, however, it is the most troublesome of punctuation marks. Its overuse and misuse also obscure meaning more than the misapplication of any punctuation marks. Regardless, this mark of punctuation, more than any other, can help to clarify the meaning of writing.

Granting a *copyright* is how the law protects people who create original works of authorship. It gives the copyright owner the right to determine who can use his or her work and how. This right can be sold or licensed to someone else. It can be bought in advance for work someone has hired you to do, as in *work for hire*. The copyright exists as soon as the original work is created in a tangible form. Ideas and thoughts cannot be copyrighted, but once on paper, on a disk, in an e-mail, or in computer code, they are copyrighted. A copyright established after 1978 lasts until seventy years after the author's death. Copyright information is easily available on the Internet and in books and other resources. Locate the U.S. Copyright Office at http://lcweb.loc.gov/copyright and the Copyright Website at www.benedict.com:80.

18 Readings, Contests, Productions, and Other Opportunities

The Next Step

Once you have the play written, there are numerous possibilities for getting it produced and eventually published. Never send off a first draft, however. No matter how good you may think it is, a week later, you will begin to see some of the faults in this draft. You will have ideas about rewriting it as soon as you get some feedback from others. Therefore, wait until you are sure the play is as good as you can make it before sending it off.

Just as there are many talented actors who don't get acting jobs, there are many talented playwrights who don't get produced. If you wish to succeed, you must keep working and writing. You must also not take the rejection of your script personally. You must learn how to market your work and yourself effectively. You must be aggressive: Find the information and follow the guidelines set forth by every theatre, contest, or other opportunity.

Most commercial productions of new plays in recent years have come from nonprofit theatres, either regional theatres found in major American cities or off-off-Broadway. New York has many small theatres devoted to new plays. Each has its own philosophy and mission. Some theatres only look for plays for children, some do only musicals, and others will not even consider either one. Some theatres are looking for clean, entertaining, small-cast, one-set comedies. Others are looking for experimental, cutting-edge works. Some contests are primarily for women or for Hispanics or Asians or other special groups.

There is no point in submitting a children's play to a theatre that doesn't produce this type of work or in sending a play to a contest for women if you are a man. Most theatres will not accept a play that is not submitted by an agent. Most agents will not represent you until you have a track record. It's a catch-22 that requires you to learn the ways of the current theatre scene and how to develop a track record. If your play wins a contest or two, is selected for development at a conference or festival, or is given a staged reading by professionals, then you may at least get it read by an agent or a director.

Play development is a major step in the process for many theatres. This involves a company taking a script and working on it with the playwright so that its flaws are corrected and it connects with an audience. Part of this process is also making sure that the play that emerges is as close as possible to the playwright's vision. Rewrites are set in motion by discussions between the playwright and the director before rehearsals begin. Once in rehearsal—in collaboration with the director, designers, actors, and so on—the playwright continues to rewrite. Readings are given so that the writer can hear what's on the page and the director can get a firm grasp of the play. The actors involved in the process may also contribute their thoughts and feelings about the characters. The writer often begins to write with the voices of particular actors in his head.

Rather than send out scripts haphazardly, it is generally best first to write a letter to agents or theatres telling them about the play. The letter should briefly describe the story of the play, note the numbers of characters and sets, the style, and the history of the play (if it has had readings, a workshop production, or won any awards). If you have written other plays that have had some success, you might give a bit of your background in a short paragraph or attach a one-page résumé. It is essential that you understand the mission and follow the guidelines of each agency or theatre. That information is readily available in many sources.

In this chapter, we will explore some of the major sources of information for submission guidelines, discuss the kinds of production opportunities available, and examine kinds of theatre companies, contests, fellowships and grants, agents, colonies and residencies, workshops, and publishers.

Sources of Information

A number of publications provide information about the submission guidelines of specific theatre companies and contests, fellowships and grants, agents, colonies and residencies, workshops, and publishers.

The Dramatists Sourcebook is published every two years by Theatre Communications Group (355 Lexington Avenue, New York, NY 10017–0217). This book is available at Amazon.com, Barnes and Noble, Borders, and other bookstores. If you can't find a copy on the shelves, you can order one. Since this guide is very complete and updated every other year, it is a great reference to have. You can also become a member of Theatre Communications Group (see later in this chapter). The benefits include (1) a subscription to *American Theatre Magazine,* which publishes many new scripts each year; (2) a discount price for *ArtSearch,* a bimonthly listing of jobs available throughout the United States, and (3) a discount on the purchase of various publications, including *The Dramatists Sourcebook.*

Backstage is a weekly newspaper published in New York. Outside New York, it may be obtained by subscription. This publication covers stage, film, and TV, providing information on all the auditions for actors every week for Broadway and off-Broadway theatres, regional theatres, touring companies, summer stock, outdoor dramas, film and TV. It also includes many features on playwriting opportunities, agents, how to find what you need in the city at reasonable prices, reviews of plays, and everything else important to the theatre professional.

Other excellent sources of information are available to writers when they join the Dramatists Guild, the professional union for playwrights, composers, and lyricists (see later in this chapter). It publishes *The Resource Directory*, which lists conferences, festivals, contests, producers, publishers, and theatres as well as agents, attorneys, colonies and residences, emergency funds, fellowships and grants, membership and service organizations, and workshops. Members of the Guild are invited to attend informative and insightful symposia, held nationwide.

There are also a variety of books that may be helpful, such as *Marketing Strategies for Writers*, by Michael Sedge (published by Allworth Press, New York); *The Script Is Finished, Now What Do I Do?* by K. Callan (published by Sweden Press, Studio City, CA); and Louis E. Catron's *Writing, Producing, and Selling Your Play* (published by Prentice-Hall). They all give useful information about submitting your script.

Information about copyright and other legal and business aspects of playwriting can be found online and in the following sources: *The Copyright Book*, by William S. Strong (published by the MIT Press, Cambridge, MA); *The Rights of Authors, Artists, and Other Creative People*, by Kenneth P. Norwick and Jerry Simon Chasen (Southern Illinois University Press); and *Producing Theatre: A Comprehensive Legal and Business Guide*, by Donald C. Farber (published by Limelight Editions).

Memberships

Some of the larger theatre cities—such as New York, Los Angeles, Chicago, Atlanta, Austin, St. Louis, Minneapolis, Philadelphia, and Boston—have organizations that provide playwrights a supportive environment to develop and present their work. Some are national in scope; others are regional, state, or local. A few of the major organizations are described in the following sections, but for a larger overview of support groups across the United States, check one of the information sources noted previously, such as *The Dramatists Sourcebook*.

The Dramatists Guild

The Dramatists Guild of America is the only professional association for playwrights, composers, and lyricists. Guided by an elected council, which gives its time, interest, and support for the benefit of writers everywhere, the Dramatists Guild works to advance the rights of its more than six thousand members, spanning around the globe. Membership is open to all dramatic writers, regardless of their production history. You can learn more about the guild, including how to join, by going to the group's website: www.dramaguild.com.

Any writer who has completed a dramatic script may become a member of the Dramatists Guild of America and receive a wide range of benefits: business affairs advice, contract review, and publications. The business affairs department offers assistance to members on a wide range of contractual issues. The lawyers in the department will examine your contract and provide you with detailed information involving its negotiation. In certain situations, you may use the Guild's standard or model contracts, available only to Guild members. Also through the business affairs department, members may receive advice on theatre-related matters such as options, commissions, contracts, producers, publishers, agents, and attorneys.

Members also have access to third-party health and dental insurance programs and a group term-life insurance plan. Other benefits include a Dramatists Guild credit card, free or discounted theatre tickets to certain New York productions, national hotel and travel discounts, and access to the Guild's Frederick Loewe Room in the heart of the theatre district for use in readings and auditions.

The categories of membership in the Dramatists Guild are as follows:

1. *Active members* have been produced on a first-class/Broadway, off-Broadway, or mainstage of a regional theatre (LORT) contract. Active members have full voting privileges and annually elect representatives to the council (board of directors). An application must be accompanied by a copy of a review or program from the qualifying production. Annual membership dues are $125.

2. *Associate members* are all other theatrical writers, without precondition of production or publication, who may be elevated to active members when the criteria is met. An application must be accompanied either by a completed script written by the applicant or by a program or review of a production. Annual dues are $75.

3. *Student members* must be currently enrolled in an accredited writing degree program. An application must be accompanied by a letter from the program's senior administrator indicating the expected date of graduation. Student members are eligible to become associate members upon graduation. Annual dues are $35.

The Dramatists Guild offers monthly symposia on numerous issues every year. Past symposia have included interviews with Stephen Sondheim, Marsha Norman, Terrence McNally, Arthur Miller, and many others; the secrets of applying for playwriting grants; panel discussions with emerging writers; the business side of writing for theatre; and getting your work produced in the United Kingdom.

Theatre Communications Group

Theatre Communications Group (TCG) is a national service organization whose mission is "to strengthen, nurture, and promote the not-for-profit American theatre." TCG serves over 425 member theatres and has 17,000 individual members. Its programs and services include *American Theatre Magazine;* the ArtSEARCH employment bulletin; plays, translations, and theatre reference books; grants to theatres and theatre artists ($4.4 million in 2001–2002); workshops, conferences, forums, and publications for theatre professionals and trustees; research on not-for-profit theatre finances and practices; arts advocacy; and the U.S. Center of the International Theatre Institute. The cost of membership (individuals $39.95 and students $20.00) is worth it just for *American Theatre Magazine,* which provides an overview of all the professional regional theatres in the United States and often includes the complete script of a new play. The TCG website is www.tcg.org/index.cfm.

Austin Script Works

Austin Script Works, in Austin, Texas, is a playwright-centered organization that provides support for playwrights at all stages of the writing process. An associate membership is open to everyone, and benefits include participation in readings and the ten-minute play playwriting retreat, the ten-minute play showcase productions, and the Harvest Festival Member discounts are provided on all Script Works events.

Chicago Dramatists

Chicago Dramatists is dedicated to the development of playwrights and new plays. Membership provides a wide variety of services, including a professional playwright's critique of your play; classes, workshops, readings, productions, and panels; collaborative projects with other theatres and festivals; national playwright exchanges; and referrals to producers. I have found their critiques to be insightful, detailed, and helpful.

New Dramatists

New Dramatists, in New York City, is located in the theatre district not far from Times Square. As the nation's oldest playwright development center, it was created to give member playwrights the resources they need to create plays for the American theatre. New Dramatists helps playwrights through play readings and workshops; dramaturgy; a resident director program; musical theatre development and training; ScriptShare (a national script distribution program); fellowships, awards, and prizes; a free-ticket program for Broadway and off-Broadway productions; writing spaces and accommodations; and photocopying. All these services are provided free to members.

Membership is open to emerging playwrights who live in the greater New York area and to those living outside the area who demonstrate a willingness to travel regularly to New York and actively participate in that community of artists. Playwrights interested in applying for membership should check the guidelines at www.newdramatists.org/member_application.htm.

The Playwrights' Center

The Playwrights' Center, in Minneapolis, Minnesota, is a service organization for playwrights. Its programs include developmental services (cold readings and workshops using an Equity acting company); fellowships; exchanges with theatres and other developmental programs; a biannual journal; the Jones commissioning program; PlayLabs; playwriting classes; year-round programs for young writers; and the Many Voices program, designed to provide awards, education, and lab services to new and emerging playwrights of color. The Center annually awards five Jerome Playwright-in-Residence Fellowships, for which competition is open nationally; two McKnight Fellowships, for which competition is open by professional nomination; three McKnight Advancement Grants open to Minnesota playwrights; and three Many Voices Multicultural Collaboration Grants.

A broad-based Center membership is available to any playwright or interested person. Benefits of general membership for playwrights include discounts on classes, applications for all Center programs, eligibility to apply for the Jones commission and script-development readings, and the Center's journal. Core (must be a Minnesota resident) and associate member playwrights are selected by a review panel each spring, based on script submission. They have primary access to all Center programs and services, including developmental workshops and public readings. Write for Membership information or go to the Center's website: www.pwcenter.org.

Production Opportunities

Readings

The best way for a playwright to determine the strengths and weaknesses of her play is to hear it. *Cold readings* are those in which actors are gathered and read a script aloud, with no rehearsal. Following these kinds of readings, the participants and observers generally provide feedback to the writer. The playwright working on her own can enlist friends and relatives to read the play aloud in her living room.

When writers hear their plays for the first time, they notice the difference between the written and spoken word. Good actors bring new dimensions to words. They know how to use their voices. However, at this stage, there is often a discrepancy between what sounded good to the writer in his head and what sounds good on stage. There is a difference in timing. Writers have to hear their plays to know what needs compression or expansion. There are moments that happen too quickly, trivial things that take up too much time, and lines that are repetitive. These are the things that directors, actors, and dramaturges point out.

Staged Readings

Many college theatre programs, community theatres, and even local semiprofessional and professional theatres offer opportunities for readings. These range anywhere from an occasional gathering of amateur actors, who read the play with no rehearsals, to a regular sophisticated theatre series for subscribers of readings done by professional directors and actors, who rehearse the script for days and present a staged reading. In a staged reading, the actors carry the scripts for reference, but they often have had time to study the characters and work out some of the general movements. Such a staged reading with skilled actors is able to provide a good indication of whether the story works.

Workshop Productions

A workshop production is a very low-budget affair. Its purpose is to mount a production of the play with actors who are fully committed to the roles and perform the play in front of an audience to see how it works. During the rehearsal process, the playwright is able to do some rewriting and tweak the script here and there to improve it. The production values—sets, costumes, lighting, sound, and props—are minimal. Sometimes, a full set, costumes, and the rest are provided, but they are still simplified. Sometimes, the show is done in front of black drapes with stock furniture and props and basic lighting.

Other Productions

When a play is selected by a theatre for a fully mounted production, the theatre company—producers, directors, designers, actors, technicians, front-of-the house staff—seeks to collaborate with the author to bring the play to life as she envisioned. A new work may be selected for production by a college or university, an amateur or semiprofessional community theatre, or a professional theatre. Professional theatres are members of LORT (the League of Resident Theatres) and must abide by union rules. There are four levels of regional theatres, which are determined by size, budget, and other considerations. Broadway, off-Broadway, and off-off-Broadway theatres in New York are categorized basically according to the size of the theatre house—specifically, the number of seats.

A few new plays get produced on Broadway because of incredible luck, because somebody knows somebody who knows *somebody,* and because they are viewed as commercially viable. However, the majority of plays generally come up through the ranks, starting with readings, a workshop production here and there, and a production at a small regional theatre. Then, if some producers are attracted to the show and feel the play is worth the risk, they may produce it off-off Broadway or off-Broadway. An extremely successful off-Broadway production sometimes transfers to Broadway.

A new playwright should begin at the local level and try to find a theatre willing to provide a reading of his work. If, after a couple of readings and rewrites, the play is considered worthy of production, the playwright should again start at the local level and try to find an area theatre willing to produce it. Another option is to enter the play in a contest or competition for further development.

Other Development Opportunities

There are a number of major festivals, theatres, and other organizations whose primary purpose is to work with emerging playwrights. The O'Neill National Playwrights Conference and the Bay Area Playwrights Festival are two of the most well known.

Probably the most prestigious and most competitive is the National Playwrights Conference at the O'Neill Theatre Center in Waterford, Connecticut. Nine to eleven plays are selected for staged readings at the month-long conference annually in July, which is attended by professional actors, directors, and dramaturgs. A couple of my former students have had works presented at these conferences, and I attended a few sessions and a reading in 1999. Their website is www.theoneill.org.

The Bay Area Playwrights Festival, in San Francisco, is another major opportunity for playwrights. Six to twelve scripts (unproduced, full-length plays only) are selected annually and given dramaturgical attention—two rehearsed readings separated by five or six days for rewrites during a two-week festival. For those selected, there is a mandatory prefestival weekend retreat for initial brainstorming with directors and dramaturgs. For information, e-mail the festival at bayplays@best.com.

Information about other festivals, conferences, retreats, and theatres that specialize in developing new works across the United States can be found at the following websites:

Asian American Theater Company Project   www.naatco.org/index.html

Greensboro Playwrights Forum   www.ci.greensboro.nc.us/leisure/drama/gpforum.htm

Baltimore Theatre Festival   www.baltimoreplaywrightsfestival.org

Playlabs   www.pwcenter.org/playlabs.asp

Sundance Theatre Laboratory   www.institute.sundance.org/jsp/site.jsp?resource=pag_ex_home

Additional information can be found in the sources noted at the beginning of this chapter.

Contests

There are hundreds of contests for new plays every year in the United States. About 125 are listed in *The Dramatists Sourcebook,* and many others are sponsored by universities and various local arts organizations. Most of the contests have no fees, but a few have begun charging fees to pay for the readers. In most cases, the fee is nominal. The prizes are varied and include awards ranging from $25 to $3,000 or more; a staged reading or a production; and travel expenses and housing.

Even if you don't win, some of the contests will send you one-page evaluations from readers. The primary benefits for those who win, in addition to the money, are the readings and productions. This is also an indication that the play has some artistic merit. It is not unusual for a really strong script to pick up several awards. When this happens, it is easier to get the play read by agents, literary managers, and directors and considered for a professional production.

American Theatre Magazine recently published the play *A. M. Sunday*, by Jerome Hairston. It was written while he was a student at Columbia and was further developed in a series of readings in the Black Ink Series at Playwrights Horizon, the Genesis Festival at the Crossroads Theatre Company, and the O'Neill Theatre Center's National Playwrights Conference. The success of having his play worked on and read at these three competitive events helped Hairston get the play accepted and produced at the Annual Humana Festival at the Actors Theatre of Louisville.

Information about contests can be obtained in *The Dramatists Sourcebook*, publications by the Dramatists Guild, online at the websites for various theatres and support organizations, and through local and state arts agencies.

Types of Theatre Companies

As noted earlier, each theatre has its own mission and philosophy. Some focus on presenting plays for young audiences. Some are dinner theatres looking for light entertainment. Others are seeking plays that deal with social, political, and psychological issues or perhaps with multicultural issues. Still others are looking for musicals and reviews.

A few theatres accept unsolicited manuscripts, but most theatres will not accept unsolicited scripts. They require that you write a letter of inquiry and include a synopsis and a résumé. The following is a typical example:

> *St. Louis Black Repertory Company* (634 North Grand Blvd., Suite 10-F, St. Louis, MO, 63103) requires the playwright to send a synopsis, a three- to five-page dialogue sample, a résumé, and a letter of inquiry. The material this theatre is looking for includes full-length plays, plays for young audiences, and musicals. There is special interest in works by African American and Third World playwrights. Facilities include the 470-seat Grandel Theatre with a thrust stage. The best submission time is June to August. The response time is two months for a letter and two months for a script. This theatre has a touring company that presents works for young audiences.

It is important to know the mission and interest of a theatre before sending it your script. Don't waste your postage to send out dozens of scripts to theatres at random. Some theatres have such specific and narrow interests that any script that does not fit their profile will not be read. On the other hand, when your play fits exactly the kind of material a theatre is looking for, you have a much stronger

[handwritten: DRAMATISTS SOURCEBOOK LISTS THEATERS THAT PRODUCE NEW PLAYS THEN CHECK FOR RELATED PLAYS THIS SEASON]

chance of having it considered. Read *American Theatre Magazine* to see what plays theatres are presenting this year. It provides an annual listing of all the major theatres seasons of plays each fall, and each issue has additional articles on some of these theatres, plays, and other events.

Fellowships and Grants

Various fellowships and grants are open to playwrights. Study the guidelines carefully, and then follow them meticulously. Don't hesitate to ask for advice and assistance from the organizations that sponsor the grants. Make sure you proofread your application for errors, and make sure it is mailed in time to meet the deadline. Once you have written one grant request, you can often modify it to fit other grants. As with contests and productions, the competition is strong. Don't waste your time unless you really meet the requirements. There are many international fellowships and grants for which knowledge of the language and culture is important. Contact state arts councils, service organizations, and your local university, or check online for information about programs and opportunities. Information about a few fellowships and grants can be found at the following websites:

[handwritten: READ HEDDA GABLER AND HAIRSPRAY]

Arizona Commission on the Arts   www.arizonaarts.org
John Simon Guggenheim Memorial Foundation   www.gf.org
New Play Commissions in Jewish Theatre   www.jewishculture.org
Playwrights' Center Grant Programs   www.pwcenter.org
Princess Grace Awards: Playwriting Fellowship   www.pgfusa.com

[handwritten: OTHERS?]

Agents

For information about agents, check with the Association of Authors' Representatives at (www.AAR-online.org) or ask for some names from the Dramatists Guild (www.dramaguild.com). If you have just finished your first play, don't waste an agent's time. Spend your own time working to get the play produced. Enter it in contests. Find local venues and organizations willing to help you develop it. If you have had work produced or published, then write a brief letter to an agent describing your work and ask if he or she would like to read a script. Include a professional résumé that demonstrates that you look at playwriting as an ongoing career, not a hobby.

Publishers

Plays are generally not published until after they have been produced. The three major publishers of plays in the United States are the Dramatists Play Service (www.dramatists.com), Samuel French, Inc. (www.samuelfrench.com), and Broadway Play Publishing, Inc. (www.broadwayplaypubl.com). Samuel French is a worldwide organization, with offices in New York, Hollywood, Sydney, London, and Toronto and affiliates in Germany and all over Eastern Europe. The company publishes 90 to 110 new titles a year. Dramatists Play Service publishes 40 to 45, and Broadway Play Publishing publishes an average of 15 a year. Broadway Play Publishing focuses on contemporary American full-length plays and wants "writing from imaginations not from personal traumas." These publishers control the rights and royalties for most of the amateur and professional productions in the United States including plays produced in high schools, colleges and universities, community theatres, dinner theatres, and regional theatres. Musicals are handled by TAMS-WITMARK and Music Theatre International.

Once your play has been produced and polished, any one of the three major publishers may be interested in publishing it, if it is a good play and they believe there is a market for it. You can send a copy of the script and a cover letter to Samuel French, Dramatists, or Broadway Publishing, noting that you are submitting it for consideration. Do not be surprised if the script is rejected, however. These publishers have high standards. If your play is produced in a professional theatre, your chances of getting it published will be increased. Bernard Kalos, executive director of Dramatists Play Service, said, "When it's a strong work there's hope. . . . If you get a rave review, . . . you'll be all set. It's close to that simple" (Wiener, 1990, p. 22).

In addition to the publishers noted, there are many others for you to consider, if your play meets their particular interests and specialties. Many publishers only accept specific kinds of material. Find out as much as possible about a publisher's operation before sending in a script. Dramatic Publishing Company (www.dramaticpublishing.com) publishes many plays for young audiences and high schools and some plays for professional, stock, and other amateur markets. If you've written a play for young audiences, this is an appropriate place to start. Eldridge Publishing Company (www.histage.com) is interested in musicals, comedies, mysteries, and serious dramas for church, school, and community theatres.

Submitting a Script

Whenever you submit a script, enclose a cover letter, a brief synopsis of the play, a résumé, and a self-addressed, stamped envelope (SASE) for the return of the manuscript. The script needs to be bound. Any script that is too thick, hard to read, full of typos and misspellings, unbound, wrapped in a rubber band, or difficult to handle will not be read. The cover letter needs to be well written and include a brief statement identifying what the play is about, the cast size, and the kind of setting (see Figure 18.1). A poorly written letter will also turn off potential readers.

In some situations, it may also be helpful to include a letter from a theatre professional recommending your work. If you want an acknowledgment that the

GEORGE SPELVIN
56 110TH ST.
NEW YORK, NEW YORK 11009

November 21, 2005

Rafael de Acha, Artistic Director
New Theatre
4120 Laguna Street
Coral Gables, FL 33146

Dear Mr. de Acha,

I am submitting a copy of my play *Tennessee Tom* for your New Works of Merit Contest. In keeping with the guidelines, this is a full-length, nonrealistic play about Tennessee Williams. It has a simple, nonrealistic set with three areas: his office in Key West, a bedroom, and a sofa and chair sitting area. There is a cast of four men and two women.

The play takes place in one night in May in 1968, as the relationship between Tom and his latest lover comes to a violent end. Suffering from the failure of his latest play and the effects of alcohol and drugs, Tom slips in and out of reality. He is visited by demons from the past who haunt him, including his mother, his sister, and his long-time love, Frank Merlo.

The play is unpublished and unproduced. It did win the national Key West Playwriting Festival and was given a staged reading last August. With the feedback from that event, I have since revised it.

Thank-you for your consideration.

Sincerely,

George Spelvin

George Spelvin

Enclosures

FIGURE 18.1   Sample Cover Letter

script has been received, include a self-addressed, stamped postcard. Do not call a theatre or any other organization to find out if it has received or read your script. Keep a record of what you have sent out to whom and when. Do not e-mail a script unless that is specifically requested.

Summary

There are numerous opportunities to explore once your play has been written. Never send off a first draft, however. No matter how good you may think it is, you will soon have ideas about rewriting it. Wait until you have polished several drafts and the play is as good as you can make it before sending it off.

You must learn how to market your work and yourself effectively. You must also not take the rejection of your script personally. You must be aggressive. Find the information and follow the guidelines set forth by every theatre, contest, or other opportunity. Each theatre and organization has its own philosophy, mission, and goals. You need to find out what those are before submitting a script. First, you need to locate the sources. Then, consider memberships, development and production opportunities, contests, fellowships and grants, and agents and publishers. Determine the best possibilities for submitting your script. When you send it out, always include a cover letter and a self-addressed, stamped envelope.

(1) locate sources / follow guidelines

(2) consider memberships, [ara] development, production opportunities, contests, fellowships, grants, agents, publishers

APPENDIX A

Sample Course Syllabus

PROFESSOR _____

WEBSITE _____

Course No. _____ Section _____ Department _____

Credits _____ Class meeting times _____ Bldg and Room _____

Office address _____ Office phone _____

Office hours _____ E-mail _____

Overview of Assignments

T   Overview of the class, review syllabus, discuss expectations, class introductions.

TH   Read Chapter 1. Do Exercise 1-A: Write a scene in which Character A confides to Character B an inner conflict over what she wants to do and believes is morally right. This will be assessed, but not graded.

T   Read Chapter 14. Do Exercise 2-A: Write a scene in which the protagonist and antagonist battle over something personal and use a variety of tactics or play different roles to try to reach their individual objective.

TH   Read Chapter 15. Do Exercise 3-A: Write a scene in which Character A seeks to deal with a social problem in society. Character B represents the other side of the issue and opposes Character A.

T   Read Chapter 16. Video and Discussion.

TH   Read Chapter 2 and 13. Do Exercise 4-A: Consider a situation in your past that resulted in a change of perception and behavior. Write a monologue in which a character responds to such an incident. Have the character speaking in an immediate conflict in which she uses the past event to achieve a current objective.

T   Read Chapter 3. Do Exercise 5: Write the first scene of your play. Select a relevant working title and the names of your characters. Give a brief description of each one. Visualize the setting. Try to jump into the conflict quickly.

TH   Read Chapter 4. Do Exercise 6-A: For several days, jot down in a journal descriptions of people and locales that you find intriguing. Pick any two of the most colorful people and one locale and write a five- to seven-page scene in which the characters clash.

T   Do Exercise 7: Write a scenario of your play. Who is in each scene, what happens, and what is different at the end of the scene?

TH   Read Chapter 5. Do Exercise 8-A: Write a continuous scene with two sequences, one horizontal and one vertical, in which Character A tries to learn a secret of Character B's past.

T   Read Chapter 6. Do Exercise 9-A: Use the action plot, write a three-person scene with a beginning, middle, and end that builds to a climax.

TH   Read Chapter 7. Do Exercise 10-A: Write a linear scene using the stimulus/ response model. In the scene, Character A and Character B each tries to win Character C to his or her side.

T   Exercise 11-A: Select an organic object such as a twig, a piece of natural wood, a leaf, a vegetable, a fruit, a flower, or a weed. Write a conflict scene that in your mind is shaped like the object.

TH   Read Chapter 8. Do Exercise 12-A: Write a scene in which there is a physical obstacle within the locale. This obstacle must be something that affects the characters in the scene.

T   Read Chapter 9. Do Exercise 13-A: Make a list of the ten most important events in the life of a character. These are the major events that have shaped that person. Pick one event in the growing up of your character that clarifies the social aspects. Write a five-page conflict scene in which Character A uses that event to gain sympathy from Character B. (First review due.)

TH   Read Chapter 10. Do Exercise 14-A: Using the Johari window as a model of human interaction, write a conflict scene between two or three characters. Character A digs into one of Character B's secrets, perhaps exposing it to a third character, while Character B exposes Character A's blind self.

T   Do Exercise 15-A: Action is the clearest indicator of character. Write a scene in which a character makes a decision at the beginning of the scene with unexpected consequences.

TH   Read Chapter 11. Do Exercise 16-A: Write a scene in which your characters are in conflict yet bonded in a crucible they cannot leave. The cause of the conflict should be a third character not present.

T   Read Chapter 12. Do Exercise 17-A: Form a partnership with another writer. Set the ground rules for the process and work together to write a ten-minute play, ten pages long, with two characters of very different voices, backgrounds, educations, and professions.

TH   Read Chapter 17. Do Exercise 21: Complete your first draft. Thirty pages minimum. Presentation of your first draft in class. Please bring a script for each character. We will plan in advance the day for the presentation of your first draft so you will know when to bring extra scripts. We will plan to read two scripts during each class. One-half point will be taken off for every error in punctuation, format, spelling, grammar, or spacing. Anyone wanting to do extra credit may write Exercises 18, 19, and 20. These must be turned in at the first class after Thanksgiving.

T   Class presentations continued.

TH   Class presentations continued. Do Exercise 22: Your final draft will be due one week after your class presentation of the first draft.

T   Class presentations continued.

TH   Class presentations continued.

T   Class presentations continued. (Second review due.)

TH   Thanksgiving—No class.

T   Class presentations continued.

TH   Class presentations continued.

Note

Writing isn't easy. There may be a week when your effort to do an exercise is a total failure. You may end up writing a scene that doesn't fit the assignment. What is important is that you come to class with something—that you try. In some classes there will be times when it is impossible for everyone to read his or her work aloud. Sometimes you may want to share a scene. Sometimes you may not. I'll try to allow for individual eccentricities up to a point, but I want you to try. I want you to make the effort. Please don't get hung up on being perfect. There is no such thing as perfect. Seldom are first drafts of a scene absolutely wonderful. This is an environment in which to write and explore, an environment where it is okay to risk failure, an environment where you will get honest and positive feedback. You will really only learn from your mistakes.

During Class Discussions

It is important when criticizing the work of others that:

1. You respond with positive comments about what you liked and why, what stimulated you, what touched you.
2. You discuss what didn't work for you and why, what seemed inconsistent or underdeveloped or clichéd or out of character or didn't hold your attention or seemed confusing. Do not critique the author, critique the work.
3. Be careful about telling another writer how to write his or her piece by explaining what you would do or how you would rewrite it. Just respond to the work. Let the writer decide how and what to rewrite or change. If you have a suggestion, ask the playwright if he or she would like to hear it.

4. Each of you should check your ego at the door. You should remain silent and listen unless asked a direct question. Do not defend your work or explain or make any comments about its meaning. The argumentative playwright who doesn't listen will short circuit responses and not hear feedback. Shut up and listen, take notes if you wish, and then use what you find valuable and discard the rest.

Objectives

Each student should develop the ability to:

1. Understand and evaluate the literary form of the play.
2. Acquire knowledge of the techniques of linear and nonlinear structure.
3. Develop an understanding of character development, conflict, dialogue, and dramatic action.
4. Realize the relationship between drama and human life.
5. Put the above into practice through the writing of exercises, culminating in the development of a complete script.

Types of Assignments

1. Be responsible for assigned readings.
2. Analyze and evaluate writings of others in class.
3. Prepare written assignments for playwriting exercises.
4. Write a one-act play.

Other Expectations

Students will be expected to see at least two theatre productions and write a two and a half page, double-spaced review of each one (see the website for guidelines).

Tickets are available for productions of _____

You may also usher and see shows free. Contact _____

Attendance

Since this class is designed to provide helpful feedback to writers, attendance is extremely important. Each major assignment needs to be prepared before class and then read and discussed in class. Students who miss a class should consult with the instructor to discuss their work. No more than one unexcused absence is allowed. Excused absences are those due to illness, accident, or death in the family and must be documented. It is the student's responsibility to notify the instructor of the reason for an absence. Excessive absences will result in a lower grade. One point will be subtracted from the final grade for every day missed.

Tardiness

Students are expected to be in class on time. Tardiness will not be tolerated because it interrupts the class activity, it is rude, and it shows a lack of respect. I will allow you to be tardy no more than three times. After three, don't bother to come to class if you are late.

Journal

Each student will keep a journal (simple lined notebook is fine) and write a minimum of one page at least twice a week. The journal should include descriptions of people and events observed, snatches of conversation (dialogue) overheard, descriptions of unusual settings, and anything else that you think may be useful, as well as reflections on your writing.

Required Text

Clark, Leroy. *Writing for the Stage.* Boston: Allyn & Bacon, 2006.

Grading

Grading in a creative writing class is naturally subjective. It is imperative that assignments be done on time, because this is a course in which each assignment builds on the last one in many cases. The final grade will be based on three areas: meeting deadlines, completing the work on the individual exercises, and completing the first and the final draft of your play. The grading will follow a point system such as follows. However, the exact number of points may change if assignments are changed or omitted. Extra credit scenes 1 to 10 points each. The reviews will be 10 points each.

Assignment Points

Attendance and class participation	20 points
Two reviews, 10 points each	20 points
Sixteen individual exercises, 10 points each	160 points
First and final draft, 100 points each	200 points
TOTAL	400 POINTS

Grade Points

A	400–360 points
B	359–319 points
C	318–278 points
D	277–237 points
F	236–0 points

Plays

I encourage you to read the following plays:

How I Learned to Drive by Paula Vogel
Long Day's Journey into Night by Eugene O'Neill
Getting Out by Marsha Norman
A Streetcar Named Desire by Tennessee Williams
Killer Joe by Tracy Letts
Fences by August Wilson
The Miracle Worker by William Gibson
Zoo Story by Edward Albee
The Beauty Queen of Leenane by Martin McDonagh
Proof by David Auburn

APPENDIX B

Outcomes and Assessment

Sharing with Others

The approach I have found most successful from my experience in teaching is to have students write the exercises and bring enough copies with them to class so that they can cast the monologues and scenes with other members of the class and have them read aloud. First, the reading itself allows the author to hear what he has written in the mouths of others and to judge for himself what works and doesn't work. Second, the reading allows everyone in the class to know the work, and when everyone in the class is familiar with what everyone else is writing, they all learn by example. Third, reading puts everyone in the same boat, so to speak. Everyone's work is displayed. Everyone participates. Everyone gets to know one another. There is a conscious effort to create a trusting and supportive environment, in which observations and responses are shared and personal attacks and rants are sharply discouraged.

Following the reading of a monologue or a scene, the teacher should lead a discussion. Students are encouraged to ask questions and to respond to the work. It is important when criticizing the work of others that students address both the positive aspects and the weaknesses. The writer learns from both types of responses.

Usually, at the end of the semester, when students have completed the first drafts of their final projects, I bring in actors to read the plays during several class periods. Skilled actors are better able to bring the characters to life and provide the playwright with insights into how the play is working and how it is not. Actors are also very adept at critiquing a work. They are able to use the skills they have learned in analysis—the techniques of finding motivation, using tactics, and developing characters—to provide the playwright with insights into where they were confused or lost or what didn't make sense to them.

Learn by Doing

A playwright may begin reading this book or taking a playwriting class with no idea in mind of a specific play she wishes to write. However, as she writes various exercises and learns about the craft, the writer will find certain characters that take off. Some scenes and characters will rise to the top, and eventually the ideas and the shape of a play will emerge. After completing six to eight exercises, the writer has usually discovered the play he or she wants to write.

As stated in the sample course syllabus (Appendix A), writing isn't easy. There may be days when a student's efforts to do exercises seem total failures. They may end up writing scenes that don't fit the exercise. What is important is that they write; that they come up with something; that they try.

Discourage students from getting hung up on being perfect. There is no such thing as perfect. Seldom is the first draft of a scene or a play absolutely wonderful. Students should try to approach the class as an environment in which to write and explore, an environment where it is okay to risk failure, an environment where they will get honest and positive feedback. Encourage students to develop their own support groups from their families, friends, other teachers, and theatre professionals.

Assessment

Assessment is the process of gathering and discussing information from multiple and diverse sources in order to develop a deeper understanding of what students know, understand, and can do with the knowledge as a result of their education experiences. The process culminates when assessment results are used to improve subsequent learning.

Through the feedback from the class after the reading of a work and with the written comments of the teacher, it is expected that students will use these assessments to improve their writing of future pieces and/or to rewrite and improve specific works.

Assessment is far more useful than grading. There needs to be a guide for qualitative judgments about student work that provides both criteria and standards of attainment for those criteria. The following are some guidelines and criteria for the assessment of student work for each exercise:

Criteria	Average	Proficient	Distinguished
Content	Fulfills purpose of assignment. Generally well done but some elements lack clarity, depth, or detail.	Fulfills purpose of assignment. Shows clear development of conflict and character.	Fulfills purpose of assignment in a clear and compelling manner. Excellent development of conflict and character. Shows depth and detail.
Characters	Clearly defined but may have problems such as too stereotypical, too much on one level, or not believable.	Orchestrated, clearly polarized, and distinct individuals. Believable.	Well-orchestrated, polarized characters. Believable. Rich in detail. Distinct and unique. Three-dimensional. Individuals.

Dialogue	Generally works but voices are not sufficiently different. Too wordy, sketchy, or commonplace. Speeches are too long, too many ideas per speech. Not consistently believable.	Dialogue is appropriate for each character. Believable.	Each character has a distinct voice. Distinct differences in vocabulary, sentence structure, and rhythm. Contains at least one "gem" of a line.
Plot and Structure	Generally has a beginning, middle, and end but doesn't completely work. Ending may be unsatisfactory. Conflict may not be strong enough. Stakes may not be high enough.	Has a clear inciting action, strong and rising conflict, variety, and a satisfactory ending.	Well-developed beginning, middle, and end. Provides a strong rising conflict and variety. Provides surprises, takes us to places we didn't expect. Strong ending.
Format and Mechanics	Generally follows correct format but too many inconsistencies, typos, comma errors, spelling errors, and other mechanical mistakes.	Follows format consistently. Few spelling, punctuation, and other errors.	Follows format consistently. Spelling, punctuation, and grammar are correct.
Improvement	Makes same mistakes over and over. No discernible improvement.	Corrects past mistakes. Makes new mistakes. Shows improvement.	Makes few mistakes. Corrects past errors. Asks questions and seeks to avoid new mistakes.

See also Figure B.1, a checklist that's based on these criteria.

Grading.   The primary function of grading is to communicate as accurately as possible the extent to which students have learned what the course is designed to teach. Grades are the final evaluative message, but they may have little impact on actual learning. A grade is an end product, a summation, the letter or number documenting to what extent the student learned the course material.

Grading in a creative writing class of this kind is naturally subjective, but hopefully, the criteria and guidelines provided here will give you a clearer understanding of expectations and evaluation. It is imperative that students complete assignments on time, because playwriting is an activity in which each step builds on the last one.

Student Name _____   Faculty Member _____   Grade _____

Criteria	1	2	3	4	5
Content					
Fulfills purpose of assignment in a clear, compelling manner.					
Shows depth and detail.					
Shows clarity of thought.					
Characters					
Clearly defined.					
Well orchestrated and polarized.					
Believable and well developed.					
Distinct and three-dimensional individuals.					
Dialogue					
Each character has a distinct voice.					
Distinct differences in vocabulary, sentence structure, and rhythm.					
Dialogue helps develop character.					
Language is appropriate.					
Style is consistent.					
Plot and Structure					
Well-developed beginning, middle, and end.					
Clear inciting action.					
Development of strong rising conflict.					
Exposition brought in only when needed.					
High stakes.					
Variety in mood, structure, and rhythm of scenes.					
Provides surprises, takes us to unexpected places.					
Strong ending.					
Staging					
Stage worthy.					
Understands reality of theatre.					
Setting, props, costumes, and actions doable.					
Format and Mechanics					
Follows professional format consistently.					
Uses appropriate punctuation.					
Uses appropriate grammar.					
Uses correct spelling.					
No typos or other errors.					
Improvement					
Shows discernable improvement.					
Corrects past mistakes.					

FIGURE B.1   Evaluation Checklist

Expectations for a Sixteen-Week Semester or a Ten-Week Course or Workshop. An instructor should select the exercises that will meet his or her expectations for the course. He or she may choose exercises from each level: Beginning, Intermediate, or Advanced. The assignments could be the same for either ten weeks or sixteen weeks, depending on the instructor's use of class time for reading the plays aloud at the end of the term. For a ten-week term, it might work better to read all the plays outside class, perhaps as a public showcase. At the Beginning level, ask for a complete one-act play, thirty pages minimum, by the end of the semester, demonstrating a mastery of the skills and techniques covered within the course. At the Intermediate level, ask for a longer one-act of about forty-five pages. At the Advanced level, ask for a sixty- to seventy-five-page full-length play. However, you can vary the length as you see fit. For example, for the Beginning level, the focus could be on writing a ten-minute play, limited to ten pages.

BIBLIOGRAPHY

Albee, Edward. "The Playwright's Craft." *Dramatists Guild Quarterly,* Autumn 1993.

Albee, Edward. *Who's Afraid of Virginia Woolf?* New York: Dramatists Play Service, 1962.

Aristotle, (trans. Theodore Buckley). "The Poetic." In *European Theories of the Drama.* New York: Crown, 1965.

Berne, Eric. *Games People Play.* New York, Ballantine Books, 1964.

Benedetti, Robert L. *The Actor at Work,* 8th ed. Boston: Allyn & Bacon, 2000.

Benedict, David. "If You Want to Put Bums on Seats, Then Put Bums on Stage." *London Observer,* March 10, 2002. Available at: http://observer.guardian.co.uk/review/story/0,6903.664667,00.html

Bergson, Henri-Louis. "The Comic Element." In *European Theories of the Drama.* New York: Crown, 1965.

Brown, Dennis. *Shoptalk.* New York: Newmarket Press, 1992.

Bryer, Jackson R. (ed). *The Playwright's Art.* New Brunswick, NJ: Rutgers University Press, 1995.

Chekov, Anton (trans. Stark Young). *The Cherry Orchard* in *Masters of the Modern Stage,* Haskell M. Block and Robert G. Shedd (eds.). New York: McGraw-Hill, 1962.

Clurman, Harold. *On Directing.* New York: Simon & Schuster, 1997.

Cole, Susan Letzler. *Playwrights in Rehearsal.* New York: Routledge, 2001.

Cowden, Tami D., Caro LaFever, & Sue Viders. *The Complete Writer's Guide to Heroes and Heroines.* Hollywood, CA: Lone Eagle, 2000.

Cox, Michael, "What Every Nurse Needs to Know about Rave Drugs." *Advance for Nurses,* May 2002.

Crain, Caleb. "Nicky Silver." *Men's Style,* December 1995.

Dietrich, John E., & Ralph W. Duckwall. *Play Direction,* 2nd ed. Englewood Cliffs, NJ: Prentice-Hall, 1983.

Dramatists Sourcebook (23rd ed.). New York: Theatre Communications Group, 2004–2005.

Durang, Christopher. *Betty's Summer Vacation.* New York: Grove Press, 1999.

Egri, Lajos. *The Art of Dramatic Writing.* New York: Simon & Schuster, 1960.

Epstein, Julius, Philip Koch, & Howard Koch. *Casablanca Script and Legend.* New York: Overlook Press, 1992.

Esslin, Martin. *The Theatre of the Absurd.* New York: Penguin, 1986.

Frey, James. *How to Write a Damn Good Novel.* New York: St. Martin's Press, 1987.

Grebanier, Bernard. *How to Write for the Theatre.* New York: Crowell, 1961.

Grimm, David. *Kit Marlowe.* New York: Dramatists Play Service, 2001.

Guare, John. "Conversation with John Guare." *Dramatists Guild Quarterly,* Winter 1992, pp. 6–14.

Gussow, Mel. *Edward Albee: A Singular Journey.* New York: Simon & Schuster, 1999.

Harling, Robert. *Steel Magnolias.* Garden City, NY: The Fireside Theatre, 1986.

Henderson, Mary C. *Mielziner: Master of Modern Stage Design.* New York: Watson-Guptill Publications, 2001.

Henley, Beth. *Crimes of the Heart.* New York: Penguin, 1982.

Hull, Raymond. *How to Write a Play.* New York: Writers Digest Books, 1983.

Ibsen, Henrik (trans. Eva La Gallienne). *Hedda Gabler.* New York: Random House Modern Library, 1951.

Ibsen, Henrik (trans. Michael Meyer). *Peer Gynt.* Garden City, NY: Anchor Books, 1963.

Istel, John. "The Naked Truth." *American Theatre Magazine,* July 2003.

Lautenberger, Fran. "Costume Advice for the Playwright." Personal communication, July, 2002.

Malevinsky, Moses. "The Science of Playwriting." *In How to Write a Damn Good Novel,* James Frey. New York: St. Martin's Press, 1987, pp. 34–35.

Mamet, David. "Mamet on Playwriting." *Dramatists Guild Quarterly,* Spring 1993.

Margulies, Dennis. "Writers and Their Work." *Dramatists Guild Quarterly,* Autumn 1995, pp. 2–11.

Marlowe, Christopher. *The Tragical History of Doctor Faustus* in *The Complete Plays.* New York: Penguin Books, 1969.

Meyer, Nancy, and Richard Meyer. "'After the Fall': A View from the Director's Notebook." In *Theatre, Annual of the Repertory Theatre of Lincoln Center,* Barry Hyams (ed.). New York: Hill and Wang, 1965.

McKee, Robert. *Story: Substance, Structure, Style and the Principles of Screenwriting.* New York: Regan Books, 1997.

Michaelson, Judith. "Woman Playwrights and Their Stony Road." *Los Angeles Times,* November 6, 1988, p. 7.

Mielziner, Jo. *Designing for the Theatre.* New York: Bramhill House, 1965.

Miller, Arthur. *All My Sons.* New York: Dramatists Play Service, 1974.

Miller, Arthur. *Death of a Salesman* in *New Voices in American Theatre.* New York: Random House, 1955.

Minot, Stephen. *Three Genres: The Writing of Poetry, Fiction, and Drama,* 7th ed. New York: Prentice-Hall, 2001

Odets, Clifford. *Awake and Sing* in *Famous Plays of the 1930s.* New York: Dell, 1959.

O'Neill, Eugene. *The Long Voyage Home* in *Seven Plays of the Sea.* New York: Vintage Books, 1972.

Perret, Gene. *Comedy Writing Step by Step.* Hollywood, CA: Samuel French, 1990.

Price, Thomas. *Dramatic Structure and Meaning in Theatrical Production.* San Francisco: EMtext, 1992.

Ramsey, Dale. "Albee, Weller, Blessing on the Playwright's Craft." *Dramatists Guild Quarterly,* Autumn 1993, pp. 6–14.

Saroyan, William. *The Time of Your Life* in *Famous American Plays of the 1930s.* New York: Dell, 1959.

Shakespeare, William. *Romeo and Juliet* in *The Complete Works of William Shakespeare,* Hardin Craig (ed.). Chicago: Scott, Foresman and Company, 1961.

Shepard, Sam. *Curse of the Starving Class.* New York: Dramatists Play Service, 1976.

Sheridan, Richard Brinsley. *The Rivals.* Boston: Walter H. Baker, 1896.

Silver, Nicky. *Fat Men in Skirts.* New York: Dramatists Play Service, 1964.

Stoppard, Tom. *The Real Inspector Hound.* New York: Samuel French, 1968.

Sweet, Jeffrey. "Ethics and Responsibilities." *Dramatists Guild Quarterly,* Summer 1986.

Thomas, Ludwig. *7/11.* Unpublished manuscript. 1991. Wichita State University.

Vassallo, Philip. "The Reasons to Write." *Dramatists Guild Quarterly,* Autumn 1994.

Vogel, Paula. *How I Learned to Drive* in *The Mammary Plays.* New York: Theatre Communications Group, 1998.

Vogel, Paula. "Interview with Elizabeth Farnsworth" *The NewsHour with Jim Lehrer,* April 16, 1998.

Wasserstein, Wendy. "Conversation with Wendy Wasserstein." *Dramatists Guild Quarterly,* Winter 1994, pp. 6–15.

Whitehurst, William. Personal interview. November 12, 2002. Florida International University.

Wiener, Sally Dixon. "The Word on Play Publishing." *Dramatists Guild Quarterly,* Autumn 1990.

Williams, Tennessee. *The Glass Menagerie* in *Six Modern American Plays.* New York, Random House, 1951.

Williams, Tennessee. *A Streetcar Named Desire.* New York: Dramatists Play Service, 1953.

Wilson, August. *Fences.* New York: New American Library, 1986.

INDEX